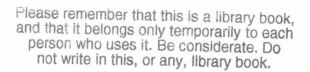

FAMILY
BONDS

FAMILY BONDS

ADOPTION AND

THE POLITICS

OF PARENTING

Elizabeth Bartholet

HOUGHTON MIFFLIN COMPANY
Boston   New York

For information about permission to reproduce selections
from this book, write to Permissions, Houghton Mifflin Company,
215 Park Avenue South, New York, New York 10003.

Library of Congress Cataloging-in-Publication Data

Bartholet, Elizabeth.
Family bonds : adoption and the politics of parenting /
Elizabeth Bartholet.
p.   cm.
Includes index.
ISBN 0-395-51085-6
1. Adoption — United States.   2. Adoption — Law and legislation —
United States.   3. Intercountry adoption — United States.
4. Intercountry adoption — Law and legislation — United States.
I. Title.
HV875.55.B38   1993   92-43666
362.7'34'0973 — dc20   CIP

Portions of Chapters 2, 6, and 7 were first
published in different form in articles by the author.
See Notes for complete citations.

Printed in the United States of America

BP 10 9 8 7 6 5 4 3 2

For
Derek,
Christopher,
and
Michael

ACKNOWLEDGMENTS

I am deeply grateful to the many people who gave me advice, assistance, and support in connection with my work on this project.

I want especially to thank the friends and colleagues who helped me in the formative stages, and those who faithfully read drafts of many chapters at later stages, all of whom helped in myriad ways to shape the final product and gave generously of their ideas and their time: Bob Bennett, Susan Brown, David Chambers, Nancy Dowd, Jerry Frug, Mary Joe Frug, Michael Meltsner, Martha Minow, Deborah Stone, Harriet Trop, and Ciba Vaughan.

Many others gave generously also, reading and commenting on drafts, sharing information and insights gained in their own work or personal lives, and providing other support. I want to thank all those who contributed, especially Helen Alston, Philip Alston, Sydney Altman, Rick Barth, Judy Blume, Betsy Burch, Mike Chamberlain, Abe Chayes, Carol Coccia, George Cooper, Marlene Fried, Mary Ann Glendon, Joan Hollinger, David Kennedy, Duncan Kennedy, Randy Kennedy, Kevin Klose, Catherine Krupnick, Betty Laning,

Phyllis Lowenstein, Laura Maslow-Armand, Frank Michelman, Bill Pierce, Todd Rakoff, Alan Stone, Gerald Torres, Jim Vorenberg, and Martha Wright.

I want to thank all those at Houghton Mifflin who worked with me on this project. Their knowledge, professionalism, and good humor have made the publication process a pleasure. Special thanks go to my editor, Ruth Hapgood, whose keen eye, feel for audience, and general good sense were invaluable. I am also grateful for the extraordinary care, skill, and sensitivity with which my manuscript editor, Liz Duvall, worked on the final manuscript. Others at Houghton Mifflin who made important contributions include Barbara Henricks, Sue Tecce, and Irene Williams. Former editor Mike Janeway's early enthusiasm for this project was important in getting it off the ground. Thanks also to Niva Elkin for her care and thought in preparing the index.

Carol Igoe and Donna Schultz devoted extraordinary efforts to production of the various drafts, and I thank them for their long hours, their patience, and their commitment to the project. I am also grateful to the many law students who contributed to my understanding of the issues.

Finally, I want to thank my family. I am grateful to my mother for the constancy of her interest in and support for my work. My brothers Ivy and Chauncey have been there for me at every stage, calling me in Peru to cheer me on during the adoptions, setting up the crib on my return with child to Cambridge, talking to me about the idea for this book, and reading drafts of the manuscript. I am also grateful to the various members of my extended family for all the many forms of support they have shown.

And above all, I want to thank my son Derek, who first introduced me to the pleasures of parenting, for his careful review of the manuscript, his related comments and counsel, and his general support in connection with the life and work reflected in this book.

CONTENTS

INTRODUCTION

In the fall of 1985 I flew from Boston to Lima, Peru, to adopt a four-month-old child. Some eighteen years earlier I had given birth to my first child. During the last ten of those years I had struggled to give birth again, combating an infertility problem that had resulted, as is often the case, from my use of a contraceptive device during the intervening years.

I had been married when I produced my first child, but divorced when he was just a few years old. Some years later I decided that I wanted more children, regardless of whether I was married. But I found that I was unable to conceive.

I subjected myself to every form of medical treatment that offered any possibility of success. I had operations to diagnose my problem, I took fertility drugs and charted my menstrual cycles and my temperature, and I had sexual intercourse according to the prescribed schedule. I had surgery to remove scar tissue from my fallopian tubes. And I went through in vitro fertilization (IVF) on repeated occasions in programs in three different states. As a single person in my early forties, I was officially excluded from every IVF program in the country that I was able to find out about. Almost all had a maximum age cutoff of forty, and all limited their services to married couples. But I was determined. I begged my way into programs that were willing to consider bending their age rules, and I presented myself as married, with the help of a loyal and loving friend who was willing to play the part of husband. Not being used to a life of fraud, I spent much of my IVF existence terrified that I would be discovered.

I wanted to have another child, and I was obsessed with the need to produce it myself. But IVF did not work for me, and I moved on to adopt.

The adoption experience changed me profoundly. It changed my life and my thinking about life. It changed my understanding of parenting and my view of the law, even though I had been a parent and a lawyer all my adult life. And it changed the focus of my professional energies, because I found myself intensely interested in what I had lived through during my struggles to become a parent, and deeply troubled by the way society was shaping parenting options and defining family.

It was, of course, to be expected that adoption would change my day-to-day life. I went back to Peru in 1988 and adopted another infant, and so am now the mother of two young children. My days start with small warm bodies crawling into my bed, my floors are covered with miniature cars and trucks and Lego pieces, my calender is ascrawl with the kids' doctor appointments and play dates. All this is familiar from twenty years ago, as are the middle-of-the-night coughing fits, the trips to an emergency room to stitch a bloody cut, the sense that there is not enough time to fit it all in.

But I could not have expected these two particular magical children. I could not have predicted the ways in which they would crawl inside my heart and wrap themselves around my soul. I could not have known that I would be so entirely smitten, as a friend described me, so utterly possessed. And I could not have anticipated that this family formed across the continents would seem so clearly the family that was meant to be, that these children thrown together with me and with each other, with no blood ties linking us together or to a common history, would seem so clearly the children meant for me.

The process I went through to form this family affected my understanding of many issues that I had dealt with during my lawyering life. I had, for example, thought of the law largely in terms of its potential for advancing justice and social reform. In the adoption world, I experienced the law as something that functioned primarily to prevent good things from happening. You need only to step through the door of this world and look around to realize that there are vast numbers of children in desperate need of homes and vast numbers of adults anxious to become parents. It seems overwhelmingly clear that efforts to put these groups of children and adults together would create a lot of human happiness. But the legal systems in this and other countries have erected a series of barriers that prevent people who want to parent from connecting with children who need homes. So, for example, the legal system helped push me away from considering adoption during all those years I pursued infertility treatment. And for five months in Peru the legal system required me to live through the peculiar form of torture reserved for foreign adoptive parents. Having made my way through the adoption barriers to find Christopher and Michael at the end, I can have no personal bitterness. I came out where I feel I belong. I am also glad that I had the opportunity to come to know and love the land in which my children were born. But I am deeply conscious that the huge majority of people who would delight in the opportunity to parent some of the world's children will not be able or willing to make their way through the barriers that the law has set in their path. The myth is that the legal structure surrounding adoption is designed to serve the best interests of the child. Actually experiencing the system as an adoptive parent shattered this myth for me.

The adoption experience also affected my understanding

of the discrimination issues on which I had focused my professional energies, first as a civil rights lawyer and then as a law professor. Experiencing the system as a victim-participant gives insights that you cannot get as a simple observer or even as an advocate for victims. In addition, discrimination in matters affecting the family is generally treated quite differently from discrimination in such areas as housing or employment. Living through an adoption forces a person to think about whether there should be such a sharp distinction.

Because of my civil rights background, my initial reaction to the adoption world was one of shock. I was familiar with a world increasingly governed by the principle that such factors as race, religion, sex, age, and handicap should not be determinative. In the adoption world, just such factors are central in deciding who gets to parent and be parented. Moreover, the discrimination, if that's what it should be called, is quite overt. Prospective parents are rated in terms of desirability *primarily* by their race, religion, marital status, age, handicap, and sexual orientation. Children are similarly rated, with race, religion, age, and handicap being key. "Desirable" parents are then matched with "desirable" children, and "marginal" parents with "marginal" children. The least desirable simply lose out altogether, as do those for whom there is no same-race or same-religion match. Parents with money can bypass the rating system and get a child with the kinds of features they want and are able and willing to pay for. The price they pay will depend on the child's market rating, with the price for a white child being significantly higher than that for a minority child. Race and money: the longer you spend in the adoption world, the more you realize the power of these two factors. Yet in the rest of our communal life we have come to accept as one of our most basic principles that race should not matter, and a cardinal principle in adoption *theory* is that babies are not for sale.

The adoption process also forced me to think on a personal

level about discrimination. When you have to fill out a form for the adoption agency that asks what disabilities you could accept in a child — mental retardation, blindness, a missing limb, Down syndrome — you think about the meaning of disability in a new way. If you check the box on the form that says "none of the above disabilities," you are pushed to think about whether your act of discrimination is fundamentally the same as or different from the act excluding a disabled person from employment or housing. If your goal is to adopt children who fall in the "healthy infant" category, as my goal was, you may spend many guilty hours questioning whether this goal is consistent with your sense of yourself as a loving human being and a fit prospective parent.

Adoption transformed my feelings about infertility and my understanding of what parental love is all about. For years I had felt that there was only one less-than-tragic outcome of my infertility battle, and that was to reverse the damage that had been done to my body, the damage that stood in the way of pregnancy. I had felt that there was only one really satisfactory route to parenthood, and that was for me to conceive and give birth. I had assumed that the love I felt for my first child had significantly to do with biologic connection. The experience of loving him was wrapped up in a package that included pregnancy, childbirth, nursing, and the genetic link that meant I recognized his eyes and face and personality as familial. Adoption posed terrifying questions. Could I love in the same way a child who had not been part of me and was not born from my body? Could I feel that totality of commitment I associated with parental love toward a child who came to me as a baby stranger? Or did the form of attachment I had known with my first child arise out of the biologic inevitability felt in the progression from sexual intercourse to pregnancy to childbirth, and out of the genetic link between us?

I discovered that the thing I know as parental love grows out of the experience of nurturing, and that adoptive parenting is in fundamental ways identical to biologic parenting. I have come to think of pregnancy and childbirth as experiences that for me were enormously satisfying but that seem of limited relevance to the parenting relationship. I do not see biologic links as entirely irrelevant to parenting, but neither do I see an obvious hierarchical system for ranking biologic and adoptive parenting. There are special pleasures involved in parenting the child who is genetically familiar, and there are special pleasures involved in parenting the children whose black eyes and Peruvian features and wildly dissimilar personalities proclaim their genetic difference.

I can, of course, be seen as specially privileged by virtue of having experienced both kinds of parenting. It may therefore be hard for those who have never borne a child to identify with me. If, for example, there is some primal need to project oneself into future generations by reproduction, I have had the luxury of satisfying that need. But it does seem to me that not much is gained by leaving a genetic legacy. You do not in fact live on just because your egg or sperm has contributed to another life. It is unlikely that the anonymous sperm donor takes significant pleasure in knowing that his genes are carried forward to the next generation in the person of some unknown child wandering the earth. The sense of immortality that many seek in parenting seems to me to have more to do with the kind of identification that comes from our relationship with our children, and with the ways in which that relationship helps shape their being.

This is not to say that *becoming* a parent through adoption is comparable to *becoming* a parent through giving birth. I found many aspects of the adoption process terrifying or unpleasant or some combination of the two. It was an entirely unknown world to me, as it is to many. In addition, society has conspired to make adoption extraordinarily difficult to accomplish.

Adoption involves choice on a scale most of us don't generally experience. You can't fall accidentally into adoption, as you can into pregnancy. You exercise choice down to the wire. Choice forces you to think about what you want and to take responsibility for the consequences of your decision. And the choice to go forward with an adoption means a lifelong commitment, which simply isn't true of other choices that most of us make. If you make a mistake in choosing a house, a job, or even a spouse, you can get out of it. Few of those who consciously enter an adoptive parenting relationship would feel comfortable opting out of their commitment.

While choice is difficult and uncomfortable for most of us, there are obvious advantages for both children and parents in parenting that results from conscious choice. In the world of biologic parenting, all too many children are raised by parents who neither planned for nor wanted them, and the evidence shows that this is problematic for both the parents and the children. As a parent, I found that one of the gratifying aspects of the adoption process was the satisfaction that came from the sense that I was exercising choice and taking control over my life. Although adoption has been made far more difficult and more frightening than it needs to be, adoptive parenting is an achievable goal, at least for those with the time, energy, resources, and will to pursue it. When I wasn't in the depths of despair and depression in Peru, I relished the Wonder Woman role I had cast myself in, and delighted in my ability to overcome seemingly insuperable obstacles. The contrast with the infertility struggle is compelling. If your goal is to have a biologic child, there is no way that you can take control. No matter what you do or how long and hard you try, there is a good likelihood that you will fail. If your goal is to become a parent, you can do it through adoption. There may be a thousand obstacles, but you can triumph over them.

I write this book for people struggling with some of the issues I encountered in my journey from infertility through adoption. I write it for those who have suffered the pain of infertility, for those who have been subjected to the indignities and the recurrent despair of unsuccessful infertility treatment, and for those who have endured the absurdities of the

adoption system. I write it for single people and others classified by the system as marginal parents, who may wonder if
they can or should adopt. I write it for those who might adopt
but for ignorance and fear.

I write this book also for those in a position to make or
influence policy. Current policy with respect to parenting
options reflects a powerful bias in favor of biologic parenting.
As a society, we define personhood and parenthood in terms
of procreation. We push the infertile toward ever more elaborate forms of high-tech treatment. We are also moving rapidly
in the direction of a new child production market, in which
sperm, eggs, embryos, and pregnancy services are for sale so
that those who want to parent can produce a child to order.
At the same time, we drive prospective parents away from
children who already exist and who need homes. We do this
by stigmatizing adoptive parenting in myriad ways and by
turning the adoption process into a regulatory obstacle
course. The claim is that no children are available for adoption, but the fact is that millions of children the world over are
in desperate need of nurturing homes. The politics of adoption in today's world prevents these children from being
placed in adoptive homes. This book argues that current policies make no sense for people interested in parenting, for
children in need of homes, or for a world struggling to take
care of the existing population.

Adoptive family relationships are often built on a foundation of human misery. Birth parents generally surrender children for adoption or abandon them because they feel forced
to do so by poverty or discrimination or the chaos that results
from war or some other disaster. Many of those interested in
becoming adoptive parents feel forced to undertake this form
of parenting by infertility. In an ideal world, we would eliminate the social ills that force some to give up the children they
bear and that deprive others of their fertility. But the argument of this book is that in the world in which we live today
and will live tomorrow, the social ills with which we are

familiar do and will exist. Adoption should be understood as an institution that works well for birth parents, for the infertile, and for children. The further argument is that adoption should not be seen simply as a partial solution for some of the world's social ills. Adoption should be understood as a positive alternative to the blood-based family form.

The politics of adoption is complex. Traditionalists often portray themselves as proadoption, and in today's world many who see themselves as progressive attack adoption as an exploitative institution. But the traditionalists tend to promote adoption simply as a preferred alternative to abortion. They do little actually to support adoption as a legitimate choice, either for the infertile who want to parent or for women who give birth but do not want to parent. Traditional understandings of the meaning of family and the proper role of women in the family help make adoption the last resort that it is, and they help shape the institution of adoption in ways that reinforce the notion that the ideal form of family is the idealized husband-wife nuclear family of the past.

Progressives are often concerned with adoption's potential for exploitation of the poor and single birth mother by the well-off adoptive couple, as well as exploitation of racial and ethnic minority groups and the Third World by the dominant white cultures and the industrialized West. Adoption certainly holds the potential for exploitation, but it is not *inherently* exploitative. It can be understood as liberating, and structured in ways that expand options for the oppressed in our society. For women, adoption can be seen as an important part of reproductive autonomy. Adoption adds to the choices enjoyed by the fertile, enabling those who become pregnant but do not abort and do not want to parent to give their children to others for parenting. We could add to the sense of choice by constructing adoption so that a woman could make the decision to relinquish her child without undue guilt. We now bombard birth mothers with the message that they should raise their children themselves at whatever cost.

"True" mothers don't give away their children any more than they sell them. "True" women are supposed either to abort or not to abort, depending on the observer's politics, but never to "abandon" their children. It would be liberating for women and for their children if we were to enable birth parents to think more positively about giving their children to those who cannot bear children but who want to provide the nurturing piece of parenting. Adoption also, of course, adds to the choices enjoyed by the infertile. It is now constructed as a last-resort parenting choice, vastly inferior to biologic parenting. This reinforces for the infertile the message that they should be fertile, and for women the message that "true" women get pregnant and give birth. A more positive construction of adoption would help free the infertile from the obsession to restore their sense of personhood by obtaining a medical fix.

This book argues that a more positive construction of adoption would be liberating not simply for birth parents, or for the infertile who want to parent, or for the children who need nurturing homes, but more broadly. Adoptive families are different in some interesting ways from families based on a blood link. Understanding the positive features of adoption could open up our minds to rethinking in important ways the meaning of parenting, family, and community. I feel that the experience of adoption has done this for me. My goal in this book is to share that vision.

I write this book, finally, for the children of the world. I write it to honor those particular children who became mine, and to give thanks.

FAMILY
BONDS

ONE

Becoming an Adoptive Parent

FROM BOSTON TO LIMA

A Telephone Call
"Come, I have a beautiful baby waiting for you." It is Monday, July 29, 1985. Yvonne de Loli, an adoption lawyer in Peru, is talking to me on the telephone. I have called her because my plans to adopt from Brazil have just fallen through. I had reached the top of the Brazilian program's waiting list and even been assigned a child when a judge in Brazil closed down the program. There had been no scandal. This was, by all reports, an entirely ethical program, run by a woman who had for many years been finding homes for abandoned children as well as for the children of women who could not afford to raise them. It was closed down as part of a general move by Brazilian judges hostile to the idea of adoption by foreigners, especially North Americans. The child assigned to me was removed from the temporary home where he waited with other children for adoptive placement, and was sent to an orphanage. It was a classic story of international adoption.

I had Yvonne's name from friends who had adopted twins

from Peru; they were the only people I knew of who had adopted from that country. I was interested in Peru because I knew it allowed adoption by singles over forty, my category as a prospective adoptive parent. And I had a romantic feeling about what I knew of Peru — fuzzy impressions of an amazing Incan civilization and dim memories of a childhood friend's tales of visits to Machu Picchu and of life in Lima, where she grew up. Indeed, I had thought of adopting from Peru early in my exploration of possibilities, but had been scared off by the difficulties that my friends had endured accomplishing their adoptions.

I telephoned Yvonne on this particular day because I was ready to adopt. I had spent several years thinking vaguely about adoption and much of the past eight months working my way through all the steps necessary for a foreign adoption. I had gotten pretty far in resolving my various fears and doubts and had finally decided that I could only know what adoption would be like by doing it. When the Brazilian program fell through, it seemed that my carefully constructed but fragile parenting plan might just dissolve, and I felt a certain despair. My adoption agency had no other program for singles and was advising me and others simply to wait for Brazil to open again. I knew from my sources that that might never happen, and I suspected that the agency would have little else to offer singles in the near future. There are many barriers in the way of adoption, and they can seem insuperable in the case of a single forty-four-year-old. I was also afraid that if I waited any longer, I might lose some of the conviction and determination that had enabled me to get this far. Although I talked to almost no one about my adoption plans, I nonetheless felt bombarded by messages that I was doing something really quite crazy. I was afraid that I might let myself be persuaded if more time went by. So I called Yvonne, feeling that I must act if I really wanted another child.

But now I get more than I am ready for from this lawyer to whom I have just introduced myself on the telephone. There's a baby waiting. Do I want it? If so, I should come down within the week. She will "hold" the baby until I get there. He is a few months old. I immediately picture a thin waif with large brown eyes in a sad face, looking through the bars of a crib — rather like the babies I will see later in the room for *abandonados*, abandoned children, in a hospital in Lima. He looks immensely appealing, but I start protesting that I really am looking for a newborn, feeling panic at the actuality of what I had thought I wanted. She tells me that a pregnant woman is due to deliver the next day and that I can have her baby instead. I tell her that I will think all this over and call the next day.

That night I debate with myself what to do, talking it through with good friends who are visiting from Chicago, a couple who are in the middle of their own struggle with infertility. The woman says, "Go for it." The man advises caution. Why rush into this? Why not take my time, explore alternatives? I conclude that it would be rash and impulsive to race off to Peru. But I call the next day and within moments am discussing the documents that I will need to take with me. Six days later I am on the plane to Lima.

Preparing to Go

Happily, there is almost no time to think. I have six days to get my adoption papers together and to make arrangements to leave and to live in Lima for the two months or longer it will take to complete the adoption. I must arrange for the transfer to Peru of the immigration documents that I have sent down to Brazil for my future child's visa. I must put together a set of documents required by the Peruvian adoption authorities: birth certificate, marriage certificate, divorce certificate, fingerprints, proof of residence, proof that I have no police record, report from a doctor on my physical health, report from a psychiatrist on my mental health, letter from my employer, letter from my minister (something of a problem, since I haven't been to church for years). All these and more have to be prepared and then taken to the appropriate officials in the appropriate order to be stamped. I must get in touch with my seventeen-year-old son, Derek, who is off on a trip, and get him back to Cambridge so that I can help make final arrangements for him to begin his freshman year at college in California a few weeks from now.

The list of things to do goes on and on. Days, I simply move through it. I race from the Cambridge police station to my adoption agency, to the United States immigration office, to the Massachusetts secretary of state's office, to the Peruvian consulate, carrying my burgeoning file of documents. At night I check off the things I have done, make new lists, and talk on the phone, making plans and arrangements. Then I fall into bed for a few hours' sleep, only to jump up early and start running again. Occasionally I pause to wonder what I'm doing and whether I'm just acting out some strange role I have given myself. By now there's a powerful momentum, and I know that I will keep moving. But there's no sense of appropriate excitement or happy anticipation.

I have to arrange with my employer for this unexpected departure and for a leave of unknown duration. I am lucky to have the kind of job I do, teaching at Harvard Law School. It is painfully obvious that an international adoption would simply not be possible for most people in less privileged employment situations. My teaching schedule gives me flexible hours and summers off from teaching to plan my work as I will. I have had to spend a lot of daytime hours this past year investigating adoption possibilities and compiling documents, getting myself fingerprinted and examined, and taking the other steps necessary to complete the "home study," which certifies me as a fit adoptive parent. I had planned my adoption for the early summer, and even though that plan didn't work out and it is now midsummer, I still have a month before classes start. I am additionally lucky because I have been able to schedule myself for only one course in the fall semester, which I am to teach jointly with another professor. I see the law school dean during this whirlwind six-day period, and he approves a partial leave for the fall semester, with the understanding that my coteacher will start the course and I will join him in the classroom as soon as I can get back from Peru.

During my meeting with the dean, who is an old friend, I mention that I still need to figure out how to get a letter from a minister certifying my good character. He picks up the phone and arranges for me to meet with the minister for Harvard University. I spend a poignant hour with this man, telling him about myself, my life, why I'm worthy of raising one or perhaps two of the children waiting for me in Lima. (I have begun to think that I might just adopt both babies Yvonne mentioned, since I might want eventually to have two, and this adoption business is so difficult it is hard to imagine going through it twice. Or perhaps I have already begun to feel that I do not want to choose between the two babies.) I talk a bit about the only real connection I have had with his church — the period some twenty-five years earlier when, as a Harvard undergraduate, I was a relatively faithful attendant at Memorial Church services. At the end he tells me that he considers me part of his flock and writes me a letter testifying to my suitability to bring up children, thereby covering the contingencies. I am deeply touched and picture myself bringing my child or children to meet him when we return and going to his services on a regular basis. (I never did become a regular churchgoer, but I went with the children to a Christmas Eve service one year and took great pleasure in introducing them to this wonderful man afterward.)

As I gather all my documents I have them "notarized," a process in which a notary public attests to the validity of the signature on a document. I then take them to the Massachusetts secretary of state's office to have them "verified." A state official affixes to each document a fancy green stamp signifying that the person who notarized the document is indeed a notary public. Then I take the documents to the Peruvian consul's office in Boston to be "authenticated" or "legalized." In this process the consulate certifies that the previous notarization and verification have indeed taken place as required. I fear — with reason — that if I don't have every document in exactly the right form before I go, I will have to come back from Peru without my child and start the process again. I go through every page of every document with the woman on duty at the consulate. She doesn't seem really sure which documents are required. Moreover, two kinds of legalization are available, a simple kind involving a stamp and a fancy kind involving a stamp together with her writing something, and she isn't sure which kind I need. I pay the extra money involved for the fancy legalization, and I wait for an hour while she laboriously legalizes every page of every document in question. I say jokingly to the stranger with me in the waiting room that this will undoubtedly be the first of many such scenes in this adoption process. But I have no idea of just how many such scenes there will be. I have no idea that my adoption cases in Lima will generate hundreds of pages of documents or that I will spend endless hours watching ancient typewriters crank them out and watching various officials sign and stamp them. The Peruvian birth certificate I will ultimately receive for each adopted child will have some dozen stamps and signatures demonstrating that Peru's minister of the interior and its minister of the exterior, Lima's chief of police and its mayor, as well as numerous others, have all signed off on the adoption by duly recognizing that one another's signatures are valid.

Derek comes home on Friday, three days before I am to leave. I think of him as the inspiration for what I am doing. Parenting him has been the central satisfaction in my life, and my determination to become a parent again regardless of the obstacles is fueled by the power of my feelings for my first child. But this week I am obsessed with my own adoption-related activities and emotions. It is hard to focus on Derek's needs as he contemplates going off to his first year at the faraway University of California at Berkeley. I feel some guilt over not being entirely here for my first child as I rush about in this new parenting pursuit.

By Saturday my documents are in order and I am able to spend several hours on vital shopping. I buy a Berlitz Spanish phrase book (I know no Spanish) and a couple of guidebooks (I've never been to Peru or, indeed, to Central or South America). I buy diapers, compromising on size since I'm not entirely sure what size baby I will have. I spend a long time in the supermarket examining bottles and nipples, unable to figure out which nipples go with which bottles or how these new plastic-bag disposable bottles are supposed to operate. I examine an aisleful of formula options with the same bewilderment. I nursed Derek and never let a drop of formula touch his lips. I buy an assortment of bottles and formulas, figuring that I will have time in Peru to unscramble how it all works. I buy Dr. Spock and Penelope Leach on child care. I borrow some baby clothes. It doesn't feel right to buy baby clothes; I don't entirely believe, or can't let myself believe, that I'll end up with a baby. But I do buy several receiving blankets — they are powerfully linked in my mind with the first days of Derek's life.

On Sunday, my last full day at home, I pack. And I talk to Derek a bit about his plans for college.

On Monday I go to the bank and take out $6,000. Sitting in the chair beside the bank officer's desk, I place $4,000 under the insoles of the sneakers I will wear on the flight to Peru, and the other $2,000 in two separate moneybags under my clothes. I have been told that I should bring in cash all the money that I will need to pay the adoption lawyer and to live in Lima for the two months that I can expect to be there. I have also been told that it is dangerous to walk the streets of Lima with more than a few dollars on your person. This is my way of reconciling the messages.

I go to my office, where I write a note telling family and friends the address in Peru where I can be reached "for the foreseeable future." I sign the first will I have ever written. Two years later I will sign a new will the night before I am to leave for Peru for my second adoption. On some level I must wonder if I will ever return from these ventures. Derek takes me to the airport. We have almost an hour to spare, and so we get a cup of coffee and have a chance, finally, to almost relax. I feel the need to cling to this last experience with him before I go. At the gate, a stranger offers to take our picture. The photograph says a lot. Derek has a supportive arm around my shoulder. I look strained and haggard, more like someone on her way to a nursing home than the eager mother-to-be of an infant.

Why was I so afraid? Why wasn't I rejoicing that I was finally about to fulfill my long-frustrated desire to have another child? I think I was experiencing fears and doubts shared by many who consider adopting. Did I really know what I wanted? Did I really want to parent at this age and stage of my life? Did I want to do this thing called adoption? And, the worst question of all, how could I ever know, in this strange world of parenting choice, that a particular child was the "right" child?

Flight into the Unknown
On the flight to Lima, my feet feel hot and sweaty from the $4,000 sneaker padding. I study my Berlitz phrase book, and the woman seated next to me helps with the pronunciation as she sees me struggling. I learn that she was born in Peru, which strikes me as extraordinary and wonderful. I tell her my story, conscious that in the next weeks I will need to make friends with many strangers. We discuss what I will name the child. I have always loved the name Christopher, but wonder about choosing a name that would provide more of a cultural link. She delights in the name and pronounces it the way I will hear it for the next eight weeks: "Crees-toe-fehr."

We arrive at 3 A.M. in the confusing tumult of the Lima airport. My new friend helps me through customs. I scan the faces of those meeting the plane and see a large, respectably dressed woman searching for someone she seems not to know. It is Yvonne. She greets me and hustles me past the immigration authorities with a word to an official she apparently knows. Her face and presence are somewhat reassuring. I am suddenly embarrassed at my outfit. The sneakers, baggy black pants, and bulky sweatshirt draped over my moneybags had seemed perfect to ward off strangers after my riches, but they feel totally inappropriate for this next stage of my venture — dealing with the lawyer who will determine my parenting fate. I will have to make up with talk for how I look. I will quickly have to demonstrate my charm, my respectability, my professional connections — my basic worthiness to parent and to be treated decently in what I have been warned is a world in which North Americans can be treated very badly.

Yvonne's husband is waiting with the car. We drive to downtown Lima and then around various lighted plazas. I finally realize that they are taking me on a sightseeing tour. I find it so astounding that they could think I would be interested in the sights of Lima right now that I have trouble even making interested noises. I have been wondering all this time whether we are on the way to "my baby." Finally we park and take the elevator up in what appears to be an apartment building. They lead me to an apartment on the thirteenth floor. As they show me around, I realize that this is where I will be living. It is hideously dreary. Yvonne tells me that one bedroom is occupied by an Italian couple who have also come to adopt. We leave my bags in the other bedroom and go upstairs to a quite elegant apartment on the twentieth floor, where Yvonne and her husband live.

Yvonne takes me in to her kitchen table and offers me coffee. It seems to me quite evidently a time for whiskey, not coffee. I have finally arrived, after what may have been the most stressful week of my life. I have had no sleep this night and very little sleep the previous nights. We are apparently about to talk about the baby. I truly need a drink. I graciously accept the coffee.

So we begin the negotiation of my life. It seems that we are to decide here and now on which baby will be mine. I worry that with the lack of sleep my wits may not be adequately together for this negotiation, but in fact my brain feels wired. My mind dances about, planning maneuvers and trying to figure out the meaning of Yvonne's maneuvers. The problem is that I don't know the specific goal. I want the "right" baby, but I don't know which is the right one, or even how to describe what would be the right one. The task is made harder by my deep discomfort that by "right" I may mean "best." She begins to talk about the timing. Do I need to get back to the United States soon? Yes, I have to get back to teach my course at the Harvard Law School. (It's important to show that I'm important. I also do want and need to get home as soon as possible, and I know that she has a lot of control over how long things take.) Conversation then begins to focus on the newborn, whose adoption would for various reasons be simpler. I give up the time-is-important gambit. I don't want the choice of baby to turn on which one will be easier to adopt. I'll stay as long as necessary.

The talk rambles on — about me, my job at Harvard (it's becoming clearer by the minute how much Harvard impresses my lawyer), me as a mother. I get out of my wallet pictures of Derek, pictures dating from infancy up until recent years. Yvonne begins to talk of the older baby now — how much he looks like Derek, how special he is. It seems that the older one is the right one for me. I believe it. It makes sense to me, since this conclusion has grown out of our conversation about Derek and his pictures. But I insist that I want to see both babies. I don't like this business of choosing a baby, but if there is to be a choice, I want it to be mine and not Yvonne's. It's settled — so I think — that at noon both babies will be produced.

I go downstairs to the thirteenth floor and the door marked

134 and enter what will be my home for the next two months. I lock myself into my bedroom. (It seems important to protect myself and my money against the dangers of Lima.) The sagging bed almost fills the room. There is a window on one side, with gray clouded glass and metal edges. It seems permanently closed, and my life feels encompassed by the four dingy plaster walls. I crawl into the bed, intensely and miserably lonely. I wonder how I have managed so to mess up my life as to land myself alone in this hideous bedroom in this strange city on this unknown continent. I think enviously of the Italian couple in the next room, and wonder how I could ever have thought that I wanted to venture into this adoptive parenting world without a man.

I toss around in the bed for an hour, telling myself that I need sleep to face the day and the decisions it will bring. Finally I jump up and go into the bathroom to take a shower, locking my money and precious documents in the bedroom behind me. The cold water spigot is broken, so I shower by leaping in and out of scalding water. I go into the kitchen. In the refrigerator there are two bottles of mineral water and some coffee, which must belong to the Italian couple. Desperate for some sense of comfort and normalcy, I try to make coffee, hopeful that the Italian couple will understand. I can find no coffeepot, no coffee filters, and indeed no kitchen supplies at all except a couple of pots, some plates, and some tableware. I finally locate some napkins and devise a filter, but it dissolves with the boiling water into my cup. I find a tea strainer, which gives a sense of civilization but fails to keep the coffee grounds out of the coffee. I settle for coffee with grounds, a brew I get used to during the next few days.

I then begin a morning of telephoning. Discovery of the telephone the night before had been the one bright note in the survey of the apartment. It was to be my lifeline to the world for eight weeks. I call Fred, an old friend from the States. I had learned just before I left Boston that he and his wife, a Peruvian by birth, would be in Lima for the week. And

I call Oriola, a Peruvian woman who lives in Lima and is a relative of close friends of mine at home. In calling Fred and Oriola, I realize how desperate I already am for some sense of connection to my prior world. When I tell Oriola, who has never heard of me until this telephone call, that I will probably be in Lima for two months, she says in a tone I will never forget, "How wonderful," and goes on to explain how pleased she is that she will have this chance to get to know me. In my pitiful condition, I am quite overwhelmed by this warm welcome.

My emotions are raw. My nerves and senses seem entirely exposed. For the next several weeks I will exist this way, bouncing from one emotional state to another, as I collide with external events.

The babies are not at Yvonne's at noon, nor at one. I learn over the next weeks that an appointment for a set time with Yvonne means at best that she will be there sometime in the next few hours, or that night, or perhaps the next day.

As I'm waiting, I suddenly focus on the fact that I might have a baby in my care within hours and I haven't begun to figure out how I will feed it. I settle down on the sofa with the books and feeding equipment I have brought with me. Dr. Spock has lengthy sections on various ways to mix and sterilize formula. The cans of formula have their own directions for mixing and sterilizing. Then there are instructions for how to put these new disposable bottles together and how to mix and sterilize with them, since they are actually plastic bags and can't be boiled like traditional bottles. It all seems extraordinarily complicated. I fight off a growing sense of panic by telling myself sternly that someone who has managed to get through the fancy educational institutions I have attended should be able to figure out how to feed a baby without poisoning it. After struggling for an hour, I feel that I have a handle on the theory. I conclude that I will use the traditional bottles, since the sterilization system for these seems pretty straightforward. Then I confront the reality of the kitchen.

There is no pot with a lid that fits, no pitcher for the sterilized formula, and of course no tongs or bottle holders. Every surface in sight is filthy. There is no sponge, no rag, no paper towel. There is nothing to clean with except a bar of soap.

At five o'clock I get a telephone call telling me that "my baby" is at Yvonne's. I go out my apartment door, take the elevator to the twentieth floor, and start to walk down the hallway to her apartment. I see myself as in a movie. I replay scenes from the past ten years — deciding to have another child, discovering my infertility, pursuing infertility treatment, and finally exploring adoption. It has all led to this walk down a grimy public hallway toward a door marked 204. It seems that time should stop or at least slow down to allow breathing space for what is about to happen. But my feet keep walking down the hall, and when I ring the bell the door opens.

There is a baby, held in someone's arms, looking right at me and smiling. He is resplendent in a white knit sweater and pants. I reach out and he is put in my arms. His smile charms me. People seem to encircle us, and their voices bombard us with sound that only half pierces my consciousness. "Isn't he beautiful?" "He's such a good baby." "He has such a good disposition." "He's so smart." "You're so lucky." "Look at the way he smiles at you." He looks well fed and cared for, not at all the sad-eyed, thin-faced *abandonado* of my imagination. I begin to pay attention to the people around us and am introduced to Señora Maria, who, it appears, has been taking care of him. I figure — rightly, it turns out — that this may be my only chance to find out something about the past couple of months of his life. I ask her the questions I have prepared for this moment. She seems kind and caring, and I feel comforted about his early life.

Eventually the baby sleeps. I'm offered a meal, so I lay him down on a blanket and join Yvonne, Señora Maria, and some others, whose identities I haven't yet figured out, at the dining table. More talk. I make it clear that I still want to see the other baby. It's important to me that I make the choice. After dinner, sometime toward midnight, Yvonne suddenly announces: "Come, in this moment we go." I pick up the baby and follow her to the door. Señora Maria and Bonnie, a friend of Yvonne's who also functions, I will learn, as her chauffeur, come with us. Yvonne leads us down to the apartment building's basement garage, where we climb into an ancient orange Volkswagen bug, with Bonnie at the wheel. Leaving the garage involves roaring up the narrow passage from the basement to the street as fast as Bonnie can gun the engine. I will undergo this experience dozens of times in the next eight weeks, and will never understand whether she has any way of knowing that no other car is headed down the passage at the same time. We race through the night, dodging among the cars with wild abandon.

I have no idea where we are going, but it seems likely that it has something to do with the other baby. I will learn that although Yvonne's English is quite good, she has no great interest in enabling her adoptive parents to understand what is happening. She prefers simply to issue her classic mandate — "Come, in this moment we go" — and sweep them along in her wake.

We arrive at what turns out to be Señora Maria's house and all settle down in the living room, where she graciously offers us coffee, as if we have come for a social visit. Someone then removes the baby from my arms and takes him off into a back room. That person reappears with a newborn wrapped in a blanket and deposits this baby in my lap. I sit looking down at the tiny sleeping face of the child born just after my first call from Cambridge. There is no agony of choice. The first baby is already mine, although I did not entirely realize it until this moment. I think briefly about bringing both babies back home, but immediately realize that I will not do this. Emotionally, I am already overwhelmed by what I am doing, and on a rational level I know that I would rather come back for another child when the first is a few years old. Knowing all this, I still have trouble giving the baby back. How do you say that you want to return a human being without its sounding like a Bloomingdale's transaction? How do you hand a baby back without feeling that you are rejecting it, and how can you reject a helpless creature that lies trusting and content in your arms? I know I can't continue to hold the baby if I'm going to give him back, so I finally mutter something, stand up, and hold him out to be taken. There are tears on my cheeks as he is removed. Yes, I'm tired, after some forty hours without sleep. But I had begun to connect with this tiny creature during the moments that I held him. I think of this scene often when I hear arguments about so-called surrogate mother contracts — arguments that women should be able to commit themselves to not developing a bond with the child growing within them for nine months, arguments that if they change their mind, their prior agreement to give up the child should be enforceable against them. After all, they should have known how they would feel, and a contract is a contract, even if it is a contract not to bond, a contract that denies the bonds that may have formed.

They bring the child I will call Christopher back to me, we drive off in the orange Volkswagen, and at about 3 A.M., almost exactly twenty-four hours after my arrival at the Lima airport, I take him home to my apartment. I change him into clothes I picked out in Cambridge for him to wear. My little room still seems a weird place to be, but I am flying high.

THE ADOPTION PROCESS

I'm standing before my judge at the Jugado de Menores (the Juvenile Court), holding Christopher, with Yvonne and Oriola beside me as my lawyer and translator, respectively. I repeat the oath after the judge: "I swear that I will provide for this child's needs and take care of him as if he were my own." As in a marriage ceremony, I commit myself "till death us do part." I look at this little stranger and wonder at my sense of ease in taking these vows. I think about arranged marriages in other societies.

It is Thursday, August 8. I arrived in Lima early Tuesday morning and took Christopher home early Wednesday. Life has moved fast.

The judge walks to the back of her office and dictates to her secretary, who taps out the provisional custody order on his ancient typewriter. It is now legitimate for Christopher to live with me. Officially he has been living under the care of a religious order. That fiction enabled Yvonne to get him released from institutional care into the warm hands of Señora Maria. It will take eight weeks of legal proceedings for the final adoption decree, which will make me officially his mother.

Oriola and I steal a look at the papers on the judge's desk, and Oriola whispers a number, which I write on my wrist. It's the baby's hospital record number. I have asked the judge to order the release of the medical records of the baby and his mother. Eight weeks later, this legal route will produce nothing more than a one-paragraph statement from the Hospital Santa Rosa confirming that the baby was indeed born there. But with the number I have copied onto my wrist, a hospital nurse who is a friend of friends will be able surreptitiously to locate and hand-copy the records for me. This is against the rules, of course, but seems the only way to get information that might be important for Christopher.

So it goes in Lima. You learn that the way to function is to avoid the law if at all possible. A book called *The Other Path,* an allusion to the terrorist group Sendero Luminoso, or Shining Path, documents the way in which the law is strangling Peru's economy, and describes the burgeoning underground economy as central to current and future productivity. There is a similar adoption underground for Peruvians who know what they're doing. I was told by a well-connected Peruvian whom I met during my stay that she and her husband "adopted" their son simply by arranging for the hospital to list her as the mother on the birth certificate.

The day before this legal ceremony, I began my new role as adoptive mother. There is a play-acting quality to my feelings as I wash and dress and feed this baby. He still seems a bit like someone else's child. By noon I find this so unnerving that I beg Yvonne's cook to watch him so that I can have an hour alone. I sit in the serene dining room of the Hotel Crillon, a wonderfully civilized place I have discovered next door to my apartment building, and spend the hour engaged in a painful, lonely search of my soul. I wonder what is wrong with me that I have not immediately and completely attached to this wonderful child. I wonder whether I am worthy to be an adoptive parent. It's a hard hour, but I feel oddly better when I go back for Christopher.

That same evening I meet Oriola for the first time. As she drives me back to my apartment building, I ask if I can give her the money I have brought with me. It's unnerving to keep it locked in my little room, hidden among the diapers and the cans of formula. I go upstairs while she waits below in the car. I carefully place $4,000 in my sneakers and my passport and airline ticket in a garbage bag. Then I step out of my apartment into the hallway, with Christopher in my arms, guarding the garbage bag. As the door slams behind me, the lights go out in the hallway. It's entirely black. I make my way by touch to the emergency stairs. Then I hear someone running on one of the floors above me and wonder if this person has put out the building lights as a prelude to robbing those inside. I go down the thirteen flights as fast as I dare, terrified that I will fall and bash my new baby's head in. In the blackness I go past the lobby floor and end up in the basement garage, and I have to climb back up to reach the lobby. When I get out onto the street, there are so many people and cars that it takes me a while to realize that there are no lights out here either. I walk up and down looking for Oriola, not quite able to believe that

I am carrying all my valuables on the streets where I was told never to walk with more than a few dollars. In the blackness I fall into a hole, and as I cradle the baby's head, I recall having noticed the two-foot-deep potholes that riddle the sidewalks of downtown Lima. Presumably they housed gracious trees in earlier, elegant times.

Finally I give up on Oriola and respond to a stranger who is trying to explain what has happened to *la luz*. He leads me back from the street to a more protected area by the apartment building. His earlier approaches had frightened me, but now I see that he has been trying to help. I sit on the steps of the building in front of the iron gate, which has been locked during the blackout. I begin to wonder when the baby will get hungry and what I will do then. The Hotel Crillon will have milk but no bottles. Finally the lights come on, people cheer, the gate is opened, and we are allowed to go back upstairs. As I walk down the hallway toward our door, I hold the baby to me and tell him that we will make it through the rest of what Lima and life have to offer.

I open the door to a ringing telephone. It's Oriola, asking in an amused voice if I enjoyed my first terrorist blackout. She fills me in on current events. The Shining Path, the most powerful of Peru's terrorist groups, has recently become active in Lima. This night they attacked the power stations and threw out the lights in whole sections of the city. A bomb had exploded near my apartment building. Oriola had taken off for home in her car because there is a lot of theft and other crime on the streets during blackouts. Her cheerful amusement now is an example of the attitude that enables her to keep going in this city where life gets harder by the day.

The phone rings again, and it's Derek, calling from the United States. This is our first conversation since my arrival in Lima. I recount the key events of the past days. He sounds pleased to have a brother. I'm touched but almost puzzled to hear him say at the end, in a worried voice, "Take care of yourself." I'm on top of the world now, and finally ready to celebrate this new child. It is close to midnight, and I realize suddenly that I haven't eaten for most of the day. I search the kitchen for provisions. Later I sit in bed, chewing on a dry roll and sipping bottled water. I luxuriate in my good fortune.

During the next week we do a lot of adoption work. I will get a telephone call from Yvonne — "Come, in this moment we go." I'll rush, until I learn better, to fill my shoulder bag with the appropriate documents for the day, to pack up Christopher's food and diapers, and to wrap him in a blanket against the cold fog of Lima's winter. Then we're off to Yvonne's apartment to wait for an hour or so, usually with some assortment of adoptive parents and others dependent on Yvonne's grace. Finally we descend to the basement, climb into Bonnie's orange Volkswagen, and roar up the ramp to plunge into the crowded streets.

We visit the police station, where I'm fingerprinted and the baby is footprinted. A police doctor performs a physical "examination." He has an ugly look about him, and when he takes me off alone to an empty room with a table equipped with stirrups, I'm afraid. But all he does is sit me in a chair, question me about the state of my health, and ask to see any scars. In the company of three adoptive couples and their babies, Christopher and I visit a psychiatrist, who processes us in twenty minutes apiece, using much of his time with me to discuss his visits to the United States. The police pay a surprise visit to my apartment, as does a social worker. Initially I am at a loss as to how to deal with these visits without a translator, but I soon realize that my phrase-book Spanish is good enough for the level of investigation involved. I am puzzled when the social worker wants to count and examine the rooms in this temporary apartment and then am suddenly embarrassed at the appearance of what for bureaucratic purposes counts as my home. She must know that Christopher won't be living here in his adopted life, but she fills out her form, duly indicating the number and state of the rooms.

The adoption world of Lima begins to feel familiar rather

than terrifying. I become quite comfortable at the adoption court, a collection of wooden structures around a courtyard. I get used to mixing the baby's formula and feeding him there, in the midst of a swirling mass of dark-skinned Peruvian faces, interspersed with occasional white adoptive parent faces, watched over by the ever-present guards with their machine guns at the ready. I begin to think of these guards as people who are there to protect me rather than threaten me.

At week's end I feel that we must have made a lot of progress and the case will surely be completed in another couple of weeks. I don't realize that all we have done is play our part in the opening round of the adoption process. Now we'll wait for the various bureaucrats to play theirs. If we're lucky, they will produce the paperwork that will let us move on to the next round. And so it will go for two more months.

This same week I establish some control over my domestic life. I have learned to communicate with Roger (pronounced "Rohair"), who lives in a tiny room in my apartment and works for Yvonne as a law clerk and all-purpose assistant. He brings me matches for the gas stove, toilet paper from Yvonne's apartment, rolls to eat, and bottled water to drink. (It will be another week before I discover a grocery store in the area.) The Italian couple has moved out and left me their espresso coffeepot. I have obtained from Yvonne's household a cleaning rag and some powdered soap. I have cleaned the kitchen counters and laid out on them some of the baby clothes I brought with me that are too small for Christopher. They serve as drying surfaces for dishes. And I have moved from my dreary bedroom into the room vacated by the Italian couple, which feels palatial by comparison. I spend almost every minute that I'm not out doing my adoption work busy at my domestic tasks. I tend to the baby when he's awake. When he's asleep I make the formula, wash and sterilize the bottles, wash our laundry in the kitchen sink, and hang it to dry in the pantry. We have only a few changes of clothes, and it takes three days for them to dry in the cold fog that blows in the windows. (I have learned that the gray fog that greeted me my first morning in this apartment is all that Lima's winter has to offer. The sun simply does not shine for eight straight months.)

I am delighted with my new prowess, and I enjoy my domestic life. I talk occasionally to friends from the States who telephone, and as I get more organized I manage to find time to write home and to record pieces of my life in a journal I have started. These things help with the loneliness. But the nights are hard. There are only two table lamps in the large L-shaped space, almost bare of furniture, that is the living room. As the dark settles in, I find myself playing with Christopher in a small circle of light on the floor, and I feel very alone and anxious for the time to pass. Telephone calls are hugely exciting. Sleep is a relief.

The next week, my second in Lima, is dominated by Christopher's illness. When I first met him he had a slight cough. By now it's a regular hacking, deep in his chest. I'm sick too, and as the damp cold settles in at night I put my baggy black sweatshirt on over my sweater and still find myself shivering. On Saturday evening, August 17, I walk Christopher for hours, listening to him cough like an old man whose lungs are dying. I melt at the smile he gives between coughing spells. Late that night I call Oriola to see if Lima has such a thing as an emergency room that is open on weekends. There is one, so at least I know that there is a place to go if the baby gets worse during the night. As I walk, holding this coughing child, I'm conscious that this is my oldest brother's birthday and a former lover's wedding day. I'm convinced that I am doing what I want to do, but I feel that it shouldn't be so hard. I have visions of happy people in the sunshine, laughing and talking and hugging as they celebrate with friends and relatives back home.

We survive the night and go to the emergency room in the morning. The doctor says that Christopher has bronchitis and I have sinusitis. We're given drugs to take, and I'm sure things will now be all right. But four days later Christopher is still coughing, and I suddenly decide that he's looking worse, not better. His chest sounds thick with phlegm, and his breathing is ghastly. I wonder if the bronchitis has turned into pneumonia, and whether the doctor was right in thinking it was bronchitis in the first place. I don't trust the drugs we're using or the doctor who prescribed them or the country's system of medical care. I'm suddenly afraid, really afraid, that Christopher could die. I call Oriola in desperation. She assures me that she will talk to the doctor right away — she will have him paged at the hospital if necessary — and she promises to come that night after work to look at Christopher. She tells me that all babies are sick in Lima in the winter. It's the fog. He will be all right.

I hang up the phone persuaded that she's right, that Christopher will live, and tears pour down my face. And I realize that somewhere in these two weeks the falling-in-love process that I now think of as adoption has happened. I am Christopher's mother. It no longer really matters what goes on in the legal process or how long it takes. I won't let him go.

Later I watch him playing, smiling and giggling between coughs. I am the complete rationalist, with no religious or mystical leanings, yet I find myself wondering at the miracle that after all the years of wandering I found my way to this particular child, this one who was meant to be mine.

After two months of legal proceedings, I complete the adoption process and fly with Christopher back to Boston. Two years later we return to Lima to adopt Michael. I live through a new set of highs and lows. I experience the same kind of mysterious and magical connecting with this new and entirely different child. I live through another two-month adoption process and then we three return to our Cambridge home. Back in the United States, I spend the next years watching these children grow and thrive, reveling in my life with them. I also spend a lot of time thinking about how difficult society makes it for adults and children to enjoy this form of family, and wondering whether it could be different.

TWO

Parenting Options for the Infertile: The Biologic Bias[1]

SHAPING WOMEN AND THEIR CHOICES

Adoption is the choice of last resort for most infertile men and women who want to parent. If asked why this is true, many would say, "Because it is natural to want your own child."[2] But it is hard to know what is natural, given the fact that society weighs in to *make* adoption the last resort. And it is not clear that we should characterize parenting decisions as the product of choice. We are all conditioned from early childhood to equate personhood with procreation and procreation with parenting.

The fertile almost never consider adoption, and the infertile are unlikely to consider it until they have reached the end of a long medical road designed to produce a biological child. This road has lengthened as the medical possibilities have expanded. The infertile seem increasingly eager for what the medical experts have to offer. It is the *treatment* of infertility that has increased in recent years, not its overall *incidence.*" Visits to physicians for infertility services increased almost threefold from the 1960s to the 1980s, while infertility rates remained stable.[3] It is generally only after people have explored the possibilities for infertility treatment and either rejected or exhausted the various medical options that they give adoption serious consideration.

My own story is simply one example of how the biases built into the system help make adoption the last resort for so many. I went to doctors when, in my mid-thirties, I first began to fear that I had a fertility problem. I knew nothing about adoption at the time — or rather, I had the same collection of limited and inaccurate information that most people have. I "knew" that there were essentially no children available and that the waiting lists for any children who were available were impossibly long. I did not know whether single people could adopt, nor did I know any easy way to find out. I had heard a lot of horror stories about adoption, many of them involving the agencies that were supposed to arrange adoptions. And I had a lot of fears about adoption — fears of what I knew, of what I thought I knew, and most of all of what I didn't know.

I talked about my parenting options to no one except a tiny handful of friends and family members from 1976, when I started seeing fertility specialists, until 1985, when I flew to Lima for my first adoption. The pain and shame of infertility silenced me. It seemed natural to look first to the medical experts for help, since I was already in their waiting rooms and since my initial instinct was to repair my body so that it would again be capable of conceiving a child. Once on that medical track, I found it hard to get off. Repeated failures resulted in renewed determination to succeed. I had achieved other things that were difficult. I could and would achieve pregnancy, even against all odds.

In 1978 I sat in my paper gown on my fertility specialist's examining table for what I thought would be a final visit. Tests had demonstrated that the tubal surgery he had performed some months before had failed to repair my fallopian tubes. I was at the end of the existing treatment road. There was no such thing as in vitro fertilization in the United States and would not be for years. Through my tears I said that I had just read that the first IVF baby had been born as a result of an experimental program in Great Britain. I told my doctor that if by any miracle his hospital was able to develop an IVF program before my body had stopped producing eggs, I wanted to be first on the waiting list. He laughed, but I was not joking. He asked me what I would do now, and I said I was thinking about adoption and wondered if he could give me any help or advice. He said adoption really wasn't possible anymore. Massachusetts had outlawed private adoptions, and that was a good thing, too — all those young girls being pressured to sell their babies, what a terrible business that had been. He said adoption really didn't work out well, anyway — he knew some sad stories. And I was too old to be a mother. No, he really couldn't help me.

I began clipping newspaper articles on adoption, but I didn't find out much, and it didn't seem worth pursuing if I wasn't married. Interestingly, I had never hesitated about pursuing infertility treatment as a single, and none of the many doctors who had dealt with me had raised a question about it.

Against all expectations, IVF did become available in the United States within just a few years. In the spring of 1983 I was on the telephone to programs around the country, in search of one that would admit me and that did not have a prohibitive waiting list. I was almost forty-three and could not afford to wait. I begged my way into a program in Connecticut, and by the time that IVF attempt failed I had found a program in California that would admit me immediately. When I woke from anesthesia in California to discover that that attempt had also failed, I was able to fly home to enroll in a program in my home state of Massachusetts, which had decided to consider applicants from the over-forty age group. I felt lucky, as this was certainly more compatible with my work and other life. I settled into IVF treatment in earnest, and went through several treatment cycles in the course of the next year. In the nearly ten years that I struggled with infertility, I spoke to dozens of different doctors, nurses, administrators, and social workers in connection with a number of different treatment programs. I dealt with people who treated their patients like human guinea pigs, and I dealt with people who did their all to give nurture and comfort. No one ever asked me to think hard about what I was doing and why. No one ever advised me to seek counseling to deal with my feelings about infertility. No one ever suggested that I consider adoption as an alternative to further treatment, or proposed ways to find out more about adoption. All of this was entirely understandable. These were medical programs, and the people involved thought in medical terms. They were working to press beyond the frontiers of knowledge and make it possible for the patients knocking down their programs' doors to achieve what they desperately wanted to achieve: pregnancy.

But in the summer of 1984 I finally did take some steps on my own to explore adoption seriously. I called adoption agencies, obtained their brochures, attended their general information sessions, and became involved with a support group called SPACE — Single Parents for the Adoption of Children Everywhere. I took an adult education course called "Building Your Family through Adoption." I sought out people who had adopted. And I broke the rules by starting the home study process, the process by which adoption agencies determine whether applicants satisfy their criteria for parental fitness. A cardinal requirement is that applicants demonstrate that they have "resolved" their feelings about infertility. By definition, you haven't resolved your feelings about infertility if you are still involved in treatment to reverse the condition. But I didn't see how I was going to sort through my feelings about infertility and parenting, or understand whether I wanted to be an adoptive parent, without taking some more steps to understand what adoption might mean for me. The logical steps to take included working with the agencies that were in the business of putting together adoptive families. Therefore I was prepared to tell the agencies what I had to in order to start the home study process. As a result of these exploratory steps, I developed for the first time some sense of what adoption was about.

And then I got lucky. I ran out of money. IVF treatment was excluded from health insurance coverage during this period, and I had cursed my fate and timing, as it seemed likely that the exclusion would eventually be eliminated. I had been paying the going price, $5,000 for a full treatment cycle. I had about run through what savings I had.

I woke one morning in March 1985 — I learned later that it was the month, and for all I know the very day, my son-to-be was born — and lay in bed thinking that I didn't want to use up my remaining funds on IVF. I would need them if I was to adopt. And I didn't want to use up any more time and energy or any more of my life on the fertility pursuit. I wanted a child, and I wanted to move on. I called my IVF program that day and said that I was not going to go forward with another treatment cycle.

I was one of the lucky infertility patients, because I *did* move on to adoption and to parenting. Treatment enables only a limited number of the infertile to conceive and bear children, and it helps prevent many from ever considering adoption as a form of parenting. By the time people exhaust their treatment options, many who might once have been interested in adoption do not have the will, the energy, or the resources to get through the many barriers that society puts in the way of becoming an adoptive parent.

I now look back in amazement at the person I was, traversing the country from one IVF program to another in search of an infertility fix. I am bemused at my shifting notions of the "natural" and of "choice." It had seemed to me natural to pursue biologic parenting, even when the pursuit led me into the high-tech world of IVF, where the doctors and lab technicians largely took over the business of conception, "harvesting" the eggs that they had cultivated in the woman patient's body and inseminating them in glass dishes. It had seemed also that I was choosing when I made the decisions to move on to new stages of treatment. Indeed, I had felt thrilled with the sense that I was pushing against the social and biologic constraints that prevented a single woman with damaged fallopian tubes from giving birth. Now I look back and see a woman driven by the forces that had told her since birth that she should go forth and multiply, that her ability to bear a child was central to her meaning as a human being, and that "real" parenting involved raising that biologically linked child.

THE INFERTILITY PROBLEM

A staggering number of people suffer from infertility. Surveys indicate that in this country, close to five million women (or their partners) have "impaired fecundity," meaning that it is difficult, impossible, or dangerous for them to achieve pregnancy and childbirth. Roughly one in seven of all couples trying to conceive are unable to do so.[4] Many say that these surveys underestimate the problem. The pain the infertile suffer has been documented in numerous studies and anecdotal accounts.[5] For many the discovery of infertility cuts to the very core of being, destroying their sense of self-worth, and indeed of self. Although men and women share almost equally in the responsibility for couples' inability to conceive, it is the women, overwhelmingly, who have given voice to their suffering. In a better world, women would not experience infertility as a devastating disfigurement and the destruction of sexual identity, but in this world, many do. It is women who bear the brunt of infertility treatment efforts. There is still not much that the doctors can do for male infertility problems. It may also be that men would not subject themselves to the burdensome and intrusive forms of treatment that women endure in the interest of conceiving and bearing children.

The infertile are potentially a significant resource for children in need of homes, but at present only a limited number of them adopt.[6] Society drives the infertile away from adoption and toward efforts to reproduce with a wide array of conditioning mechanisms and regulatory structures.

MAKING ADOPTION THE LAST RESORT

The medical profession has a near-monopoly on the information given out as people discover their infertility and explore and exercise options. When people who have been trying to have a baby realize that something may be wrong, they usually consult their family doctor or their gynecologist, and then, if they can afford it, a fertility specialist. The specialist educates them about the range of treatment possibilities and, if they are willing and financially able, begins to lead them down the treatment path. A couple may start with temperature charts and scheduled sex and move on to fertility drug treatment. They may then decide on an exploratory laparoscopy, which can reveal pelvic adhesions on the woman's fallopian tubes. Tubal surgery may follow, and then tests to see whether the tubes remain open. If the woman still does not become pregnant, the couple may explore and pursue IVF or related high-tech treatment methods.

This treatment scenario has become a common one, and as people move through it, their chief advisers at every step are likely to be doctors. The advice doctors give is inevitably biased toward the treatment option. Doctors think of it as their job to know and advise about the various medical possibilities. Few see it as equally their job to explore with patients why they are considering medical treatment, whether continued treatment efforts are worth it, or when enough is enough. Fewer still see it as their job to help patients work through the advantages and disadvantages of treatment as compared with parenting through adoption. Doctors once played a major role in helping infertile patients connect with pregnant patients interested in surrendering their children for adoption. But the specialized fertility experts in today's treatment world have little interest in or knowledge about adoption.

It is only in the IVF programs that any form of counseling is apt to be provided as part of the treatment process. However, IVF counseling has generally been designed to serve the needs of the IVF programs, with a view toward screening out problem patients. In the better programs, counseling may provide some understanding of the nature of the IVF process and of the chances for success, but it is extremely unlikely to provide any opportunity to explore feelings about infertility or alternatives to treatment.

The adoption world does essentially nothing to reach out to the infertile to educate them about adoption possibilities. Indeed, adoption agency rules operate to push the infertile away and thus to prevent them from obtaining the information they need to consider adoption at an early stage. The accepted ethic among adoption workers is that prospective parents must resolve feelings about infertility before they pursue adoption. The idea behind this makes some sense: people *should* try to understand their feelings about infertility and grieve over any loss that that infertility represents before they become adoptive parents. They should not enter into adoption thinking of their adopted child as a second-best substitute for the biologic child they still ache to produce. But it may be impossible to know what part of the pain of infertility relates to a desire to parent, and whether this desire will be satisfied by adoption, without knowing what adoption is about. An understanding of adoption may thus be essential to resolving feelings about infertility. Adoption agencies are potentially one of the best sources of that understanding. It is in completing the various steps of the application process that the infertile are likely to get a real comprehension of the specific options available as well as of their own feelings about adoption. However, if they admit to any real doubts about adoption or to any ongoing concerns about infertility, they risk getting an unfavorable rating at the end of the home study process. Many who think that they might be interested in adopting will conclude that the appropriate course is to start the home study process only after they *know* they are ready to adopt.

There are some organizations and support groups, such as Resolve, that are designed to provide information and counseling to the infertile. But they have limited resources and influence, and so far appear to be reaching limited numbers.

So the information package that is being handed out to the infertile is biased in the direction of medical treatment. The problem is exacerbated by the fact that those receiving the package have little independent basis for understanding their options. The stigma associated with infertility means that those affected rarely discuss their problems openly. Many talk only to their doctor. Many are reluctant to be seen at public sessions where they might learn about adoption.

Other factors contribute to the medical tracking process. The infertile are bombarded with messages that reinforce the idea that it makes sense to consider adoption, if at all, only as a last resort. They are lured into IVF by aggressive advertising, characteristic of the free market world in which medical treatment takes place. They are simultaneously pushed away from the adoption world by negative messages from myriad sources telling them that adoption is an inherently inferior form of parenting.

The infertile can, of course, obtain meaningful information about adoption if they are sufficiently persistent. But many will not have the time, energy, and determination to find out enough about both the treatment and the adoption possibilities to truly understand at an early stage what their options are.

* * *

If the infertile do manage to get accurate information about their various parenting options, they find that our society gives vastly preferential treatment to people seeking to produce children rather than those seeking to adopt.

First and foremost, those seeking to reproduce operate in a free market world in which they are able to make their own decisions subject only to financial and physical constraints. Those seeking to adopt operate in a highly regulated world in which the government asserts the right to determine who will be allowed to parent.

As a result, those seeking to reproduce retain the sense that they are normal rights-bearing citizens. No one asks them to prove that they are fit to parent. They are perceived as having a God-given right to reproduce if they are capable of doing so. Those in the business of providing infertility services do not see it as their role to regulate access to parenting. The IVF practitioners who made the initial decision to exclude singles from their programs did so in large part because in an era when IVF treatment was highly controversial, the risk-averse course was to limit services to married couples. But IVF programs never enforced their rules excluding singles with the moral fervor typical of the adoption agencies, as my own experience illustrates. Today, as the IVF treatment industry has become more established, many programs are beginning officially to open their doors to singles.

Those entering the world of adoption agencies and home studies quickly realize that they have no right to become adoptive parents. Parental screening is the essence of what traditional adoption is all about, with the government determining through its agents who should be disqualified altogether from the parenting opportunity and then how those who are qualified should be rated for purposes of allocating the available children. There are no privacy rights in this world, either. The entire point of the home study process is to find out whether the most intimate events and relationships of a person's life have produced someone fit to parent. It is true that there are significant differences between the screening process in agency adoptions and that in independent adoptions. Prospective adopters with enough money can buy their way around the traditional agency home study process. But many who would like to adopt do not have this kind of money, and even in independent adoptions, the government demands at least some minimum showing of parental fitness.

The parental screening requirement is a very real deterrent to many who might otherwise consider adoption. People don't like to become helpless supplicants, utterly dependent on the grace of social workers, with respect to something as basic as their desire to become parents. Screening also adds to the financial costs of adoption. Because it takes time, prospective parents must endure the related delays in forming a family. Screening turns the process of becoming a parent into a bureaucratic nightmare in which documents must be endlessly accumulated and stamped and submitted and copied.

Regulation also sends a powerful message about the essential inferiority of adoption as a form of parenting. By subjecting adoptive but not biologic parents to regulation, society suggests that it trusts what goes on when people give birth and raise a birth child but profoundly distrusts what goes on when a child is transferred from a birth to an adoptive parent. The specific nature of adoption regulation constantly reinforces the notion that biologic parenting is the ideal and adoption a poor second best. Adoptive families are thus designed in imitation of biologic families. Prospective parents are screened because as adoptive parents they are suspect. They must be carefully matched with the right children because of the assumed risk that adoptive parenting won't work out. Ideally, they should be matched with the kinds of children they could have produced. And so forth.

Society also discriminates in financial terms, giving preferred treatment to those who choose child production over child adoption.[7] People covered by health insurance are reimbursed for many of the costs involved in infertility treatment, pregnancy, and childbirth. Although insurance plans have so far typically not covered IVF treatment, the trend is in the direction of expanding coverage to include it.[8] Treatment and childbirth expenses that are not covered by insurance are tax-deductible if they exceed a certain percentage of income. By contrast, those who adopt are generally on their own in paying for the adoption, and only limited subsidies are available for those who adopt children with special needs.[9] There is no equivalent to insurance coverage for the expenses involved in adoption, nor are those expenses generally deductible for income tax purposes. Employment benefit policies also favor child production over adoption. Employers that provide health insurance and childbirth leave usually do not provide equivalent benefits for those who become parents through adoption.

This discussion only begins to touch on some of the many ways in which society demonstrates its support for biologic parenting and its suspicion of adoptive parenting. We have been conditioned from birth to believe that we should be fertile and should reproduce. Women are taught from birth that their identities are inextricably linked with their capacity for pregnancy and childbirth and that this capacity is inextricably linked with mothering. We are all bombarded on a daily basis with messages that childbirth is infinitely better than adoption as a route to parenting.

CORRECTING THE BIAS

It makes no sense for a society that thinks of itself as sane and humane to be driving people in the direction of child production rather than adoption. It makes no sense for the children out there — those who have already been born and who will grow up without homes unless they are adopted. A sane and humane society should encourage people to provide for these existing children rather than bring more children into the world.

It makes no sense for the adults out there, either. Of course the infertile are begging for treatment, and of course those who manage to produce a child will say it has all been worth it. But they have been conditioned to feel that pregnancy and childbirth are the only solutions to their problem. Those who give birth are not in a position to know what they would have done with the years they spent in doctors' offices or what the experience of parenting an adopted child would have been. And most people who go down the treatment road will not succeed in producing a child. A recent government report estimates that only about one half of those who pursue an extensive series of treatment programs, including tubal surgery and two IVF cycles, will produce a child.[10] Of those who do not, some will move on to parent through adoption. They will often ask themselves later why they wasted all those years on the treatment treadmill. But most of the unsuccessful infertility patients will never become adoptive parents. Many will find that after years of struggling to conquer infertility, they are too old, or too tired, or too poor, or too broken in spirit, to begin another uphill battle, and that of course is what adoption is. Many people are in their late twenties or early thirties by the time they discover they have fertility problems, and in their late thirties or early forties by the time they have exhausted their treatment options. This is old in the adoption business, and while adoption may be possible, it is much more difficult than it is for people ten years younger. The choices are more limited, and more money and time and effort are needed to pursue them. Those who have been through years of infertility treatment may still want to parent but have nothing left with which to fight for that privilege.

So we need to correct the biologic bias to give children a better chance and to give adults more genuine choices. Many forces at work today seem designed instead to exacerbate this bias — to push the infertile ever more forcefully away from adoption and toward reproduction. There is, for example, significant hostility to transracial and transnational adoption, the forms of adoption that involve the great mass of children who need adoptive homes. The adoption search movement, involving adopted persons and the birth parents who have relinquished children for adoption, has focused new attention on the alleged problems of the adoptive family. Search movement advocates argue that biologic links are of central importance to parenting, and that all parties to adoptive arrangements suffer by virtue of the break in genetic continuity that infertility and adoption represent. This new negativity helps make adoption additionally suspect, both for individuals making life choices and for a society making policy decisions. At the same time, the technological possibilities in infertility treatment have exploded, and this means that there is a somewhat greater chance for the infertile to produce a biological child. It also means that they may spend their entire adult lives trying. So for most women with damaged fallopian tubes, the treatment road that used to end with tubal surgery can, with the advent of IVF, go on for many years more. The increasing availability of insurance exacerbates the problem. Having to pay upwards of $5,000 per IVF cycle has functioned as a significant brake on the IVF industry. The infertile are likely to pour into IVF programs in huge numbers if insurance pays the bills. Once in, many will find it hard to make the decision to get out. The treatment process has its own momentum. The sense of inadequacy that makes the medical route appealing in the first place is reinforced by every failure. The fear that you may have wasted yourself and your life becomes greater as the investment becomes greater, and feeds the compulsion to keep going.

We need to shift directions. The project is daunting, since it involves restructuring our understanding of infertility and of parenting. But some pieces of the project are easy to identify.

We need to make counseling available on a widespread

basis to those suffering from infertility, so that early in their struggles they can begin to deal with feelings of loss and inadequacy, can try to unravel what part of their pain, if any, relates to a desire to parent, and can begin to puzzle out what parenting is and should be about. We also need to make meaningful information about various parenting options available early, so that they can gain some real understanding of what it would mean to pursue infertility treatment and what it would mean to pursue adoption. The counseling and the information should come from groups that are not tied to or part of any medical establishment. We need to create new support organizations for the infertile. Adoption agencies and organizations should become much more active in outreach efforts.

We also need radically to reform the regulatory system that structures adoption. When the infertile *do* get an accurate sense of their options, adoption should not look like such an uphill struggle. We need to change our laws and policies so that they facilitate rather than impede the process of matching people who want to parent with children who need homes. And we need simultaneously to question current practices that push the infertile to pursue treatment.

In the remaining chapters I give a more concrete sense of what seems to me to be wrong with the way we are now shaping people's understanding of parenting. I contrast adoption's degraded status with my own vision of adoption as a positive family form. And I suggest some ways in which we might think of restructuring adoption and other parenting options.

THREE

Adoption: Tales of Loss and Visions of Connection

THE CHILD WHO HAD TO BE RETURNED

I am in the hallway waiting area of Inabif, the Peruvian government agency through which I adopt Michael. I am waiting to go to Viru, a shelter for children whose biologic parents cannot care for them.

I first met Michael ten days ago at Viru, bundled up in a blanket with only his tiny, four-week-old face visible. I took him home the next day to the apartment in suburban Lima that I rented for this second adoption. Within twenty-four hours I found myself tearing through the streets in a taxi, mopping his feverish body with a wet cloth and terrified, as I saw his eyes lose contact with mine and begin to stare off into the middle distance, that he would die in my arms before we got to the emergency room. At the hospital he was wrapped entirely in a wet towel and his feet were placed in a pan of ice water. I watched the puzzled but surprisingly cheerful little face that peered out from the monkish hood the towel formed about his head, while we waited for two hours as his temperature slowly came down. Sometime during that taxi ride, or in that hospital room, I became hopelessly attached. I fell entirely in love during the next few days, as I nursed him back to health and watched the first winsome smile light up his still weak face as he lay on his blanket on our sofa, looking at me.

I am now engaged in what will be an eight-week process of legalizing our bond, our connection. This process of making him "my child" as a matter of law will be an agonizing one, in large part because of the threat that this person who already feels like part of me will be taken from me. By law he still belongs to his birth parents, and to the Peruvian adoption system.

I am to go to Viru today to deliver to its director a copy of the court order granting me provisional custody of Michael. Obtaining this order the day before was a triumphant moment and gives me some assurance that things are at least temporarily on track. I wait at Inabif for my social worker, since she will have to escort me to Viru. One always waits at Inabif, sometimes for an hour or two, sometimes for longer. The waiting area is a short, wide hallway, with three doors leading to adoption agency offices and one leading to a police department office. Others who are seeking to adopt are almost always waiting also, sitting on the benches lined against the walls or standing. Having left Michael and Christopher back in the apartment, I spend the time as I usually do, talking to the other adopters, hearing their stories, commiserating with some, advising others, and above all trying to pick up clues to help me through this process: What judges are known to give trouble to foreign adopters or to singles? What problems have others had working with my social worker?

I approach a woman who is holding an infant, and I begin my usual round of questions for someone I take to be relatively new to the adoption process, since I have not seen her here before. How old is your child, is it a girl or boy, how long have you had him or her? These are the fun conversations. These women have a now familiar new-adoptive-parent glow about them. But when this woman looks up, her eyes are sad and pained, and she shakes her head, saying nothing. I retreat, not daring to violate her private sorrow but puzzled and curious. She doesn't look the part of a birth mother here to relinquish her child for adoption. She is dressed too well, is accompanied by an apparent husband, and does not look Peruvian.

My social worker, Maria, finally emerges from her office and rattles out something in Spanish, gesturing to indicate that this woman and I should come with her. Another woman and the husband follow as we go down the steps and past the police guards at the entrance, to squeeze into a tiny gypsy cab for the trip to Viru. (I am relieved to find we are actually going there as planned, since at least half the times I go to Inabif it turns out that, for never-explained reasons, whatever was supposed to happen on my case that day will not happen.)

In the taxi I discover that the second woman is Peruvian and speaks Spanish. She is there to help the couple, friends of hers from Italy, who are here in Lima to adopt a child. They speak only Italian. I am able to talk to their Peruvian friend as I have by now developed a modest ability to communicate in Spanish. I started this second adoption trip with only the survival Spanish I picked up during the first adoption, supplemented by a few language classes in Cambridge. But the Inabif adoption process has proved a good school. Inabif permits no lawyer intermediaries, so I have to work directly with the agency personnel and the various other bureaucrats involved. They speak only Spanish, and Inabif's one translator is rarely available to me. With the help of the pocket phrase book and pocket dictionary I brought with me, and constant practice sessions with the taxi drivers who drive me about town for my various adoption-related appointments, my Spanish has improved enormously. When the price for not understanding or not being able to express yourself can be a misstep that means the loss of your child, the incentive for learning to communicate is high.

The couple's friend tells me that they were assigned this six-week-old girl eight days ago and took her home to live with them, but yesterday they were told that they would have to give her back. The reasons have not been made clear to them, and there are many possibilities. Some legal complication may have developed, meaning that the child cannot be freed for adoption. The birth mother may have changed her mind. But I have learned by now to be suspicious of these stories about adoptions that have to be called off, children that have to be returned. In many cases the only problem is that someone in the system has not received a "gift."

This couple has been told only that the child they have is no longer free for adoption and that when they return her they will receive another. The new child will also be a girl. The exchange is to take place today.

I look at the woman and child crowded next to me in one of the ancient Volkswagen taxis that fill Lima's streets. The woman's eyes are fixed on the child's face. The baby is dressed perfectly, with attention to every detail. She has white lace-edged socks and pink satin shoes. A traditional Peruvian lace band is set in her jet-black hair. The woman pats dry each spot of sweat on the child's face with a soft cloth. The sadness is overwhelming.

At Viru, I deliver my court order and we stand around waiting for whatever will happen next. We are in a bare courtyard surrounded by one-story office structures and slightly taller buildings that house the children. The Italian woman sits down on a bench with the baby, apart from the rest of us. She offers a bottle of water. She pushes a few stray hairs off the baby's forehead.

Feeling that I should not watch her pain any longer, I turn away and notice a group of very young children being led single file from a building across the courtyard to an opening in the wall that separates us from a smaller courtyard. The children go through while the adult in charge returns to the building. I wander over to look through the opening. The

dusty courtyard holds a few broken swings and a few working ones, one broken tricycle and one that looks functional.
There are large mudholes in the swing area, full of unpleas-
ant-looking water. The children look to be from three to six
years old. There is no older person in sight. I watch as some
kids wander aimlessly and others laugh and run about. I
fantasize about taking one or two of them home with me, if
someone would just say the word.

Screams draw my attention to a chase, and I see one of the
bigger kids knock a little one flat, sit on him, and begin to
punch him. I stand immobilized, afraid that if I step in I will
get in trouble with the authorities who still control Michael's
fate. Another child runs up, pulls the big one off, and lifts the
little one to his feet. The little one walks off to sit, still sobbing,
on one of the deserted swings.

I turn back to my group in the first courtyard, thinking
about what it does to children to grow up policing themselves
in the courtyard of Viru. I think of the many people I have met
who would be ecstatic if they could take one of these children
home. I wonder why there seem to be no efforts to find
adoptive homes for children like these. I learn later that most
of the children at Viru, like most children in foster care in our
country, are not technically free for adoption. Many have birth
parents who may never visit and have no apparent capacity to
function as parents, but who have not taken the formal steps
necessary to free their children for adoption. Some may not
want to lose their children entirely. Others might simply not
have been asked to give the matter any thought.

As I approach my former companions, I notice the woman
clinging to her husband, weeping into his shoulder. He holds
on to her, his face buried in her hair. The baby is nowhere in
sight.

After a few moments we are motioned into an office. More
time passes, with the woman still quietly weeping. Then a
Viru attendant walks in with a blanketed infant, which she
places in the woman's arms. The woman uncovers the face

and we all look. It is another adorable six-week-old face, perfect and serene in sleep. The woman covers it and sits expressionless. An hour later, after various bureaucratic procedures have been completed, we crowd into another Volkswagen taxi for the return to Inabif. The child's face remains covered the entire time, except for once or twice on the bouncy taxi ride when she cries and the woman does what she needs to do to stop the crying. She will undoubtedly connect eventually, but now is too soon. She is still mourning.

I saw other adoptive parents in Peru lose the children they had come to think of as theirs. Until I climbed on the plane with Christopher and Michael for the flight home, I lived in fear that this might be my experience. Although I did not get to know any birth parents, I heard stories of the women who surrender the children they have carried for nine months — stories of women weeping softly in the courtroom where they formally relinquish their children, swearing that this action is voluntary and uncoerced. Most of these women have no good options. Keeping the child may mean loss of their job as a live-in maid, or loss of their man, or another mouth to feed in a family that lives with hunger. There are also stories of the pleasure that some women seem to take in the life they are giving their child, as they look at him or her cradled in the arms of the eager parents from the faraway, mythical land of opportunity.

Adoption stories are stories of connection, loss, and new connection. They are stories filled with tragedy that need not be. We could do more to prevent the initial losses and to facilitate and nourish new connections.

A VISION OF ADOPTION'S POTENTIAL

Adoption as we know it often arises out of situations of loss and destruction, sadness and despair. The birth parents who surrender or abandon children generally feel forced to this action by circumstances that range from problematic to devastating. The nations that send children abroad for adoption are generally Third World countries convulsed by poverty and violence. The children themselves start their lives with the loss of the parents who would normally provide essential love and nurturance. Many suffer significant deprivation in their early lives. Many are marked by disability, illegitimacy, or race as outcasts in the societies into which they are born. Many of the people who become adoptive parents have experienced the loss represented by infertility. Often they have spent years reexperiencing that loss as they pursue fruitless treatment efforts.

These tragedies, like others, hold the potential for transformation and rebirth. Adoption can give birth parents a chance to gain control over their lives. It can open up a future that might include pregnancy and parenting experiences for which they will be prepared. In the meantime, adoption enables them to provide their child with the kind of nurturing home that they are not now in a position to offer. Adoption can give the infertile the parenting opportunity they have ached for, as well as a new perspective on the meaning of their lost fertility. Adoption can give children the love and nurturance they need to heal any early wounds and to flourish.

Adoption can also stimulate some new thinking about family and community. Adoptive families are by definition families linked not by blood but by intended parenting and a social commitment that crosses bloodlines. Often these families are built across lines of racial, ethnic, and national difference as well. The law of adoption focuses on the potential negatives, building on speculation about what might go wrong in families not based on biology, but the evidence indicates that in fact adoptive families work very well. We might learn a great deal by focusing on the potential *positives* in adoption, speculating about what might go particularly *right* in these families, and why.

Since like many adoptive parents I experience unique positives in the adoptive relationship, I now look at the "normal" family from this perspective and ask questions I never used to ask. Why, for example, should biology be considered as determinative of parental rights as it now is? Why should it be so hard to remove children from abusive parents? Why should the privacy of the biologic family be so sacrosanct?

These questions occur in part because adoptive parents have to earn the chance to parent. While much in the parental screening process seems to me wrong, the notion that parenting is a privilege and not a right seems appropriate.

These questions occur also because adoptive relationships have a more contingent quality than the traditional biologic family. Adopters become parents to particular children as a matter of conscious choice — choice that might not have been made. By contrast, those who give birth tend to experience the parenting of their children as a given — a natural and inevitable relationship. Adoptive families know that there is another set of parents, whether they are dead or alive, whether they are known to the adoptee or not. Adoptees can choose whether or not to pursue their biologic or ethnic roots, whether and to what degree to try to relate to birth relatives or countries or cultures. In some societies adoption is designed so that they can choose to return to their birth families if life in the adoptive family becomes unsatisfactory. Students of these societies say that both adoptive and biologic family relationships are conceived of as far more fluid and flexible than in our society.[1] My postadoption self wonders whether children in our society might not be better off if parenting relationships here were more qualified by choice and subject to change, with children encouraged to form a broader range of intimate connections and empowered to opt out of bad relationships.

Adoption separates the biologic from the nurturing part of parenting. For adoption to work for the various parties involved, the nurturing aspect has to be understood as central to the meaning of parenting. Adoption pushes us to ask questions about whether our society has structured parenting in a way that gives appropriate recognition to nurturing.

An adoption perspective stimulates other questions about parenting norms. Why do we think of it as extraordinary and not ordinary to love as "our own" children born to others? Why do we consider it "unnatural" for a woman to surrender a child for others to raise if she is not prepared to parent and they are? In some societies, those who can become pregnant feel an *obligation* to consider giving the child they produce to others who want to parent but cannot produce their own.[2] In the African American community and in many societies in other parts of the world, there are strong traditions of shared parenting within an extended family group, and informal adoption is common.[3]

Adoptive parenting by definition involves the parenting of children who are not "us" but "other." It leads us to think more deeply about how much "normal" parenting relationships suffer from assumptions that "our own" children will or should look like us or like better versions of ourselves.

Adoptive families can teach us something about prejudice and discrimination. Many of those who seek to become adoptive parents are single, older, or disabled. Many are gay or lesbian. The adoption system discriminates against all these groups but nonetheless permits some of their members to parent children for whom no other homes are available. The studies indicate that these adoptive families function very well. We might learn to question some of our assumptions about what makes for good parenting if we took a closer look at these families. Many of the children who are available for adoption are from racial minority groups, and many have severe mental or physical disabilities. Large numbers of these children are adopted by white middle-class couples, who make up the vast majority of the waiting adoptive parent pool in the United States. The studies indicate that these families function very well also. We might learn something about our capacity for community if we took a closer look at these families, whose members seem to be successfully transcending racial and other differences.

We could structure our laws to recognize adoption's positive potential as a family form and to make it work to expand life's potential for birth parents, their children, and the people who want to parent. At present we seem to be doing just the opposite.

A SNAPSHOT OF ADOPTION'S REALITIES

Our society's current laws signal adoption's inferiority to the biologic family and proclaim the dangers allegedly inherent in raising children apart from their birth families. Almost all the rules are designed either to ensure that a child is not improperly removed from the biologic family or that a child is not placed with an inadequate adoptive family. There are no rules, or at least none with any teeth, that give children a right to a nurturing home or that limit how long they can be held in limbo.

Our laws design adoptive families in imitation of biology. The central symbolic event is the issuance of a new birth certificate for the child and the sealing of the old certificate, together with other adoption records. The goal is to ensure that the birth parents, the child, and the adoptive parents can all proceed with their new lives as if the child had never been born to the original parents. The clear implication of this "as if" model of adoption is that adoption is an inferior and not quite real form of family which can at best aspire to look like the real thing.

The central legal event in adoption is issuance of the adoption decree, which completely severs the legal relationship between the child and the birth family, transferring to the adoptive family all rights and responsibilities. Legally as well as symbolically, it is as if the child were born to the adoptive parents. This promotes a rigid separation of the birth from the adoptive family, reinforcing notions that the true family is the closed nuclear family and warding off as much as possible any sense that adoptive relationships might be more contingent and less proprietary than traditional parenting relationships.

The "as if" adoption model produces parental screening policies that confirm traditional prejudices. The home study process favors married couples who look as if they could have produced the child they will adopt. It tends to screen out prospective parents who do not fit traditional notions of what parents should look like; among those disqualified or ranked at the bottom of eligibility lists are singles, older parents, gays and lesbians, and people with disabilities. The rules for matching waiting children with prospective parents are designed to maximize sameness and avoid what is seen as dangerous diversity within families. Originally the goal was literally to match — to give prospective parents children with similar physical features and similar mental characteristics, so that the parents could pretend to the world and even to the child that this was their biologic child. In addition, the idea was (and to a great degree still is) that adoption has the best chance of working if the child is as much like the parent as possible. After all, how can you expect a smart parent to relate to a not-so-smart child, or a musical parent to relate to a baby jock? What would happen to the talented child in a family of pedestrian minds? In today's adoption world, the matching ideal has given way significantly to reality: there are relatively few healthy babies in this country to match with the mass of eager prospective parents. But interestingly, traditional matching principles are very much alive with respect to race. Powerful policies in force throughout the nation restrict adoption across racial lines, reinforcing notions of the importance of racial barriers.

Our adoption system has failed to live up even to its own limited vision. The promise to serve children's best interests and to provide them with at least a rough imitation of a biologic family has never been taken seriously. Laws and policies that are supposed to protect children have created barriers to adoption that function effectively to prevent children from getting the kind of protection they most need — a loving, nurturing, and permanent home. Scratch the surface of the system and it becomes obvious that adults' interests regularly trump children's. The system's rules proclaim that parents must be screened for fitness and that money cannot be used to obtain children, because children should not be treated as property to be sold to the highest bidder. But the reality is that prospective parents with money can and do bypass the screening system to obtain the children who are thought to be most desirable. The reality is that children *are* treated as property, owned by their biologic parents and their racial, ethnic, and national communities. Many children grow up in foster and institutional care because we are reluctant to cut the biologic cord so as to free them for adoption, even in situations where there is little hope for a viable life with their birth family. And children abandoned by their biologic parents are claimed as the property of particular adult communities and openly spoken of as national or community "resources," to be disposed of in ways deemed to serve the community interest.

FOUR

Adoption and
the Sealed Record System

"I'M GOING TO GET ANOTHER MUMMY"

When Christopher had been with me in the United States for
about a year, I decided to adopt again. I had raised Derek as
an only child, and this time around I wanted the experience
of family that involved more than one child. Derek was certainly still part of the family, and he and Christopher had
developed a wonderful relationship, but he was grown and
away in California at college.

The decision to go back to Peru for this second adoption
was an easy one, despite the predictable difficulties. Peru was
familiar territory now, and I had come to love the country and
had made some close friends during my months there for
Christopher's adoption. Also, I figured that it would be good
for Christopher and his new sibling to have Peru in common.

I was due for a term off from teaching at full salary. I
decided to use this sabbatical for the second adoption so that
I would not have to worry about trying to schedule the Peruvian part of the process to fit into my summer vacation. I

arranged to fly to Lima with Christopher after my fall classes ended, just in time to spend Christmas in Peru. Derek was on a bicycle trip in Latin America, having taken the fall term off from college, and he would meet us there for Christmas. Then I would start the second adoption. I had scheduled my sabbatical for the spring of 1988, so was not due back at the law school until the fall.

During the weeks before we were to leave I tried to prepare Christopher, who was now two and a half years old, for the experience of having a new sibling. I told him that we were going to Peru to find a baby to adopt to be his brother or sister. We talked a lot about the "teeny little baby" we would find and how Christopher would help take care of it. He seemed happy enough about the prospect, and would cup his hands to show how big the baby would be, indicating something about the size of the school guinea pig. We talked about how much fun the baby would be and how Christopher would feed it a bottle.

Two nights before we were to go, I was reading Chris a story in his bedroom. When I finished, I kissed him goodnight and started to walk away. His voice stopped me as I reached the door: "Mom. When we get to Peru, I'm going to get another mummy." I experienced instant panic. He was already thinking of the dreaded "other mother." For him, going to Peru meant having the chance to find her. How was I going to deal with this? What should I say to him? I wasn't ready for this conversation.

In the next second I realized that I had misinterpreted. He was too young to understand that there really was another mother, even though I had told him that he was adopted. He was simply afraid that he was going to lose the mother he had to this new child who was coming into our lives. His way of dealing with that fear was to tell me that he would get another mother, just as I was going to get another child. Surely this was what was going on.

Much relieved, I sat down on his bed and talked to him

about how much I loved him and always would, and how there was plenty of love to go around, and there was no way in which he would lose out on love just because this new child was coming into our lives — all the usual messages of assurance that parents give when new siblings are on the way. We talked more about the teeny little baby whom he would help take care of and who would grow into a playmate. He listened and he let me leave the room.

The next night, our last before flying off to Peru, I read him another story, kissed him goodnight, and reminded him that I would be waking him up at dawn to go to the airport. As I reached the door his voice called out: "When we get to Peru, I'm going to find a teeny little mummy."

Adoptive families live with the reality that there is another mother, another family. The question is how to understand that reality. Should the birth mother be seen as "the real mother," and as such a threat to the parent-child relationship established in the adoptive family? Should she be locked away as part of the adopted child's no longer relevant past, or sought out and invited to participate in his present and future life? Or should she be recognized as a real but somewhat distant relative, who might be of no more than historic importance to the child but might also be a source of significant connection and comfort?

My own experience over the years of living as part of an adoptive family has made me less fearful of that other mother, readier to open the door to her presence in our lives. It has also made me think about the role that closing out the birth family plays in creating the sense that the birth mother *should* be seen as a threat to the adoptive mother — in conditioning our belief that the ties that bind are ties of blood.

TRADITIONS AND TRENDS[1]

The tradition in this country through most of this century has been to sever all links with the birth family when the adoptive family is formed. The court creates a new parent-child relationship between the adoptive parents and the adoptee and simultaneously seals the records that document the transfer of the child from the birth to the adoptive family. The child is issued a new birth certificate, which reads as if he or she had been born to the adoptive parents. The original birth certificate goes into the sealed file. For legal purposes the child is effectively reborn, with all legal and relational links to the past destroyed. The sealed records are supposed to ensure against any reconnection with that past. Members of the birth and adoptive families, along with the public, are denied access to them. The adoption agencies cooperate by keeping confidential any information that might enable birth families to figure out where their children have gone and adoptive families to figure out where their children have come from. The records are sealed not simply for the duration of the adoptee's childhood but permanently, to be opened only on a showing of "good cause," which is generally defined as a demonstration of overwhelming necessity.

Societies in other times and places teach that adoption does not need to be constructed this way. The sealed record tradition is actually short-lived in the history of adoption as an institution. In early Roman times, adoption was for a period designed as an open relationship in which the adoptee knew and would inherit from both the biologic and the adoptive parents. In many societies today adoptions are arranged informally among the private parties, with the government taking no action to sever or to redefine parental links.[2] In the United States, adoptive arrangements were similarly informal until the latter part of the nineteenth century, and it was not until the 1920s that states began to pass laws designed to separate birth and adoptive families. Informal adoption continues to flourish in many communities in the United States today, as children are transferred on a temporary or long-term basis from one parental figure to another within a kinship or community network.[3]

The sealed record system stands in significant contrast to the manner in which our society structures other complex family relationships. It is no secret that relatively few families today fit the nuclear family image on which the adoptive family is modeled — the stable husband-wife couple raising their children on an ongoing basis to the exclusion of any other significant parental figures. Some children are raised in this kind of family, but most are raised by single mothers or divorced parents, either alone or in combination with some succession of mates. The legal system ordinarily makes no attempt to write out of existence, by sealing records or other such mechanisms, the various parental figures who walk out of their children's lives, such as the divorced parent who relinquishes custody. It is only in regulating adoptive families — families formed in the absence of any blood link — that the government feels that it has to seal records so as to figuratively destroy the existence of the family that *is* linked by blood.

The trend in this country is quite clearly in the direction of greater openness. The push for change is coming primarily from adult adoptees and birth parents — usually birth mothers, since birth fathers are rarely heard from. The openness proponents, together with their self-help and advocacy organizations, constitute what is known as the search movement. They have focused attention on the problems they see as inherent in the sealed record system and on the importance they attribute to the search that enables birth parents and adoptees to connect with each other.[4] The changing adoption market has also enabled many birth mothers who want openness to insist on it. The enormous demand for infants to adopt means that birth mothers can do a lot to establish the terms on which they will surrender their children, and many have been pushing for more openness.

This move has resulted in recent years in some changes in the legal framework governing adoption. A few states have enacted legislation that gives adult adoptees an absolute right to access to their original birth records. Most states have enacted some kind of mutual consent system for releasing identifying information (naming the parties) to birth parents, adoptive parents, and adoptees, once the adoptees have reached the age of eighteen or twenty-one. As of 1991, more than thirty states had such legislation, with some states opting for passive registry systems, in which the various parties to the adoption can register their consent to or interest in contact, and others opting for active registry systems, in which the state facilitates a process for finding out whether the relevant parties will consent to a desired contact.

In addition, a significant amount of *de facto* openness has developed. Many birth mothers have been using their new bargaining power to obtain varying degrees of openness, ranging from a simple exchange of identifying information to elaborate agreements for ongoing correspondence and visitation. Also, search movement organizations have developed the search methodology to a fine art, enabling large numbers of adoptees and birth parents who want to locate each other to find their way through and around the sealed record rules.

A burning issue in today's adoption world is whether to move any further in this direction. Nearly everyone agrees on the importance of providing adoptive families with what is categorized as nonidentifying information about the birth family: health, genetic, and social information. But there is no consensus on where we should go from here with respect to identifying information. The National Committee for Adoption, an organization of adoption agencies that constitutes a powerful lobbying force, is adamantly opposed to any significant deviation from the sealed record system. It has gone along with proposals for passive mutual consent registries, but these registries have been notoriously ineffective in enabling adoptees who want to make contact with their birth families to do so.

The sealed record system continues to stand as a significant barrier between the birth and the adoptive family in most adoptive arrangements. Records continue to be sealed on a permanent basis as part of the adoption process. Almost all states deny the adult adoptee and the birth parent any access to the records unless the other party has consented, and some states require consent by the adoptive parents as well. Few states have created effective systems to assess whether birth parents or adoptees would consent if they knew their counterparts were interested in obtaining information or in arranging for a meeting. Most state and state-licensed agencies continue to arrange adoptions on a confidential basis and refuse to open up the records that would permit birth and adoptive families to get in touch with each other.

THE CURRENT DEBATE

The debate over the future of the sealed record system is fierce, with the opposing advocates at one another's throats. But the themes sounded on both sides of the debate are strangely similar: biologic links are of vital significance to parenting; adoption is a flawed institution, and the families that it creates are both flawed and fragile.

For search movement advocates, the idea that biology is central to parenting is a reason for openness. They argue that adoptive families built on secrecy, on a denial of the birth family's existence, are sick at the core. They contend that adoptees who are cut off from knowledge of their biologic heritage suffer "genealogical bewilderment." They advocate the search for the birth family and what is called the reunion with that family as the road to recovery for today's adoptees and birth parents. They advocate elimination of the sealed record system and greater openness in communication between birth and adoptive families as the road to a healthy adoption system in the future. For many people in the search movement, openness is only a partial solution to the adoption "problem." They contend that the biologic link between parent and child is so important that the very institution of adoption should be eliminated or at least radically altered. They argue that birth mothers should not be put in situations that force them to surrender their children, and urge that society make greater efforts to preserve biologic families. In situations in which the birth family absolutely must relinquish day-to-day custody, they believe that guardianship arrangements should be substituted for adoption, so as to preserve a legal parenting link as well as an informational link with the birth family.[5]

For adoption traditionalists, the centrality of the biologic link is a reason to maintain the closed record system. They take a more positive view of adoption, arguing that it makes sense in many situations for birth parents to surrender their children for others to raise. But their claim that sealed records are essential to make adoption work reveals a similar sense of suspicion of the arrangement. They argue that sealed records are needed to protect the privacy of the birth parents, to enable the birth mother to put the past behind her and move on to a new life. They argue that sealed records are also needed to protect the privacy and integrity of the new adoptive family, preventing the confusion inherent in the existence of another set of parents and protecting the adoptee from unpleasant revelations about the circumstances surrounding his or her birth and surrender. Implicit in these arguments is the sense that there is something deeply shameful in giving birth to a child that one is not prepared to raise and in the decision to surrender, and that there is something very threatening to adoptive families about the existence of blood-linked relatives.

THE MIXED MESSAGES INHERENT
IN A MOVE TO OPENNESS

For those who believe in adoption as a valid family form, the sealed record system should be deeply problematic. Sealed records and the creation of a new birth certificate mean that adoptive families are founded on a lie — a claim that the original birth never took place and that the adoptee was instead born into the adoptive family. Implicit in the lie is the assumption that the adoptive family is in fact a flawed and inferior family form. If it was as good as the biology-based family, there would be no need to lie. If it was permissible for birth mothers to relinquish children they felt unable to raise, there would be no need for them to seal off their past. If the parent-child relationship in the adoptive family was as powerful and legitimate as other parenting relationships, there would be no need to seal the adoptive family off from threats that birth parents might appear on the scene to usurp the parenting role.

Greater openness seems a good move from this perspective. Adoption should be understood as a positive alternative to biologic parenting, not as a desperate last resort, either for birth parents or for the infertile. Adoptive families should be understood as healthy, functioning families, not as fragile entities that will fall apart if a "real" mother walks in the front door. The attempt to erase the birth family is destined to place adoptive families on the low end of a family hierarchy. Greater openness would free people to see that adoptive families are not simply viable but hold some special strengths as a family form.

Of course, greater openness might be thought to create a threatening sense of difference for adoptees as they grow up — a sense that there is something wrong with their family because, unlike other children, they have this other family to think about. But *most* children today grow up with a changing cast of characters playing various parenting roles as the years go by, with single parents living with some combination of relatives and friends and mates and with birth parents divorcing and moving out as stepparents move in to share or dispute parenting functions. In today's world, it is not at all clear that the sealed record system functions to reduce the adoptee's sense of difference. In fact, by treating the adoptee's extended family network so differently from other children's, the system seems to signal that there is something uniquely problematic and shameful about the particular complexity that has to do with adoptive status.

All this argues for reversing the current presumptions about identifying information. At present we seal adoption records and allow parties to the arrangement to obtain the information only upon a demonstration of good cause. We should move to a system of open records and allow the parties to request closure upon a demonstration of good cause.

While greater openness seems the appropriate move for the future, the politics of adoption today make decisions about what steps to take *now* very complicated. In the current context, a move to embrace openness might further denigrate rather than affirm adoption. The pressure for openness is coming from a movement that is profoundly hostile to adoption as a family form. In addition, today's world is one in which we are all bombarded on a regular basis with messages that reinforce the significance of biologically linked parenting. In this world birth parents *are* something of a threat to the viability of adoptive families. In a future world in which the stigma surrounding adoption and infertility has been eliminated or at least significantly reduced, opening records should send a signal that birth family links are real and relevant but not of necessary and central importance to an adoptee's personhood or to parenting relationships. The establishment of an open-record system today might send a very different signal.

Complicated issues also arise in thinking about just how powerful the connection between birth and adoptive families should be in any new regime of openness. It seems right to structure adoption as an independent family form rather than as a poor imitation of the biologic family in its idealized nuclear form. But freeing ourselves from the traditional model forces us to think about what should be central to the concept of family. We might want to embrace the idea of openness with respect to *information,* creating a system in which birth and adoptive families are free to know each other and to establish relationships throughout the adoptee's childhood as well as in adulthood. But we might reject any notion that birth and adoptive parents should share *control,* or attempt to divide the legal rights and responsibilities of parenting. By ridding ourselves of the notion that adoption should be designed to duplicate the biologic nuclear family, we would be forced to think about which aspects of that family model we want to appropriate and which we want to reject. We would be forced to think about the ways in which adoptive families should be similar, as well as the ways in which they should be different.

My idea of what an open regime would look like is quite different from the vision implicit in the claims of the search movement. If there were open access to birth records, I do not see most adoptees rushing to make contact with birth relatives. If identifying information were shared from the point of the adoption on, I do not imagine that there would be more than limited communication between adoptees and their birth relatives in most instances. But I may be wrong. Openness means that more ambiguity and contingency would be built into the adoptive situation. In some cases, the biologic relationship might prove important or even predominant. It might prove more generally important than I now think would be the case. But parenting should not imply that the parent owns the child's affections or has a right to exclude alternative relationships.

FIVE

Adoption and
the Parental Screening System

ON BEING SCREENED FOR FITNESS

It is the summer of 1984, a year before I will leave for Peru for my first adoption, and I am on my way to an informational meeting sponsored by SPACE — Single Parents for the Adoption of Children Everywhere. I need information, but I dread going. I imagine a group of seriously dreary and strange people sitting in the church basement meeting room toward which I am headed, and find the prospect of two hours in that setting hideously depressing. Single people are not supposed to adopt, and I know not one who has. I have only recently learned that it really is possible for me to adopt, and it still feels like a freakish thing to be doing.

I see myself as neither dreary nor particularly strange. I am conscious that I am indeed quite conventional in my desire to enlarge my family, although perhaps unusual in my determination to achieve that goal. I am a woman who has had one child and has always wanted and assumed I would have more. I spent my twenties in the marriage that produced this child but eventually did not work as a marriage, and my thirties and early forties exploring various relationships with men, none of which seemed to make sense for marriage and children. From thirty-five to forty-four I tried to get pregnant anyway, through natural and then increasingly high-tech methods, and I am still in the throes of in vitro fertilization treatment. I am taking what seems like the logical next step by exploring adoption possibilities.

But while I am aware in some abstract sense that there is a rather large group of women out there with similar desires and frustrations, I am convinced that no one at all like me will be in that room. Adoption is a foreign and off-putting world.

In the church basement I discover a roomful of people with fully familiar human characteristics. Betsy Burch, the director of SPACE, introduces us all to the world of singles adoption. She is a wonderfully cheerful, down-to-earth person who exudes warmth, good nature, and common sense. She talks about her own adoption of two black children from foster care, the obstacles she encountered in adopting them as a single white person, and how she made it through the system. I begin the process of finding out how I will be able to adopt.

In the next six months I read several how-to books on adoption and take a course on the subject at the Cambridge Center for Adult Education. The course is taught by Judy Bailey, mother of thirteen adopted children, most of whom came from foster care and several of whom suffered serious neglect or abuse in their early lives. She tells us stories designed to warn us about the kind of adjustment problems that can occur in the adoption of older children. She tells how one of her children, on the first night he came home, stabbed her husband in the chest, necessitating a visit to the emergency room, and how another, on his first night home, threw her recently adopted infant twins down the stairs. She gives us an enormous amount of information about how to pursue an adoption. In our last class she passes around some family photographs, filled with toothy grins and shining faces, and tells us of her children's current accomplishments in school. She wishes us well and asks us to call her when we adopt a child ourselves, so she can "light a candle in her heart" for that child. It is unlike any course I have taken.

I become part of the network of adoptive parents and potential adopters and learn how essential this network is as a source of information, assistance, and support. I spend dozens of hours with strangers, on the phone and in their living rooms, hearing their stories and playing with their adopted children. Adoption begins to seem less foreign. I can now imagine myself as an adoptive parent.

I develop a sense of how this adoption world works — how it categorizes me and how I can maneuver within its strictures. I realize that for the first time in my privileged life I am seen as having something other than a stellar set of credentials; indeed, by the objective criteria that count in the adoption world, I am ranked near the bottom of the barrel. My single status and my age will be considered the most important things about me in assessing my fitness as a parent. My apparent success in raising a child will be nearly irrelevant. Since I am able-bodied and heterosexual, I will not be disqualified altogether; instead I will be placed at the low end of the prospective parent list.

However, since I have some money, I will be able to buy my way out of the system to a significant degree. I am not limited to the public adoption agencies, which would consider me only for the hard core of hard-to-place children in foster care, typically teenage children with extremely serious disabilities. Although I cannot easily afford it, I can imagine paying something in the range of $10,000 to $12,000 to arrange an adoption. This means that if I want to adopt an infant or a young child, I will be able to. I can shop among the private agencies and among the lawyers and other intermediaries who arrange independent or nonagency adoptions to find people who are willing to place such a child with someone in my category. I can pay the domestic and foreign agency fees required for an international adoption, and I have learned that there are many infants and young children in other countries in need of homes and free for adoption. Many of these countries have adoption systems that screen out singles and those over forty, but some will permit me to adopt.

I do not have the range of options that I would have if I had more money to spend. Many agencies charge $20,000 to $35,000 to arrange an adoption, and prospective adopters can end up paying much more than that if they have to pursue a variety of paths before finding one that works for them, as is often the case. But I have at least some options, and I am lucky to live in Massachusetts, which has a relative wealth of different adoption agencies as well as parent support organizations such as SPACE and ODS, the Open Door Society.

I do not feel prepared to adopt a child with serious disabilities, and I want the experience again of raising a child from infancy. I cringe at the prospect of entering the heavy-duty competition of the independent adoption world, pedaling my résumé around the country in an effort to appeal to birth parents and beat out others scrambling for the limited number of U.S.-born babies. International adoption seems appealing by contrast, because there appears to be an actual need for adoptive parents. I begin to fix on the idea of a child from Latin America, a descendant of the Indian peoples who built the fabulous lost cities and fashioned the golden treasures that I have heard about since childhood.

With the help of my books and my advisers, I begin to concentrate on adoption agencies that are sympathetic to singles and experienced with Latin American adoptions. Simultaneously I learn how to shape my life story for the home study process, by which the adoption agency I select will assess my fitness to parent. The rules of the parental screening game apply not just to such objective factors as age and marital status but to subjective assessments of my capacity to love and nurture an adopted child. I will be required to fill out a form inquiring into details about my childhood, my relationship with my parents, my former marriage and divorce, my current romantic and sexual life, and any other aspect of myself that is thought to be relevant to my parental fitness. The rest of the process involves interviews with the person I will call my social worker, who will explore the same issues. The home study is crucial to my prospects. At the conclusion a report will proclaim me fit or unfit, screen me in or out for the agency's purposes. Assuming that I am screened in, the home study will affect how the agency will treat me — how helpful it will be, for example, in finding a particular child for me to adopt.

I learn that it is important to have had a happy childhood and a good relationship with your parents and siblings. I learn that there are appropriate and inappropriate reasons for wanting children: you don't want them out of need, but neither do you want to rescue them. I learn that I must have resolved all my feelings about infertility: I must have recognized my grief and loss but moved through those emotions to acceptance, and of course I must have given up pursuing any kind of infertility treatment some time ago.

I learn some of the special rules of the game for singles. I must have powerful links with members of my extended family, so that they can provide backup support and the ever-important male role models for my child. My work must be emotionally satisfying (so that I don't seek all my emotional satisfaction from this child) and provide financial stability, but it must leave me free to spend the first six months after the adoption at home with the child, and it must leave me significantly free thereafter for a parenting role in which I will have to make up for the absence of a father.

The rules regarding the single's sexual life and appetites are particularly tricky. I must above all demonstrate my heterosexuality. Gays and lesbians are considered presumptively unfit by most adoption agencies in the United States, so it is important to demonstrate a healthy interest in the opposite sex. But I should not be running about with a variety of men. Promiscuity is bad. However, involvement in an ongoing exclusive relationship with a man raises immediate questions as to where the adopted child will fit in and what the future of the relationship with this man will be. In my adoption course at the Cambridge Center for Adult Education, one participant was troubled about what to do with her long-term live-in lover and intended husband. They had been together for seven years, always planning to get married when they got to the point of having children. They were now at that point but had discovered that she was infertile. They wanted to adopt but were not sure whether to formalize their relationship in a marriage first. As we talked through their dilemma with our adoption-wise teacher, it became clear that rather than getting married, this couple needed to separate, since newly married couples are even more disadvantaged than singles in the adoption world. If they were serious about adoption, she should apply as a single, and since a live-in lover is generally unacceptable in the home study process, he should move out. He could of course move back in at some later point, since once a placement is made the system rarely removes a child.

I have always been a good student. I study the system conscientiously and learn my lessons well. Then I write the story of my life. It is a lovely story. Although it necessarily contains many problematic features, such as my parents' divorce and my own, the heroine emerges unscathed and indeed leads a truly blessed existence. The divorcing parents did not destroy the fabric of her nine-year-old life but managed to function even after the divorce as nurturing role models. The professionally fulfilling career she developed has landed her miraculously in a tenured (read entirely secure) job at the Harvard Law School, a job that actually requires her presence in a classroom only a few hours a week. Yes, she needs to put in additional hours in some really quite interesting professional activities, but it is extraordinary how much flexibility there is and how much time will be free for child-rearing responsibilities. The heroine is perceptive enough to recognize that there have been some really hard spots in her life that *could* have interfered with her development as an emotionally fulfilled person and prospective adoptive mother, but she has worked through her feelings about divorce and infertility and emerged wiser and more committed to parenting than she might otherwise have been. She has of course long ago fully resolved her concerns about infertility, as well as all doubts and anxieties about adoption. She stands at the end of the home study story, glowing with readiness for the experience of adoptive parenting.

Several months after submitting my application, I emerge from the home study process with a favorable report. It is now the spring of 1985, and in March I decide to withdraw from my IVF program. I am as ready as I figure I will ever be for adoption, short of actually plunging down that path. However, I am still filled with doubts and anxieties as I take the plunge and begin the process of finding the particular child who will be mine.

I have received no real help from the adoption agency in resolving my feelings about infertility or in thinking about the issues involved in being an adoptive parent. The whole point has been for me to suppress anything that might complicate the process of arriving at a determination that I am parentally fit. I will get no real help in locating a child, either. When the agency's adoption program in Brazil collapses, I will be penalized for my uppity attitude in trying to find out whether it will ever reopen and for taking steps to implement an alternative adoption plan. When I fly off to Peru, I will have to sign a piece of paper absolving the agency of responsibility for anything that may go wrong. By the end of my two adoptions, I will have paid the agency $6,500 for the original home study and $4,500 for the home study update required for the second adoption. These fees are only the beginning. In Peru I will have to spend five more months and many more thousands of dollars having my fitness to parent further assessed before becoming the legal adoptive parent of Christopher and Michael.

When I first became pregnant during my long-ago marriage, I was deemed to have a sacrosanct right to parent. Whatever struggles I may have had with my marriage, and whatever doubts I had about its future, were considered entirely my private business. During the years that I sought infertility treatment so that I could produce another child, no one asked me to demonstrate my fitness to parent. It was only when I sought to parent an already existing child produced by others that the government stepped in, asserting that I must understand that I had no rights whatsoever to engage in this form of parenting and that if I was even to be considered for the privilege, I must humble myself before the bureaucrats and demonstrate my fitness according to their rules. The theory is that the best interests of the child demand the screening of adoptive parents, but this makes sense only if you think that there is something deeply suspect about parenting a child born to another. Why would anyone think that those who consciously plan to adopt someone else's child pose more of a risk than those who fall unwittingly into pregnancy? What real threat do adoptive parents pose to children who cannot in any event be raised by their biologic parents — to children who are being raised by foster families or in institutions or on the streets?

One night in Peru I have a dream about this adoption world. In my dream there is an enormous barricade made up of rocks and rubble topped with walls and fences. A mass of people crawl all over it. Some are hard at work building bridges and tunnels and roads that will enable people to cross over. Others are hard at work destroying bridges and blocking tunnels and building new fences and piling rocks on the roads. At the bottom of the barricade on one side are some others selling their services to eager adoptive parents. And on the far side are thousands of children.

I was able and willing to go through the adoptive process.

For many, the financial and emotional barriers to adoptive parenthood — barriers created in large part by the screening system — are simply too high.

ASSESSING THE SYSTEM'S FITNESS

Screening for parental fitness is a basic part of the agency adoption process. Both public and private agencies conduct home studies designed to assess eligibility for adoptive parenthood. The process also determines the ranking of prospective parents for purposes of child assignment; that is, it determines which parents will be considered for which children within an agency's jurisdiction.[1] As discussed later in this chapter, home studies are not part of the independent adoption process, in which birth parents place their children with adoptive parents either directly or through an intermediary.[2]

Defenders of the home study system claim that screening assesses such important qualities as the capacity to love and nurture an adopted child. They also claim that the child assignment, or "matching," process involves sophisticated judgments as to which particular parent-child combinations will work best. But the fact is that the screening and matching system is extremely crude and quite inconsistent with its alleged purposes.

The system ranks prospective parents from top to bottom in terms of relative desirability, which is assessed primarily on the basis of easily determined objective factors. These factors reflect the system's bias in favor of a biologic parenting model as well as a socially traditional family model. So heterosexual couples in their late twenties or early thirties with apparently stable marriages are at the top of the ladder. These are the kind of people who could, if not for infertility, produce children, and who should, in the system's view, be parents. Single and older adoptive applicants — those in their late thirties and forties — are placed lower on the ladder, along with people with disabilities. Gays, lesbians, and the seriously disabled are generally excluded altogether.[3]

Although social work practices reflect changing social realities, they tend to lag a generation or so behind. Bureaucratic rules take on a life of their own. Entrenched policies take time to reverse, and the bureaucratic mentality is averse to risk: the safe path for an adoption agency is to select parents on the basis of accepted models. Single adoptive parenting was essentially unheard of until the mid-1960s, when forty children were placed in single parent homes by the Los Angeles Department of Adoptions.[4] Many adoption workers continued to treat single-parent adoption as highly suspect, and questioned whether singles should be found eligible to parent even those children who would not otherwise find adoptive homes. As late as 1969 a respected adoption expert found it necessary to defend single-parent adoption as "not inherently or necessarily pathogenic."[5] The fact that a large percentage of all children in our society were being raised by single parents took decades to sink into the bureaucratic mind and to have an impact on adoption practices.[6]

The adoption screening system ranks and categorizes children waiting for homes, as well as parents, in order to decide how to make particular parent-child matches. The children are placed on their own desirability list, with healthy infants at the top, somewhat older and less healthy children next, and the oldest and most seriously disabled children at the bottom. Children are also classified according to racial, ethnic, and religious heritage.

In matching children with parents, the system operates primarily on the basis of what looks roughly like a market system, one in which ranking produces buying power. The most "desirable" parents are matched with the most "desirable" children, and the less desirable with the less desirable, on down the list. The "marginally fit" parents are matched with the hardest-to-place children, which often means the children with the most extreme parenting needs and demands.

The matching system also demonstrates deference to a biologic model of parenting. As I have noted, in earlier times agencies made a significant effort to give prospective parents children as closely matched as possible in looks and temperament to the birth children they might have had. While this philosophy has been tempered in recent years by virtue of necessity, it still governs with respect to those attributes deemed most important. Older parents are often precluded from adopting children more than thirty-five or forty years younger than themselves on the ground that they would not have been likely to have produced such children themselves. Black parents are given black children, and Catholic parents are given the children surrendered by Catholic birth parents.

Discrimination is thus the name of the game in adoptive parenting. Those who procreate live in a world of near-absolute rights with respect to parenting. Those who would adopt have no rights. They must beg for the privilege of parenting, and do so in a state-administered realm that denies them both the right to privacy and the "civil rights" that we have come to think of as fundamental in the rest of our communal life. Differential treatment on the basis of age, race, religion, and disability has been outlawed in almost all areas of our lives. Increasingly, the law forbids discrimination on the basis of marital status and sexual orientation. It is only in the area of adoption that our system proudly proclaims not simply the right to discriminate but the importance of doing so.[7] It is not just the prospective parents who are treated shabbily but also the children, in whose best interests the system is supposedly designed. They are categorized in terms of their marketability, with the "undesirables" handed off to those deemed marginally fit to parent.

THE ROLE OF MONEY

The parental screening system applies only to those who do not possess the money to buy their way around it. Prospective adopters with money can escape all but minimal screening. They can also exercise extensive choice among the children available for adoption, and it is they who are most likely to end up adopting the healthy infants who are most in demand. The more money prospective adopters have, the greater their ability to shop around and escape the strictures of the system.

Without money, you are limited to the public adoption agency system, which deals primarily with the children in foster care and applies the classic screening and matching criteria. With money, you can venture into the private adoption agency world, where a great variety of screening systems are used and a much larger proportion of healthy infants and young children are available. Some private agencies screen and match according to the classic home study criteria, but others are much more sympathetic to nontraditional parents. Still others are willing to place children with virtually all adoptive applicants who satisfy minimal criteria. Prospective adopters can shop among the private agencies and select the one most sympathetic to their personal profile and most likely to provide the kind of child they are looking for. Fees vary significantly, with the agencies that are most open to nontraditional parents tending to charge higher fees.

Money also gives access to the world of independent adoption, which accounts for roughly one third of all nonrelative adoption in this country. Here home studies are not required at all. Some intermediaries and some birth parents apply their own screening criteria, and nontraditional parents have a harder time adopting than young married couples do. But many of those who place children in the independent process do little or no screening, and those who are more selective have a wide variety of views on what qualities they are looking for. A great many parents who surrender infants at birth are attracted to independent adoption, so prospective adopters with enough money to explore the possibilities are able both to avoid classic screening and to find their way to a healthy newborn. The state subjects these parents to only the most minimal scrutiny in the court process that formalizes the adoption. Even when a postplacement home study is required, its purpose is to determine whether the adopter satisfies minimum fitness criteria, not to decide whether he or she ranks high enough to be assigned a particular child, as is the case in the agency process.

Independent adoptions are allowed in all but a handful of states. Even those states that outlaw them as a formal matter and require home studies prior to adoptive placement permit a form of adoption that enables those with money to bypass key aspects of the screening system. In what are known as identified adoptions, prospective adopters are allowed to find their own child as long as they satisfactorily complete a home study before taking the child home. Since they can generally exercise some choice as to who will do the study, and since they will not be compared with other potential adopters, they must satisfy only minimal standards for parental fitness.

Judged in terms of the very values it purports to serve, the screening system fails. Together with the rule against baby-buying, parental screening is supposed to ensure that children are assigned not to the highest bidder but to those deemed most fit to parent. The fact that money enables those deemed least fit to buy their way to the children who are most in demand makes a farce of the entire system.

LIMITS OF THE CURRENT REFORM DEBATE

The current debate about parental screening consists largely of a war between home study advocates, on the one hand, and independent adoption advocates, on the other. Adoption agency traditionalists promote the view that independent adoptions should be outlawed, or at a minimum regulated in ways that would make them look more like agency adoptions. In particular, they say, preplacement home studies should be required so that those who find their own children are at least screened for parental fitness before they take any child home to live. A number of recent reform proposals take this position,[8] and there seems to be popular support for calls to restrict the independent adoption "market." Any adoption scandal — a baby-selling ring, child abuse by an adoptive parent — is likely to trigger demands by public leaders and the media for laws and regulations that clamp down on independent adoption. However, this approach to reform is generally premised on the assumption that more regulation of the kind we already have is a good thing, that the current adoption agency model is a good model, and that parental screening systems function in a positive way.

Independent adoption advocates focus on the flaws in the agency model. They condemn some of the social biases inherent in the traditional screening process and note the absence of any evidence that screening actually succeeds in identifying superior parents. They also point to a variety of benefits associated with independent adoption: more services for the birth parents, more potential for communication between the birth and the adoptive parents and for other forms of openness in the adoptive arrangement, and earlier placement of children. But those who promote the advantages of independent adoption tend to ignore the question of whether it is *appropriate* to have a separate, "better" system, available only to parents with money, for the distribution of healthy white infants who have been siphoned off from the adoption agency system. If the agency system isn't working well, the appropriate solution involves restructuring that system rather than simply permitting those who are financially well off to bypass it.

Some voices have called for changes in the agency screening criteria, arguing, for example, that agencies should be barred from using such factors as age, marital status, religion, disability, and sexual orientation as the basis for categorically excluding certain groups from adoptive parenthood.[9] Some have proposed that agencies be required to screen in all applicants who satisfy a minimal fitness standard, excluding only those who are found demonstrably unfit.[10] But there is no consensus that this is the appropriate direction in which to move. In any event, these proposals would do little to change the essential nature of today's screening and matching system, which functions primarily not as a device to disqualify adoptive applicants but as a method to allocate available children to the parents deemed most desirable. Few groups are excluded as unfit, and a decision to include as minimally fit those who are now significantly excluded would mean little, since the system would place them at the bottom of its hierarchically ranked fitness lists. Reform proposals that have as their goal real changes in the system must take on not simply the eligibility cutoff determination but the entire ranking and matching setup.

AN ALTERNATIVE VISION

We now place an extremely high value on the right to procreate and the related right to hold on to our biologic product. We place no real value on the aspect of parenting that has to do solely with relationship. There is an essentially absolute right to produce a child, but there is no right to enter into a parenting relationship with a child who is not linked by blood — no right to adopt. Foster parents, stepparents, and others who develop nurturing relationships with children are deemed to have no right to maintain such relationships.[11] They and the children who may have come to depend on them are subject to the whim of the blood-linked parent. Such parents, in contrast, have enormous proprietary power over their children. Even in situations of serious abuse and neglect, the government is reluctant to interfere with parental rights. Children have essentially no rights and no entitlements, although the system is supposed to operate in their best interests. Everyone knows that their best interests require nurturing homes and parenting relationships, but it is painfully obvious that children have no enforceable rights to those things.

We could flip this rights picture, upend this hierarchical ranking of values. We could place the highest value on children and their interests in growing up in a nurturing relationship. We could place a higher value on nurturing than on procreation, and we might choose to do so in part because it seems to serve children's interests in being parented. A less radical step would be to accord at least more significant value than we now do to the nurturing aspect of parenting.

Any such revision of parenting rights and responsibilities would lead to a very different view of the role that adoption agencies should play. It would seem obvious that their primary function should be to create parent-child relationships — to find homes for children in need of nurturing parents, and to find children for adults who want to nurture. In this new world, agencies would become adoption advocates. They would commit themselves to finding a home for every child who cannot be cared for by his or her birth parents. They would reach out to find these children and the adults willing to parent them. They would encourage people dealing with infertility to consider adopting an existing child instead of undergoing treatment designed to produce another child. They would encourage those capable of procreation to consider adoptive or foster parenting instead. They might devote some resources to screening out those who are demonstrably unfit to parent, but they would be conscious of the importance of not creating barriers that would discourage people from providing homes to existing children in need. They would recognize the extensive evidence demonstrating that children are better off in permanent homes than in institutions or foster care. Their respect for adult interests in enjoying parenting relationships would make them reluctant to impose any screening requirements that do not seem necessary to protect children.

ELIMINATING THE CURRENT SCREEN

Quite obviously, this vision would mean abandoning the system of parental screening and matching that we know today. All who want to become adoptive parents would be presumed fit.

We could create a parental licensing system based on a minimalist screening principle to disqualify those found demonstrably unfit, for such reasons as a past history of serious and persistent drug or alcohol abuse, prior child abuse, apparent incapacity to provide for a child's most basic needs, serious ill health, or advanced age. Such a licensing system might be politically essential, to assure people that adoption would not result in the kinds of abuses that occurred in the nineteenth century, when some children were turned over to families who saw them as a form of cheap labor. It might also be essential to assure foreign governments and agencies that children they send to the United States for adoption will receive adequate homes. But the standards for assessing minimal fitness should be adapted from those used to decide when children can be removed from blood-linked parents. They should be similar to the standards we would use if we were to impose a licensing requirement on those seeking to procreate.[12] Any such licensing scheme should be applied to all adoptive applicants. Money should not enable anyone to bypass the screening deemed essential to children's protection.

We would scrap the more extensive screening that goes on today. Adoption workers would get out of the business of ranking parental quality and lose their power to determine which kinds of children should be allocated to which kinds of parents. Prospective parents would make their own decisions as to which kinds of children to apply for and would be served on a first-come, first-served basis. Adoption workers would facilitate matches. They would seek to accommodate the interests of birth and adoptive parents as well as the interests of those children old enough to express their own preferences. They would offer all parties advice and counseling designed to further appropriate matches and to maximize the success of adoptive relationships. But they would not have the power to play God by deciding who should be allowed to parent or what kind of child they should be assigned.

Today's form of parental screening and matching would be understood as inconsistent with the new value accorded to the relational aspect of parenting. We would not dream of telling fertile people that they have no right whatsoever to produce a child — that childbirth is a privilege to be allowed or not at the entire discretion of the government. We would not dream of telling pregnant people that when they give birth, the government will decide whether they can keep the child on the basis of whether a social worker thinks that the child looks like a good match for their particular parenting profile. We would be horrified if the government tried to deny the right to procreate to those over forty, or to the physically handicapped, or to singles. Even the kind of minimalist licensing scheme I have suggested would strike most people as outrageous and presumptively unconstitutional if it were to be applied to biologic parenting.[13] Indeed, recent proposals to encourage welfare recipients to use contraceptive devices are condemned by many as interfering unduly with the right to procreate, as are proposals to force contraception on convicted child abusers.[14]

Parental screening in the adoption area has always been justified as necessary for the protection of children. But children have much to gain and little to lose from scrapping the system.

WHAT CHILDREN HAVE TO GAIN

One thing children have to gain is what they most need — homes. The current screening and matching system creates barriers that prevent many potential parents from adopting. Some cannot afford the expense, and others are unwilling to endure the indignities, of the home study process. Still others are driven away by the seemingly endless bureaucratic requirements, or by the uncertainty about whether at the end of the process they will be permitted to parent. Others are actually precluded from adopting because they do not satisfy the screening criteria applied by the kinds of adoption agencies that they can afford. The current screening and matching system also diverts energy that agencies could spend on locating children in need of homes and reaching out to recruit adults who could provide those homes.

Another thing children have to gain is parents who are prepared to parent and to deal with any special issues involved in adoptive parenting. The home study process is supposed to provide education, counseling, and preparation. Applicants are encouraged to explore issues that might interfere with good parenting and to discuss concerns about their infertility or anxieties about adoptive parenthood. They are supposed to consider honestly what they are looking for in a child and what kinds of children they would find it difficult to parent. They are told to think hard about how they should deal with issues involving their adopted child's birth family and racial or ethnic heritage.

These issues *should* be explored by those contemplating adoptive parenthood. The problem is that agencies cannot do a good job of education and counseling in the context of a process that simultaneously is functioning to screen and match. Most adoptive parents want to score well in the process in order to improve their chances of adopting and of being assigned the kind of child that they want to parent. Those with any game-playing abilities will know that to score

well, they should *not* bring up any issues that might cause a
social worker concern. Therefore, it is likely that the very
issues that need serious exploration will get none, as the
eager adoptive applicant strives to come up with the best
possible version of a life story and a series of "right" answers
to difficult questions.

WHAT CHILDREN HAVE TO LOSE

Many traditionalists claim that what children have to lose if
we abandon the screening and matching process is appropriate parenting. The argument for parental screening rests
largely on the assumption that children are subject to special
risks when there is no biologic link between parent and child.
But there is no reason to think that adoptive parents pose
more of a risk than biologically linked parents do. Indeed, the
fact that adoptive parents have *consciously chosen* parenthood
would seem more than enough to compensate for any difficulties that might be inherent in adoptive parenting. Nor is there
any evidence that the absence of a biologic link is relevant to
the successful establishment of a parent-child relationship.
Studies indicate that adoptive families function extremely well
when compared with biologic families, and that adoptive parents are very successful in enabling their children to overcome
the effects of unfortunate preadoptive histories (see Chapter
8). There is no evidence that adoptive parents are more likely
to abuse their children than biologic parents are, or that they
are otherwise problematic as a group.

There is no reason to think that the home study process is
needed to ensure appropriate parent-child matches, either.
Education and counseling can help guide adoptive parents to
make appropriate choices. Furthermore, the reality of the current system gives the lie to claims that it serves to promote
good matches. Why give the special-needs children who pose
the greatest parenting challenges to people deemed to have
the fewest parenting capacities and resources? Why, for ex-

ample, are teenagers with multiple disabilities systematically allocated to the single-parent applicants?

The only significant argument for parental screening is based on the notion that there is a limited supply of children for adoption. Screening is said to be an appropriate way of allocating this scarce resource. If only some of those who want to be adoptive parents will have the opportunity, why not select those who will do the best job?

But the supply is *not* limited. There are many more children in need of adoptive homes than there are homes available for them. While it is true that limited numbers of healthy infants born in this country are available for adoption, more than 400,000 children were in foster care at the end of 1990, and the numbers are going up at a frightening rate. Tens of thousands of these children are free for adoption and waiting for homes. Many of them will wait for years before being placed with adoptive families, and many will grow to adulthood in foster or institutional homes.[15] In other countries there are untold millions of children in need of homes, many of whom are free for adoption and many more of whom could be free if adoptive homes were available.

In any event, there is no reason to think that the screening system can succeed in ranking parents in terms of their relative fitness. Bureaucracies are not capable of making the kind of subtle distinctions and refined judgments necessary to assess the likely quality of future parenting. They have to operate by rules and categories, and it is inevitable that if they are allowed to use age, marital status, and sexual orientation as criteria, they will use them to create rigid categories that will result in irrationally characterizing the parental fitness of many individuals.

Bureaucracies are also incapable of measuring many of the qualities and characteristics that seem most central to predicting success as an adoptive parent. Most adoption workers would agree that the home study process *should* be designed to judge such things as the nature and quality of an applicant's commitment to parenting, capacity to love children and to provide a stable and nurturing environment, sense of humor, tolerance for difference, and other factors that are similarly hard to assess and quantify. A screening system that relies on poorly paid social workers who have limited time to devote to each investigation will not be able to assess these factors adequately, assuming that even the most expensive and intrusive system we might design could. The current system fails miserably and is doomed to fail. It is simply too easy for applicants to come up with the right answers and too hard for social workers to assess the accuracy of those answers. In fact, the system doesn't even do a good job of identifying sexual orientation, an objective factor considered so significant that the "wrong" orientation is disqualifying in most screening systems. It is well known that many gays and lesbians adopt, and they do so for the most part simply by presenting themselves as heterosexual singles.

Beyond this, it is very likely that we do not know what we think we know about what makes for good parenting or happy families. Our views are necessarily shaped by a model of parenting sanctioned by biology and tradition. Single people and older people who push forward to ask for the opportunity to parent usually do not look much like the others in their categories in the general population. A large proportion of the people who are preferred because they fall into the married category will be divorced within a few years,[16] and their children will be subject to the trauma and change that divorce represents.[17] Generally, those children will effectively lose one parent, and their remaining parent will be less prepared to function as a single parent than the person who deliberately adopts on his or her own. People who choose to become parents in their late thirties and forties often testify that this is a particularly good stage of life in which to parent, because they feel less torn by the conflict between work and family and more capable of giving of themselves to a child than they did when they were younger. Some gays and lesbians maintain that for children with a same-sex or bisexual orientation, growing up with determinedly heterosexual parents can be oppressive.

The studies that exist provide no indication that the objective factors relied on by the current screening system function as useful predictors of good parenting. There is no evidence that these factors are correlated with success as an adoptive parent,[18] and there is no evidence that those who become adoptive parents by virtue of the agency screening process are more successful than those who use the independent adoption system and thereby avoid such screening.[19] Studies of some of the parents rated as marginal by the system, such as straight singles and gay singles and couples, reveal no significant disadvantages suffered by their children when compared to children raised in traditional two-parent households.[20]

Of course, these studies stop short of providing definitive proof of the current system's irrationality. They often rely on the adoptive parents' assessments of their children's adjustment — assessments that pose an obvious risk of bias. Moreover, it is extremely difficult to create adequate control groups and to define adoptive success. But these studies are all we have in the way of empirical evidence. At a minimum, they raise serious questions about the assumptions on which the agency screeners operate.

Parental screening has enormous costs from the perspective of those screened and categorized by the system. A declaration that a person is unfit, or marginally fit, to parent another human being is a serious condemnation. A denial of the opportunity to parent constitutes for many people a denial of what is most meaningful in life. The government should have to demonstrate a powerful interest in screening in order to justify such costs.

The government has traditionally asserted an interest in promoting heterosexual marriage and parenting in the context of such a marriage. But adoptive screening does little to promote this vision of the family. What it does is to drive some gays and lesbians underground to pose as straight adoptive parents, and others, together with older applicants and singles, into the independent adoption world, where they can avoid the screening system. Furthermore, it drives many of those who are fertile but would nonetheless be interested in adoption into the world of biologic parenting. Straight singles and gay singles and couples meet with no real restrictions if they seek to form families by reproduction, either naturally or with the help of reproductive technology. Increasing numbers are becoming parents through the use of sperm donors and, more recently, in vitro fertilization and surrogacy. More and more older prospective parents are resorting to IVF and related methods of infertility treatment. Even assuming that the government has a valid interest in promoting a traditional model of the family, this interest is not served by driving socially unorthodox people away from adoptive and into biologic parenting.

The state's claimed justification for adoptive screening is that it is necessary to serve children's interests. But it is hard to identify any way in which the current system furthers the goal of ensuring children the best homes. What is clear is that it deprives many children altogether of the homes they need.

SIX

Adoption and Race

EARLY FRAGMENTS FROM
ONE TRANSRACIAL ADOPTION STORY[1]

When I first walked into the world of adoption, I was stunned at the dominant role race played. I had thought I understood something about the meaning of race in our society. My life's work as a lawyer had largely involved dealing with issues of racial discrimination. But I discovered that race played a unique role in this world. It was central to many people's thinking about parenting, and it was a central organizing principle for the agencies that had the authority to construct adoptive families.

Early in the process of exploring how I might adopt, I discovered that the first order of business for the agencies responsible for matching children waiting for homes with prospective parents is to sort and allocate by race. The public and most of the traditional private agencies would not consider assigning a waiting minority child to me, a white person, except as a last resort, and perhaps not even then. The organizations and individual entrepreneurs that arrange independent adoptions, while more willing to place across racial lines, also sorted children by race. In this part of the adoption world, minority children might actually be easier for the white prospective parent to find than white children, and they were often available for a lower fee. Information sheets listing different prices for children of different races were handed out at counseling sessions for prospective parents.

I discovered also how dominant race was in the thinking of many prospective adoptive parents. The large majority of the people actively looking to adopt in this country are white, and for the most part they want white children, at least initially.

The familiar refrain that there are no children available for adoption is a reflection of the racial policies of many adoption agencies and the racial preferences of many adoptive parents. The reality is that while there are very few white children in comparison to the large pool of would-be white adopters, there are many nonwhite children available to this pool, both through independent adoption in this country and through international adoption. And there are many nonwhite children waiting in foster care who are unavailable solely because the adoption agencies insist that they cannot be placed transracially.

Racial thinking dominates the world of international adoption as well. When I began to look into the possibility of adopting from South America, I was intrigued by my agency's Brazilian program. Brazil allowed singles to adopt and allowed people my age to adopt infants. Babies were available for placement immediately after birth. I would only have to spend a week to ten days there to complete the legal procedures and could then return to the United States with my child. And there was no waiting list; I could expect to have my baby within a few months of completing my home study. Given the difficulties that a forty-four-year-old single person faces in adopting from other countries, this all seemed unbelievable. The explanation, of course, was race. Brazil had a significant slave trade in earlier years, and as a consequence, much of its population is of African descent. The children available for adoption from this program were part black. This put the program low on the desirability list for many prospective parents despite all its attractive features. Chile, by contrast, is considered a highly desirable country because it has such a white population. There are so few dark-skinned people that even the children of the poor — the children likely to be available for adoption — tend to be white.

During my two adoption trips to Peru, I discovered something about how children are rated in racial terms in their own country as well as here. Most of the children available for adoption in Peru are of mixed Indian and Spanish heritage. While there is tremendous variety in ethnic features and skin color, few of the children are white. My second adopted child, Michael, stood out as unusually white.

Several weeks after I first took Michael home with me, I sat with him wrapped in a blanket in my arms in the office of one of Lima's fanciest pediatricians. He had recovered from the fever he developed during his first twenty-four hours with me but had been suffering from nausea and diarrhea almost ever since. For a large part of this time he had been living on a water-and-mineral mixture, which protected him from dehydration but provided no nutrition. He had kept no milk down for the past five days. I had been to three different doctors in three weeks; none seemed to have any idea what to do. They told me that babies were always sick in the summer in Lima; it was the water. They also told me that babies died all the time in Lima, as if to say that if that was what was going to happen, there was really nothing that could be done.

I told this new doctor the story of Michael's troubles, trying with my words and tone to convey my sense of desperation — to make him understand that if he didn't help us, Michael might die. The doctor listened impassively. When I finished, he made no move to look at Michael, but after assuring himself that the nanny spoke no English, he proceeded to tell me that he could get me another child in a way that would avoid all the troublesome procedures of a Peruvian adoption. Women who would not keep their babies were giving birth in his hospital all the time. He could have the birth certificate for one of these children made out showing me as the mother, and the baby would be mine.

When I finally realized that this hospital baby was being suggested as a substitute for the one on my lap, I said in what I hoped was a polite but firm tone that I planned to keep this child and that I was here because he was seriously ill. I asked if the doctor could please now examine him. The doctor then shrugged his shoulders and showed me into the examining room.

I put Michael on the table and started to undress him, and for the first time the doctor looked at him. "Oh. I see. I understand. What an extraordinary child." He gave me what was meant to be a knowing look and continued Michael's physical, shaking his head in surprise as he noted, "Entirely white. Not even any Mongolian spots" (these are marks that nonwhite children often have on their backsides in early life). It was overwhelmingly clear that Michael's value had been transformed in the doctor's eyes by his whiteness. Whiteness made it comprehensible that someone would want to cure and keep this child rather than discard him.

Michael got well (although with no help from this particular doctor) and turned out to have nothing more serious than an allergy to cow's milk. But the fact that he was unusually white for an adopted child proved troubling for the rest of our stay in Lima. I was told by advisers wise in the ways of Peruvian adoptions that his whiteness made him so desirable that I would have to guard against losing him to other adoptive parents or to lawyers hungry for the high fees that he would bring. I was advised not to take him out in the city but to keep him hidden in my apartment. When I had to take him to the various police and medical examinations and court appearances that are part of the adoption process in Lima, I learned to keep his face covered with a blanket at all times. When dealing with people who had seen him or might know what he looked like, I talked constantly of how frail and ill he had been since birth, hoping thereby to discount his value.

I learned more about my own feelings about race as I puzzled through the process of creating my adoptive family. Adoption compels this kind of learning. You don't just get at the end of one general line when you're adopting; there are a lot of lines, each identified by the race, disabilities, and age of the children available, together with the length of wait and the difficulty and cost of adoption. In choosing which line to join, I had to think about race, and to think on a level that was new to me. I had to try to confront without distortion the reality of parenting someone of another race, since the child and I would have to live that reality. I had to decide whether I wanted a child who was a racial look-alike or not. I had to think about whether it would be racist to look for a same-race child or racist to look for a child of another race, as I was learning that the black social workers' organization opposed transracial adoption, calling it a form of genocide. When I decided to do an international adoption, I had to choose which country's line to stand in, and part of that choice was thinking about whether I had particularly positive or negative feelings about parenting a child of one of the different racial and ethnic groups involved, and musing about whether it was offensive or entirely all right to be engaged in this kind of thinking. When I finally did adopt, I began life as part of a Peruvian-American family, part of a brown-skin/white-skin, Indian-Caucasian mix of a family.

On my return with Christopher from my first Peruvian adoption, we emerge from the airplane in New York City to make our way through customs and immigration. There are signs directing United States citizens to one line and aliens to another. I start toward the citizens' line, conscious of the comfort of finally being back in the land where I belong, and then realize that since the child I am carrying is an alien, he and I belong in that other line, the one for those who don't belong.

When we have been back in the States for a few weeks, I find myself startled on a trip to the supermarket by a stranger's question: "Where did he come from?" I'm genuinely puzzled as to why this person would think that Christopher came from someplace other than me, as to why she would immediately assume adoption. It is as if I have to be educated to see the blatant physical differences that others see — his brown skin, black eyes, and straight, thick black hair; my fair skin, blue eyes, and curly blond-brown hair. As I push Christopher through the streets in his stroller, I am struck by the appearance of other people's children — they are pale, anemic-looking creatures, with strangely bald heads. The brown-skinned beauty who splashes in my bathtub every night has become the norm of child.

As the months go by, I begin to hear troubling comments: "Oh, he's from Peru. I didn't know they came that dark there. . . . But he really seems to be doing very nicely." I realize that I need to develop responses for the things people will say to and about him. I worry about the preponderance of blue-eyed, white-skinned children at his child care center and wonder what I can do about it. I listen with new ears to familiar discussions of racial issues. I hear the proponents of affirmative action at the child care center arguing that there should be at least one minority child in each class, talking of how the other children will benefit from the minority child's presence. I am angered in a new way by the blindness to the minority child's needs, and by the condescending tone. I learn something about the problems that children of color face as they advance into the older grades at the local school, which my oldest child attended and to which I plan to send Christopher.

Then one day, when Christopher is three and a half, he says to me across the kitchen table at dinner, "I wish you looked like me." I respond, wanting not to understand him,

"What do you mean?" And he says, "I wish you were the same color." I try to reassure him, telling him that it makes no difference to me that he and I look different — in fact, I like it that way. But my comments seem not to the point. He repeats that he wishes I looked like him, and his voice and eyes reveal his pain.

I am left to puzzle at the meaning of this pain. Is it one of a thousand pains that a child will experience as he discovers differences between himself and others — in this case, a difference between himself and his school friends, with their same-race parents? Is it, as the opponents of transracial adoption would have us believe, part of a permanent anguish caused by the sense that he does not truly belong in the place where he should most surely belong — his family? Or is it simply a signal that living as part of a multiracial, multiethnic, multicultural family will force us to confront the meaning of racial and other differences on a regular basis?

This child is as much inside my skin as any child could be. It feels entirely right that he should be there. Yet the powers that be in today's adoption world proclaim with near unanimity that race-mixing in the context of adoption should be avoided if at all possible, at least where black- or brown-skinned American children are involved.

In this chapter I discuss the barriers to transracial placement that have been erected by adoption agencies and note the destructive impact these barriers have on black children, whose lives are put on hold while they wait in foster care for months, years, and often their entire childhoods for color-matched families. I examine the law on racial discrimination and question how current racial matching policies in adoption can be squared with the antidiscrimination norm that governs elsewhere in our social lives. I explore the meaning of these policies — why it is that they seem to have made so much sense to so many people over the years, why it is that blacks and whites, conservatives and liberals and radicals, judges and legislators and social workers, have found common cause in preventing the mixing of the races in this context. My contention is that current policies are inconsistent with the oft-proclaimed principle that the best interests of the child should be determinative, and that they are inconsistent with an appropriate understanding of the role that race should play in social ordering.

Racial matching policies represent a coming together of powerful and related ideologies — old-fashioned white racism, modern-day black nationalism, and what I will call "biologism," the idea that what is "natural" in the context of the biologic family is what is normal and desirable in the context of adoption. Biologic families usually have same-race parents and children. As we have seen, the laws and policies surrounding adoption in this country have generally structured adoption in imitation of biology and reflect widespread and powerful feelings that parent-child relationships will work best between biologic likes and related fears that parents will not be able truly to love and nurture biologic unlikes. These feelings and fears have much in common with concerns among both blacks and whites in our society about the dangers involved in crossing racial boundaries. It is thus understandable that there is so much support for racial matching in the adoption context.

But the question is whether we *should* be so reluctant to cross boundaries of racial "otherness" in adoption — whether today's powerful racial matching policies make sense from the viewpoint of either the minority children involved or the larger society. It is a question of growing practical importance. Minority children are pouring into the already overburdened foster care system.[2] In the five-year period from 1986 to 1991, the number of children in foster care rose by *50 percent*.[3] There is increasing talk of bringing back the orphanages of the nineteenth and early twentieth centuries. Current policies stand in the way of placing the children in need of homes with available adoptive families. In addition, how we think about the race-matching issue will affect how we think about the growing phenomenon of international adoption, which involves the adoption by whites in this country of dark-skinned children from foreign countries and cultures. Racial matching policies also have powerful symbolic importance: how we deal with race in the intimate context of the family says a lot about how we will treat race in other social contexts.

THE HISTORY

In this country, crossing the racial line in adoption has always been regarded as highly suspect. Through the middle of this century adoption agency practice, social attitudes, and the law posed nearly absolute barriers to transracial adoption. Segregation was the order of the day in much of the country, and supporters of that order saw the mixing of the races within the family as the ultimate symbol of the outrage and degradation threatened by moves toward a more integrated society. "Race mixer" was the epithet hurled at people like myself who worked in the South in the early 1960s to break down legal barriers to integration. Most states prohibited interracial marriage at some point in their history. Transracial adoption was similarly prohibited, sometimes by explicit legislation, more generally by adoption agency policy.

The 1960s represented a period of relative openness to transracial adoption. Agencies began to place waiting black children with white parents when black parents were apparently unavailable. But in 1972 an organization called the National Association of Black Social Workers (NABSW) issued a proclamation opposing transracial adoption. It took the position that "Black children should be placed only with Black families whether in foster care or for adoption. Black children belong, physically, psychologically and culturally in Black families in order that they receive the total sense of themselves and develop a sound projection of their future."[4] Committing themselves "to go back to our communities and work to end this particular form of genocide," leaders of the NABSW pledged to put a stop to transracial adoption.

CURRENT RACIAL MATCHING POLICIES

Today most public and private adoption agencies are governed by powerful race-matching policies. There is general agreement among agency policymakers that children should be placed on a same-race basis if possible, and transracially only as a last resort.[5]

Most agencies separate children and prospective parents into racial classifications and subclassifications. Children in need of homes are divided into black and white pools, and the children in the black pool are then classified by skin tone, and sometimes also by nationality, ethnicity, or other cultural characteristics. The prospective parent pool is similarly divided and classified. An attempt is then made to match children in the various "black" categories with their parent counterparts. The goal is to assign the light-skinned black child to light-skinned parents, the Haitian child to Haitian parents, and so on. The white children are matched with white prospective parents.

This scheme confronts a major problem in the fact that the numbers of children falling into the black and white pools do not fit, proportionally, with the numbers of prospective parents falling into their own black and white pools. More than a third of the children in out-of-home placement are black, and more than half are children of color.[6] By contrast, a very high percentage of the waiting adoptive parent pool is white. Figures for the major national listing of hard-to-place children waiting for homes show that roughly two thirds of these children are black and two thirds of the families waiting to adopt such children are white.[7] A recent report on a major state foster care system shows that 54 percent of the children available for adoption are nonwhite while 87 percent of the waiting prospective parents are white.[8] These statistics can only hint at the extent of the numbers mismatch. Many whites interested in adopting do not even get on agency lists because they are told that no children are available for them to adopt.

Current matching policies place a high priority on expanding the pool of prospective black adoptive parents so agencies can place children without utilizing the waiting white pool. Programs have been created to recruit black parents, and subsidies have been provided to encourage them to adopt. Traditional parental screening criteria have been significantly revised for prospective black adopters: agencies reach out to include the kinds of people traditionally excluded from the white parent pool or placed at the bottom of the waiting lists — singles, people in their fifties and sixties, and people living on welfare, social security, or similarly marginal incomes. As a result, the pool of black adoptive parents looks very different in socioeconomic terms from the pool of white parents: black adopters are significantly older, poorer, and more likely to be single. In altering screening criteria, adoption workers have by no means repudiated these criteria as irrelevant to determining parental fitness. Black and white candidates are still assessed and ranked by these criteria, but because of the importance given to the racial factor, those at the bottom of the black list are generally preferred to all those on the white list for any waiting black child. Despite these efforts, the numbers mismatch continues. There are many more black children than there are waiting black parents, and there is a large pool of waiting white parents.

Today's matching policies generally forbid the immediate placement of black children with waiting white families even when no black families are available. Some policies specify that a definite time period — three or six or twelve or eighteen months — must pass before a transracial adoption may be considered, or after which it must be considered. Many agencies are required to hold children until active efforts to locate same-race families have proved fruitless, or until such efforts and the unavailability of a same-race family have been documented. These non-time-specific policies are thought to result in even longer holding periods. Policies amounting to absolute or near-absolute bans on transracial adoption appear common. The NABSW continues to take a firm stance against it: "NABSW steadfastly holds to the position that Black children should not be placed with white parents under any circumstances."[9] There appear to be many adoption workers who either are sympathetic with the NABSW's position or feel intimidated by its advocates and by others who oppose transracial adoption except in the most limited circumstances.

The extreme nature of current holding policies is revealed by the stories of some of the transracial adoptions that *are* allowed to take place. The director of an adoption program for minority children in New York State told me that 99 percent of his agency's placements were same-race placements. He then described one of the few transracial adoptions he had facilitated. The child had been in the foster care system for eleven years and free for adoption for eight of those years. He was finally placed transracially at the age of thirteen only because of concern that as a result of accumulated bitterness, he would probably exercise his option at age fourteen to refuse to accept adoption if it was offered. The director, a strong advocate of racial matching, felt that an exception was warranted in these unusual circumstances, but noted that he had to battle forces within the state and agency bureaucracies in order to implement the placement.

The director of another program with a specific focus on recruiting minority parents told me of a transracial adoption she had arranged. It involved a victim of fetal alcohol syndrome, who was mentally retarded. The director had held this child for three years while she looked for a minority family. When a white couple volunteered their interest in adopting him, the director hesitated, but finally agreed to see them. She eventually placed the child with them, since she was impressed by their parenting credentials and by the fact that they already had children from a variety of ethnic backgrounds.

Another director told me of a transracial placement she made in a case involving hard-to-place minority siblings. The only available minority family was interested in adopting one but not the other. Since the director felt that separation would be disastrous for the children, she placed them with a white couple. As a result she was subjected to intense criticism and pressure from the local chapter of the NABSW.

Matching policies are reflected to a degree in written rules and documented cases. In recent years, several states have enacted laws requiring agencies to exercise a same-race placement preference. Other states have regulations and many adoption agencies have written policies mandating such a preference.[10] Numerous cases have appeared in the media, in congressional hearings, and in litigation involving the removal of black children from white foster families with whom they have lived for long periods, often years. This action can be triggered by the white family's expression of interest in adopting their foster child; the agency intervenes to move the child to a same-race foster family which may or may not be interested in adoption. The white parents in such cases often have poignant stories to tell. They may have nursed through hard times a child who arrived in their home in serious distress. The child has thrived under their care and feels a close attachment, and they feel a similar attachment and want to adopt so that the child will be a permanent part of their lives. The agency can offer no alternative except a shift to a new foster family. Experts testify to the destructive effect of disrupting the only stable relationship the child has known. Whether or not the agencies are forced to back down, by public pressure or court order, these cases reveal something of the power of the racial matching philosophy, since child welfare professionals generally agree that stable parent-child relationships should not be disrupted and that foster families should get priority consideration for the adoption of children with whom they have formed such relationships.

Whereas the written policies and court cases are testaments to the strength of the racial matching philosophy in today's adoption world, it is the unwritten and generally invisible rules that are central to understanding the nature of current policies. The entire system has been designed and redesigned with a view toward promoting same-race placements and avoiding transracial placements. The rules generally make race not simply a factor, but an overwhelmingly important factor in the placement process.

THE IMPACT OF CURRENT POLICIES

There can be no doubt that racial matching policies result in delays in and denial of permanent placement for minority children. The only real questions have to do with how regularly these occur. No good studies on the issue are available. Those in a position to gather the relevant information and sponsor related research have opted not to do so, presumably at least in part because they are reluctant to reveal facts that would call into question the wisdom of current policies.

Nonetheless, we know enough to conclude that very large numbers of black children in need of homes are spending significant amounts of their childhood in foster and institutional care rather than permanent adoptive homes because of the policies against transracial placement. We know that this is what the policies *demand* if black adoptive families are not available, and we know that the black families are *not* available. We know that minority children are disproportionately represented in the population of children waiting for adoptive homes, that they wait longer than white children, and that they are less likely to be eventually placed. A recent study found that minority children waited for an average of two years, compared to an average one-year wait for nonminorities.[11] Minority placement rates were 20 percent lower than nonminority rates. The minority children were comparable in age with nonminorities and had other characteristics that, if race had not been an issue, should have made it easier to find adoptive homes: they had fewer disabilities and fewer previous placements in foster care. The study concluded that racial status was a more powerful determinant of placement rate than any other factor examined. Another report, on a major state foster care and adoption system, shows that black children accounted for 41 percent of the children waiting for adoptive homes but only 14 percent of the children actually adopted.[12] It also indicates that if race were not an issue, the minority children should have been easier to place, since they tended to be younger and to have fewer disabilities.[13]

Informed observers of the adoption scene — people who see racial matching policies in operation — believe there is a strong causal connection between the policies and the delays and denial of placement that minority children face. The most adamant critics of transracial adoption tend first to deny that there is a problem, and second to argue that the solution lies not in transracial placement but in renewed efforts to preserve and reunify black biologic families and to recruit black adoptive families. They argue that with such efforts, black adoptive homes could be found for all black children actually in need of homes. They argue further that whites would not be willing to adopt the minority children who wait, noting that most of the children in foster care are older and that they suffer from a variety of physical and emotional problems.

While the resources devoted to preserving black biologic families and to making same-race adoption work have been limited, the fact is that they are likely to remain limited. There are, and almost certainly will be for some time, too few black families for the waiting black children. By contrast, many white families are eagerly awaiting the opportunity to adopt. Although white adopters, like black adopters, tend to prefer healthy infants, recruitment efforts in recent years have demonstrated that whites as well as blacks are often willing to adopt older children and children with devastating disabilities.[14] Current racial matching policies stand in the way of tapping this ready resource for minority children.

We know that many minority children never receive adoptive homes and many others spend years waiting in foster care or institutions. We know that many prospective white adopters are interested in adopting black children as well as older children with serious disabilities. There can be no doubt that the current racial matching regime, by barring and discouraging white parents from transracial adoption rather than welcoming them in the agency doors, denies adoptive homes to large numbers of minority children.

THE EMPIRICAL STUDIES

The major argument made in support of racial matching is that transracial adoption would hurt children. Racial matching advocates have generally focused on this argument, presumably at least in part because it is seen as politically more viable than arguments based on notions of black separatism or community empowerment. Adoption laws throughout the nation demand that matching policies be justified in terms of how they affect the best interests of the child, and thus push policymakers to defend their policies on the ground that transracial placement would be problematic for the children involved.

Many claims have been made as to how and why black children would suffer if denied a same-race upbringing. However, there is virtually no evidence in the entire body of empirical research on transracial adoption that it has a harmful effect on children. By contrast, there is extensive, unrefuted, and overwhelmingly powerful evidence that the delays in permanent placement and the denials of such placement that result from current matching policies do devastating damage to the children involved.[15]

Studies that have been undertaken reflect a bias on the part of those responsible for sponsoring and conducting research. They look at transracial adoption as an exception to the accepted racial matching norm and ask questions about whether the problems anticipated by adoption professionals and NABSW critics have materialized. The general emphasis is thus on the potential *negatives* in transracial adoption. Few studies ask questions designed to assess the potential *positives*, and almost none attempt to assess the harm to children caused by current matching policies.

Despite this bias, the studies provide an overwhelming endorsement of transracial adoption. They were conducted by a diverse group of researchers that included blacks and whites, critics and supporters of transracial adoption. With astounding uniformity, the research shows that transracial adoption works well from the viewpoint of the children and the adoptive families involved. The children are doing well in terms of achievement, adjustment, and self-esteem, and they compare well with children raised in same-race families. They seem fully integrated in their families and communities yet have developed strong senses of racial identity. The studies provide no basis for concluding that placing black children with white rather than black families has any negative impact on the children's welfare.

At the same time, we do not really need comparative studies on the impact of current matching policies to know that these policies are causing serious harm to minority children. We know that these policies regularly delay and often prevent permanent placement. To the degree that we know anything about child welfare, we know that this harms children. Many studies and decades of professional experience demonstrate that continuity and stability in a child's family relationships are central to well-being, that permanent adoptive homes are far better for children than temporary foster homes, and that delay in adoptive placement reduces the chances for a successful adjustment.

This is not to say that the studies in themselves should resolve the debate about transracial adoption. The issue of how current matching policies affect the welfare of children is only one part of that debate. Another part involves issues concerning the value of preserving and promoting black families, black culture, and the empowerment of the black community. Nonetheless, most participants in the debate claim that they are motivated largely or entirely by their concern with the welfare of the children at issue. The adoption professionals, the legislatures, and the courts, which will be jointly responsible for resolving the debate, are all bound by principles that require enormous deference to the best interests of the child. The studies provide persuasive evidence that transracial adoption serves the interests of children.

The research does indicate some interesting differences in transracial adoptees' attitudes about race and race relations, which critics of transracial adoption cite as evidence that supports their position. But this evidence is positively heartwarming for those who believe that blacks and whites should learn to live compatibly in one world, with respect and concern for each other and with appreciation of their racial and cultural differences as well as their common humanity. The studies reveal that blacks adopted by whites appear more positive than blacks raised by blacks about relationships with whites, more comfortable in those relationships, and more interested in a racially integrated lifestyle. They think race is not the most important factor in defining who they are or who their friends should be. They often describe themselves as biracial or American or "human" rather than black.

These findings are taken as evidence of *inappropriate* racial attitudes by the critics of transracial adoption. But several students of transracial adoptive families have given voice to the positive implications they see in this evidence. Noting that the transracial adoptees perceive "their world as essentially pluralistic and multicolored," one report concludes that they represent "a different and special cohort, one socialized in two worlds and therefore perhaps better prepared to operate in both. The hope is that having had this unique racial experience, they will have gained a greater sense of security about who they are and will be better able to negotiate in the worlds of both their biological inheritance and their socialization."[16] Another report concludes:

> There has developed a positive black self-image, combined with a mixed black-white pattern of social interaction. It seems to us that this pattern may be one which will allow these young people to move with equal comfort in both black and white worlds, allowing them to cull what they wish from each culture, and perhaps creating bridges which will be of use to an even wider world.[17]

The fact that there are some differences in the racial attitudes developed by transracial adoptees is not surprising. These children have grown up in white families, which tend to live in either relatively white or integrated communities. They have felt a comfortable part of their white families and have flourished in what have been significantly white worlds. It is understandable that they will have developed a sense of the meaning of race that is very different from that of black children living in a state of relative isolation or exclusion from the white world. As one student of black identity writes, they "can be expected to be more bicultural than categorically black-oriented."[18]

This is understandably problematic from a black separatist or nationalist perspective. The president of NABSW wrote in the association's spring 1988 newsletter:

The lateral transfer of our children to white families is not in our best interest. Having white families raise our children to be white is at least a hostile gesture toward us as a people and at best the ultimate gesture of disrespect for our heritage as African people. . . .

We are on the right side of the transracial adoption issue. Our children are our future.[19]

But the evidence shows that transracial adoptees develop a strong sense of black identity, contrary to many of the critics' claims. These adoptees have essentially as strong a sense of black identity and racial pride as other minority children. White families do vary as to how much they help their black children feel part of the black community and proud of their black heritage, but there is no evidence that black parents do a better job than white parents of raising black children with a sense of pride in their racial background. *Nor is there any evidence that any differences that do exist in racial attitudes have any negative implications for the well-being of those raised transracially.*[20]

In addition, the studies reveal that transracial adoption has a significant impact on the racial attitudes of the white members of these families. The parents say that they have developed a new awareness of racial issues and describe their lives as significantly enriched by the experience of becoming a biracial, bicultural family. The white children in these families are apparently powerfully committed and connected to their black brothers and sisters. Both the white and the black children seem to be unusually free of racial bias, and unusually committed to the vision of a pluralistic, multicolored world in which a person's humanity is more important than his race.

In the context of a society that is struggling with the issue of how to deal with racial hostilities, the studies of transracial adoptive families are extraordinarily interesting. They show that black children raised in white homes are comfortable with their blackness and also uniquely comfortable in dealing with whites. They show parents and children, brothers and sisters relating to one another as if race were no barrier to love and commitment. They show the black adopted and the white birth children growing up with the sense that race should not be a barrier in their relationships with people in the larger social context. In a society torn by racial conflict, these studies show human beings transcending racial difference.

THE LAW

Current racial matching policies are in conflict with the basic law of the land on race discrimination. They are also anomalous. In no other area do state and state-licensed decision-makers use race so systematically as the basis for action. In no other area do they promote the use of race so openly. The federal Constitution, state constitutions, and a mass of federal, state, and local laws prohibit discrimination by public entities on the basis of race. Private entities with significant power over our lives are also generally bound by laws prohibiting such discrimination. In the past twenty-five years this body of law has grown, so that today we have guarantees against race discrimination not only in housing, employment, and public accommodations but in virtually every area of our community life.

It is true that the antidiscrimination norm has been limited by principles of respect for privacy and freedom of association. We allow people to act on the basis of racial preference in choosing their friends and companions and in forming truly private social clubs. But we also allow them to cross racial boundaries if they choose to do so. The government cannot promote racial separatism in private life. In *Loving* v. *Virginia*, the Supreme Court held it unconstitutional for the state to prohibit interracial marriage. In *Palmore* v. *Sidoti*, the Court held it unconstitutional for the state to transfer custody of a child solely because the white mother had begun living with a black man. The Court rejected arguments that removing the child from a racially mixed household was justified by the state's goal of making custody decisions on the basis of the best interests of the child. Conceding that there was a "risk that a child living with a stepparent of a different race may be subject to a variety of pressures and stresses not present if the child were living with parents of the same racial or ethnic origin," the Court nonetheless had no problem concluding that these were constitutionally impermissible considerations.

The antidiscrimination principle has been interpreted as outlawing almost all race-conscious action by the state and by the agencies that control our communal lives. There does not need to be any showing that the action is designed to harm or that it results in harm. Race-conscious action has generally been allowed only where it can be justified on the grounds of compelling necessity, or where it is designed to benefit racial minority groups, either by avoiding or by preventing discrimination or by remedying its effects. These exceptions have been narrowly defined.

The adoption world is an anomaly in this legal universe. In agency adoptions, as we have seen, race-conscious action is one of the major rules of the game. Under antidiscrimination law, the fact that race is a *recognizable* factor in decision-making is ordinarily enough to make out a case of intentional discrimination. Adoption agency policies make race not merely *a* factor but the *central* factor in the placement process.

Public adoption agencies, as well as many private agencies, are governed by legislative and constitutional provisions forbidding racial discrimination. The federal Constitution's equal protection clause and its related limit on legitimate affirmative action apply to adoption agencies, adoption courts, and the various state and local governmental bodies that promulgate laws, regulations, and other policies governing adoption. Title VI of the 1964 Civil Rights Act bans discrimination by adoption agencies, public and private, that receive federal funds. Accordingly, it applies to virtually all public and many private agencies. Many states have constitutional, statutory, and regulatory provisions that broadly prohibit discrimination by public and private agencies.

Racial matching policies fit none of the recognized exceptions to the antidiscrimination norm. There is no compelling necessity for racial matching. The number of black children available for adoption is very small compared to the size of the black community; placing more of these children with white families poses no realistic threat to the existence of that community or to the preservation of its culture. It is hard to see transracial adoption as more threatening to these interests than racial intermarriage or racial integration in public education. Official efforts to prevent intermarriage or to prevent black children from attending school with white children or being taught by white teachers have been held unconstitutional, and would be regarded as intolerable by blacks and whites alike in today's society.

Nor can we rationalize racial matching policies as legitimate forms of affirmative action, designed to eliminate or to remedy the effects of prior discrimination or otherwise to benefit blacks as a group. It is easy to argue that there has been such discrimination. Traditional agency screening procedures and criteria may well have had an adverse impact on prospective black parents in the past, depriving them of an equal opportunity to adopt. A vast array of social policies going back to the institution of slavery can be held responsible for the fact that it is black families whose children are disproportionately available for adoption and white families who are disproportionately in a position to adopt.

The problem is that racial matching policies are not like the kinds of remedial affirmative action programs that the courts have accepted as legitimate. The courts have generally insisted that such programs be limited in duration and be designed to help move society to a point where we can eliminate race as a decision-making factor. By contrast, racial matching policies require race matching on an ongoing basis, without any apparent limit in time. They are designed not to eliminate the role of race in agency decision-making in the future but to perpetuate its importance.

In addition, racial matching policies are fundamentally inconsistent with traditional affirmative action rationales because they promote racial separatism rather than integration. Both antidiscrimination law and affirmative action programs have been designed to break down segregative barriers.

Finally, and most significant, these policies are inconsistent with affirmative action rationales because they injure black children. Even those courts and Supreme Court justices most sympathetic to affirmative action have argued that allegedly benign racial classifications should be scrutinized carefully to ensure that they really are benign in impact and do not serve to disadvantage their supposed beneficiaries. Racial matching policies are not clearly beneficial in any short-term or long-term sense to blacks as a group, and they are seriously harmful to a significant part of that group — the children in need of adoptive homes.

There is no particular reason to believe that blacks as a whole would support these policies. The policies have been developed and are promoted by the leaders of one black social workers' organization in the absence of any evidence of general support in the black community and with little vocal support from any other organization. Reported surveys of black people's attitudes indicate substantial support for transracial adoption and very limited support for the NABSW's position or for the kinds of powerful matching principles embodied in today's adoption policies.[21] The apparent motivations for these policies seem complex, with white opposition to race-mixing in the context of the family playing a part. There is no obvious answer to the question of whether racial matching policies are likely to benefit or burden the black community. Black adopters are limited by race-matching policies to children of their race and skin tone. Black birth mothers are often prevented by these policies from obtaining what they may most want — immediate placement of their children in permanent homes. And it is questionable whether imposing an obligation on the black community to take care of "its own" while providing limited resources for the job does much to help that community.

What *is* clear is that current policies are harmful to the group of black children in need of homes. Programs that do concrete harm to one group of blacks in the interest of promoting what are at best hypothetical benefits to another cannot be justified as legitimate affirmative action. And in any event, adoption law throughout the nation requires that children's interests take precedence over adult or community interests.

Of course, advocates for racial matching argue that growing up with same-race parents is a benefit of overriding importance to black children. But the claim that a black person, by virtue of race alone, will necessarily be more capable than a white person of parenting a black child is the kind of claim that courts have generally refused to allow. There is no evidence that same-race placement is beneficial to black children, and there is a good deal of evidence that delayed placement causes them harm. Ultimately, the argument for racial matching policies rests on the unsupported assumption that black children will be significantly better off with "their own kind." This kind of assumption cannot be permitted under our nation's antidiscrimination laws.

DIRECTIONS FOR THE FUTURE

We should not view racial matching as an issue on which black interests are pitted against white interests, with blacks who are fighting for the rights of "their children" opposed by whites who want the children for their own benefit and by defenders of white privilege.

The issues at the heart of current racial matching policies are the significance of racial difference and the role of separatism in dealing with this difference. Historically, these policies represent the coming together of white segregationists and black nationalists and the merger of their separatist ideologies with "biologism." Arguing that biologic sameness helps make families work, adoption professionals have structured the adoptive family in imitation of biology and promoted the goal of matching adoptive parents with their biologic lookalikes. The NABSW leadership's attack on transracial adoption met with relatively ready acceptance from white social workers not just because of liberal white guilt, but because it fit with the traditional assumptions of their professional world. This world is part of a larger social context in which there has always been a strong sense that racial differences matter deeply, and a related suspicion about crossing racial lines. Both black nationalists and white segregationists promote separatism, especially in the context of the family, as a way of promoting the power and cultural integrity of their own group. Even those blacks and whites who are generally committed to integration often see the family as the place to draw the line.

From a separatist perspective, current racial matching policies make a certain amount of sense, even if they do result in the denial of permanent homes to black children who could be placed. Those who believe in maintaining the separateness of the white community can take comfort in the fact that these policies provide a near-absolute guarantee that white children will not be placed with black parents or with interracial couples. Those who believe in promoting a sense of black community can take comfort in the fact that most of the black children who do not find adoptive homes are growing up in black foster homes. They can hope that by maintaining the barriers to transracial placement, they will increase pressure on the system to devote more resources to efforts to preserve and reunify the black biologic family.

But we can recognize the importance of racial and cultural difference without subscribing to separatism. We can celebrate a child's racial identity without insisting that anyone who is born with a particular racial makeup must live within a prescribed racial community. We can recognize that individual members of various racial groups choose to define their identities and to define themselves in relationship to racial and other groups in an endless variety of ways.[22] We can believe that people are fully capable of loving those who are not biologically and racially similar but are "other," and that it is important for more people to learn to do so. We can regard the elimination of racial hostilities as more important than the promotion of cultural difference.

From this perspective, which I share, transracial adoptive families constitute an interesting model of how we might better learn to live with one another in this society. These families can work only if their members have an appreciation of racial difference and a love that transcends such difference. And the evidence indicates that these families do work.

In my view it is clear that both law and principle require elimination of the powerful racial matching policies typical of today's adoption world. No delays in placement, whether for six months or one month, should be tolerated in the interest of ensuring a racial match. Delay harms children, because at the very least it causes discontinuity and disruption. And any delay risks further delay, because the older a child gets, the harder it is to find an adoptive home. Any preference for same-race placement that causes delay or that otherwise threatens the interest of the children involved should be viewed as unlawful racial discrimination, in violation of the equal protection clause of the Constitution, Title VI of the 1964 Civil Rights Act, and other applicable antidiscrimination mandates.

The only genuinely hard question for me is whether we should allow agencies to exercise a truly mild preference, so that in situations where qualified black and white families are waiting to adopt, children can be assigned on a same-race basis. There is some reason to think that this limited form of race matching would serve children's interests. There is, for instance, reason to fear that white parents might harbor racial attitudes, on a conscious or subconscious level, that would interfere with their ability to appreciate and celebrate their black child's racial self. You have only to step into the world of adoption to realize that it is largely peopled by prospective white parents in search of white children. The urgency of their race-conscious quest seems to explain much about that world. But the picture is a complicated one. There is tremendous variation in racial attitudes among adoptive parents, and those attitudes are shaped and conditioned by messages from adoption workers and the broader society. Many white adopters start the adoption process with no apparent racial preference. Many others begin their quest thinking of a white child and turn to transracial adoption after considering their options. For them, transracial adoption may appear to be a second choice. But the fact is that for a very large number of adoptive parents, adoption itself is a second choice, forced upon them by their inability to reproduce. It is understandable that when they first contemplate adoption, they would be interested in finding a biologic and therefore a racial lookalike. They are of course conditioned by a variety of forces in our society to think of biologic parenting as preferable to adoptive parenting, and simultaneously conditioned by current racial matching policies to think that they should adopt within their racial group. All adoptions require parents to transcend the conditioning that defines parenthood in terms of procreation and genetic connection. The evidence indicates that adoptive parents are able to do so and that adoptive relationships work. The evidence similarly indicates that when whites arrive at the point of consciously choosing to enter into parenting relationships with black children, the relationships work, and indeed appear to work as well as same-race biologic relationships.

A mild same-race preference might also be thought to protect children from unnecessary pain and stigma associated with being different. All adopted children have to deal with the difference of having lost their biologic parents, and many adoption professionals feel that this puts adoptees at risk of feeling that they do not really belong. We would add to the sense of difference by placing black adoptees with white parents in what are likely to be predominantly white communities. We may believe that these children should feel that they truly belong, and research studies provide evidence that they do. But it still seems probable that many children would find it more comfortable, all things being truly equal, to be raised by same-race parents.

A mild preference for same-race placement would also seem to serve the interests of black adults who want to parent, as well as black community interests. It would counter, at least to some degree, the tendency of transracial adoption to work only in one direction, as black but not white children are placed across racial lines.

But there would be real dangers in a rule involving even a mild preference. On a symbolic level, it is problematic to have social agencies rather than private individuals deciding what role race should play in forming families and how racial identity will be defined and nurtured. The Supreme Court decided some time ago that government should not be in the business of deciding whether interracial marriages are wise. We would not want to live in a regime in which social agencies prevented such marriages, or prevented interracial couples from producing children. Moreover, the existence of families in which blacks and whites live in a state of mutual love and commitment, and struggle in this context to understand issues of racial and cultural difference, seems a positive good to be celebrated. The government should not be in the position of discouraging the creation of such families.

On a pragmatic level, it is not clear that it is possible to create a genuinely mild preference for same-race placement. There is a real danger that if any racial preference is allowed, enormous weight will in fact be given to race no matter what the formal rule of law. After all, agencies and courts commonly describe today's matching policies as if race were simply one of many factors in decision-making, with nothing more than a mild preference for same-race placement at work. Current adoption law, as reflected in court rulings and the administrative guidelines interpreting Title VI, holds that race should *not* be used in the absolute and determinative way that we know it systematically *is* used. Given adoption professionals' extraordinary level of commitment to same-race placement and the amount of discretion to make placement decisions they have traditionally enjoyed, it may well be that the only practicable way to prevent race from playing the kind of determinative role that it plays today is to prohibit its use as a factor altogether.[23]

On balance then, it seems that even a mild preference is unwise as a matter of social policy. The generally applicable legal rule that race is not to play any role in social decision-making should be held to apply in adoption as well. All prospective parents should be free to adopt children without regard to any adoption agency worker's views as to which children are an appropriate racial match. Agencies should use subsidies and other recruitment devices to reach out to prospective parents of all races to find homes for children who cannot be placed without such recruitment. They should revise the traditional screening criteria for white as well as black prospective parents, with the goal of creating a pool of people interested in and capable of providing good homes for all the children in need.

A no-preference regime would remove adoption agencies from the business of promoting same-race placement, but it would not mean that they must ignore racial considerations altogether. They could act in their educational and counseling capacity to advise prospective parents on racial matters; they could encourage parents to explore their feelings about race, and they could try to educate them about issues involved in raising a child of a different race. They could try to guide prospective parents toward the kind of child they seem most fit to raise.

A no-preference regime would not mean that agencies would have to ignore private parties' preferences with respect to race. Prospective parents and children old enough to make their own decisions could decide what role, if any, race should play in the formation of their own family. In the adoption area the state is attempting to create a relationship that is as intimate, as powerful, and as permanent as any that human beings know. It is as if it were plunged by necessity into the business of arranging marriages. It is wrong for the government to presume that a racial match is central to the happiness of every coupled parent and child, but it is equally wrong for it to insist on arranging parent-child couplings without regard to the racial feelings of the people involved.

Both common sense and the available evidence from empirical studies indicate that racial matching policies are doing serious harm to black children. Accordingly, these policies violate the principle at the core of our nation's adoption laws: that the best interests of the child should govern the placement process. They also violate the antidiscrimination norm contained in the nation's various civil rights laws and in the equal protection clause of the Constitution.

It is true, as advocates of current policies often say, that more could be done to find black families. But it is extremely unlikely that our society will anytime soon devote more than lip service and limited resources to putting blacks in a social and economic position where they are capable of providing good homes for all the waiting black children. It will always be far easier to get white society to agree on the goal of placing black children in black homes than to get an allocation of financial resources that will make that goal achievable. The danger in using black children as hostages to pry the money loose is that white society will not see these lives as warranting much in the way of ransom. Moreover, in a desperately overburdened and underfinanced welfare system, those who care about children have to take children's many needs into account as they make decisions about allocating any new funds that might be available. Money is desperately needed to provide services that will enable biological families to function so that children are not unnecessarily removed. It is desperately needed to protect children from abuse and neglect. It is desperately needed to improve the adoption process so that children who should be permanently removed from their families are freed up for adoption and placed as promptly as possible. Money is needed in these and other areas to help ensure some very basic protections for children that should take priority over the adult agenda of promoting racial separation.

SEVEN

Adoption Among Nations

SCENES FROM THE WORLD OF INTERNATIONAL ADOPTION

Some Preliminary Thoughts

My youngest child, Michael, had lived with me for two and a half years when his application for U.S. citizenship was approved. I gave a party to celebrate the completion of the last legal step involved in his and Christopher's adoptions. One wall of my living room was decorated with the dozens of legal documents that attested to some important milestones in the long journey. With their red ribbons and gold seals and the dozens and dozens of official stamps and signatures, these documents symbolized for me moments of triumph over the forces arrayed against the formation of my family. I spent hours hanging them so they would be properly displayed, although I knew that no one at the party would understand their meaning for me.

For each child the collection included the Massachusetts adoption agency home study approving me as parentally fit; the Immigration and Naturalization Service (INS) order clearing me to go to Peru in order to adopt; the Peruvian adoption court order appointing me provisional guardian (the order that enabled the child to live with me in Lima pending completion of the adoption); the final adoption decree, issued by the same court two months later (which made me the legal parent); the Peruvian passport enabling the child to leave the country; the visa issued by the U.S. consulate in Lima enabling him to enter the United States; the U.S. adoption decree, issued by a Massachusetts court; and the certificate documenting U.S. citizenship. Numerous birth certificates were also displayed on my walls. Each of my adopted children has been thrice born and has three birth certificates to prove it — the first issued at the time of his actual birth, the second after the Peruvian adoption, and the third after the U.S. adoption. The Peruvian birth certificates are the most glorious, and are stamped by the largest number of officials — some dozen in all, including Lima's mayor and Peru's minister of the interior as well as its minister for foreign affairs. The collection of documents looked imposing, but it represented only the proverbial tip of the massive bureaucratic iceberg involved in international adoption.

My adoptions were in many respects examples of smooth efficiency in the world of international adoption. It took only a year in each case, from the start of the home study process in Massachusetts to my return with the child from Peru. Peru has been known as a difficult country in which to accomplish a foreign adoption, but virtually every country presents its own set of difficulties. Some have programs with long waiting lists of prospective adopters; some have restrictive parent eligibility criteria that exclude singles and those over forty from consideration; some take from six to twelve months to process an adoption, requiring the child to wait in a foster home or an institution until the adoption is finalized. Countries that make foreign adoption relatively easy one day often close down the next. I count myself lucky to have found my way to Peru at a time when it was relatively sympathetic to foreign adoptions.

Many of those who have tried to adopt there in recent years have been required to spend eight months or more in Peru in order to complete the adoption process, and many others have lost the children they were initially assigned, as the authorities place new restrictions on international adoption.

Nonetheless, I think of these two adoptions as among the hardest, most challenging experiences of my life. There were many times that I felt scarily close to the limits of what I could handle without somehow cracking. The worst aspect by far was my terror that the child I had come to think of as my own shortly after he came home to live with me would be taken from me. I came to realize early on that I could not know until the end either when the end would come — how many months the process would take — or whether when it did come my child would be *legally* mine and free to go home with me to the United States.

The difficulties involved in my adoptions now seem of no real moment in my life. I was able to go to Peru and return as the legal parent of these two children. The five months that I was required to live in Peru gave me the opportunity to make some good friends there and to learn something about the country and the history and culture of its people. Our house in Cambridge, Massachusetts, is now filled with ponchos and llama bells and books on Peruvian art and artifacts, and I can talk to my boys about the land of their birth as something other than an abstraction. We follow the news about Peru with concern for our particular friends as well as the country as a whole.

But the difficulties amount to insurmountable barriers for most people contemplating adoptive parenthood. For financial and emotional reasons, most people are not able to abandon job, family, and the rest of their life for an unpredictable number of months to endure what it takes to accomplish an adoption in Peru or in many other countries.

When I was in Peru, I had a lot of time to think about the meaning of these barriers. I spent endless hours sitting on hallway benches at Inabif, the state adoption agency, and at the adoption court, waiting for something to happen or to be told that nothing actually would happen that day. I observed the sweet-faced young couples who sat on the benches with me as they waited day after day to see whether a child would be assigned to them. I shared the excitement of those who finally did get a child. I commiserated with those whose faces became taut with strain as the weeks went by and the adoption process for some reason or for no apparent reason broke down, and as they lived with the daily reality that the child they now thought of as theirs would be taken away.

As I sat there, I thought about the children that I saw and heard about every day. I thought of the babies in the shelter where Michael lived briefly, and the social worker's warning that if Michael had to go back there, he might die of the virus that was sweeping through the shelter (this vibrant, healthy chunk of a child, born with no more serious health problems than an allergy to cow's milk). I thought of the hospital where Christopher and Michael were both born, and my visit to its room for the *abandonados,* with cribs for eight or ten children. Babies lay in most of the cribs, some crying and some silent. In one a sad-eyed child, perhaps two years old, stood holding on to the bars, staring silently at me. They were there not because of any health problems but simply because there was no one to care for them. The hospital was impressively clean and orderly for an obviously poor hospital, and caring people worked there. But the room was clammy, cold, and drafty. There was no attendant in sight and apparently none within earshot. I was told that someone came every four hours to feed the babies and every six hours to change them (diapers are expensive in Peru). She tried to hold some of the babies for their feeding, but obviously this wasn't possible for all of them — there were too many. In between these visits the babies simply lay there, crying or quiet, staring through the bars of their cribs. I thought of the stories I had heard from a Peruvian reporter about the thousands of orphans created by the Shining Path's activities, and the plans that were being made to build additional orphanages to house them. No plans were in process to find them adoptive homes.

The INS Preclearance

I leave my Cambridge house at 6:30 A.M. to get to the INS office in Boston by seven to line up in the hallway outside the locked doors, which won't open until nine. I know from previous experience that if I wait until nine to get there, I will be given an interview number that won't be called until sometime in the afternoon.

This is the day I will submit my application for the INS "preclearance," which will permit me to go to Peru for Michael's adoption. The INS must certify that I have satisfied Massachusetts and INS requirements and demonstrated for U.S. purposes my fitness as an adoptive parent of a child from abroad. I have been through this process with Christopher's adoption, so at least I feel I know what I am doing. But with this as with other steps of the second adoption, I cannot rely on prior findings of fitness; everything must be done all over again. I bring a sheaf of documents — completed home study, fingerprint sheets, birth certificate, divorce decree, and many more.

At nine a guard opens the doors, and those of us who have been waiting — some hundred by now — file through to sit on the benches in the enormous waiting room until our numbers are called. I am surrounded by people from other countries trying to deal with their own immigration problems. At 9:15 the man who was ahead of me in line takes his papers up to the interview window and presents them. He is promptly told that they are no good; he will have to fix them and come back another time. He struggles in his broken English to figure out the problem. What is wrong? Can he fix it now? He has taken a day off from work to come in. He is sent away with no understanding of what he needs to do to have things be right another day.

I go up and present my lawyerly piles of originals and copies. The man at the window looks through them and announces that the divorce decree is no good; I need a final order from the divorce court. With all the weight of my status as an American citizen and a Harvard law professor, I tell him that this is the only order that the divorce court in New York issued, the divorce took place fifteen years ago, in 1972, and is indeed quite final, and these identical papers, including this very same divorce decree, were accepted by the INS just two years ago for the preclearance for my first adoption. The man shakes his head, unmoved. The divorce decree is still not adequate. I beg him at least to check with another INS official. He reluctantly does so and returns, saying that he will let me submit my papers but they will probably be rejected by the authorities who decide these things. I go away relieved and grateful but worried that if my papers are rejected, I will not have time to resubmit them and get them processed before my projected date of departure for Peru. As it turns out, the INS finds my papers acceptable and issues the preclearance, enabling me to move on to the next stage.

The Peruvian Adoption

I arrive in Lima's airport with a small suitcase full of documents (and with copies in a separate suitcase in case the first set is lost or stolen). I have the Massachusetts home study and the INS preclearance. I have fourteen additional documents that are required for the Peruvian adoption process, including medical reports on my physical and psychological health, character references from my employer and my minister, and police reports documenting the absence of any criminal record. Each has been notarized and translated. Each has been stamped with the seal of the Massachusetts secretary of state and legalized and stamped, page by page, by the Peruvian consulate in Boston. (I have also brought all the vital papers documenting Christopher's adoption and naturalization as a U.S. citizen, and I have brought an updated Peruvian passport in addition to his U.S. passport. I am worried about losing the first child while I am in the process of adopting the second. Most of my friends at home think that I am paranoid. My friends who have adopted from abroad do not.)

The documents I bring from the United States will do no more than get me through the entrance of the Peruvian adoption process. Peru will now do its own home study and examine my parental fitness through its own social workers and psychiatrists and police and doctors.

It is midnight when Christopher and I land in Lima. The airport scene is the familiar chaos. There is nothing resembling a line for customs, just a massive, shoving crowd. With our several large bags, we end up at the back of this crowd. Not yet three years old, Christopher is very game, and takes responsibility for one of the large bags, pushing it forward a few inches at a time. It takes two hours for us to get up to the customs officials, but I am thrilled to be here, and intensely conscious of how different it all seems from my first terrifying arrival two years ago. Adoption is known territory now. I feel at home in this crazy airport. I am pleased to be back in this country, which I have come to love. A couple who became dear friends during Christopher's adoption are waiting for us on the other side of customs. I have brought a flashlight to deal with the predictable terrorist blackouts, and a Thermos for the hot water I will use to mix formula during those long waits with the new baby in the police stations and the adoption court. I am sure that I will be able to handle the difficulties of the adoption process a lot better this time.

But international adoptions are not so predictable. This second Peruvian adoption turns out to be in many ways different from the first, and in many ways much, much worse.

After finding an apartment in Lima, I start my baby search, talking to adoption lawyers, talking to people at Inabif, and talking to more or less everyone I meet ("My friend's sister-in-law has to give up her baby — I'll call her"; "My cousin's friend works in an orphanage — I'll meet you there tomorrow"). I meet other North Americans, many of whom have been in Lima for weeks looking and waiting for a child. I am lucky. Within a week I hear of several children available for adoption, including newborn triplet girls that an Inabif social worker told me about during my first interview at the agency. It seems so clear in the adoption world of Lima that the point of life is to find babies to parent, that when I am asked if I am interested in the triplets, I actually spend some moments contemplating the possibility. But I force myself to think of the realities of life back home. I try to envision myself getting them there (carrying one in a frontpack and one in a back-pack, with Christopher pushing one in a stroller?), and I tell the social worker that I really can't handle triplets.

The next day I am told by Inabif authorities of a one-month-old baby boy. I arrange to meet him. That afternoon I rattle through the streets in one of Lima's ancient taxis to find Viru, an impressively clean and professional, although obviously poor, children's shelter. After an hour's wait, a woman appears and hands me a small blanketed bundle. I sit on the bench in the courtyard and push the blankets away a bit to find a scowling face with dark eyes under pronounced eyebrows. I smile at what a character he seems already. I take off the outer blanket and the inner blanket and the long pants and the jacket. It is at least ninety degrees in this courtyard, and it feels like an act of cruelty just to hold a baby sweltering inside all these layers, but Peruvians dress their babies warmly and I worry that I may be demonstrating parental unfitness. I watch this child grimace and yawn, and wonder a thousand wonders in this strange moment of deciding whether to become the parent of this particular child. How do you know your baby? I begin to feel oddly comfortable with his little face. The next day I tell Inabif that I would like to adopt this child. A few days later Michael comes home to the apartment in Lima where Christopher and I have been living.

Deciding to adopt Michael means that I will be working directly with Inabif, the state adoption agency, and will have no lawyer to act as a buffer between me and the Peruvian system. During Christopher's adoption I was in a perpetual state of rage and despair at my dealings with Yvonne, the private lawyer who arranged that adoption. But as this adoption proceeds, I come to think longingly of Yvonne's protective presence. That first adoption, which seemed traumatic at the time, was a smooth-running operation with no major hitches in comparison with this one.

The formal steps are essentially the same. I will be visited by a social worker to check out my home and to assess the quality of my parenting during the temporary guardianship period. I will make the rounds to be checked out by the police, the medical doctors, the psychiatrist, and others. I will make countless appearances in the adoption court.

But when the Inabif social worker comes to my house, it does not feel like the *pro forma* visit of my first adoption. I have heard from other adoptive parents that this particular social worker has removed several children from the adoptive parents with whom they were originally placed and has put a hold on the court proceedings in several other cases, leaving the adoptive parents in a state of desperate uncertainty. No one knows for sure why, but some suspect that it was because she felt she had not been appropriately treated. Does this mean they failed to provide a "gift" that she felt entitled to? It is illegal to bribe public officials in Peru, and the president is campaigning to give this legal prohibition new meaning, so it seems genuinely dangerous to think of offering anything to a social worker. But the bureaucratic and judicial systems traditionally operate on the premise that gifts will be given to smooth the way; a refusal to proffer the expected gift can be seen as niggardly or hostile, and it poses a very real risk that whatever it is you want will simply not happen.

The gift system is so prevalent that some people earn their living by hiring themselves out at a small fee to do what it takes to make the system work. When I needed to send a suitcase back to the United States, a Peruvian friend took me to the air shipping agency, where his first act was to hire such a person for a five-dollar fee. This man's livelihood depended on getting such fees from people who wanted to do nothing more than send an air freight package. In exchange for the fee he would get the necessary stamps and approvals, a process that involved giving some number of one- and two-dollar payments to a handful of different functionaries. These payments would be considered bribes in the United States, but they are simply part of what it takes to mail a suitcase in Peru. We arrived at the air shipping agency at nine in the morning. By hiring this man to hand out such payments, we were able to obtain the final permit for sending the suitcase by the close of business that afternoon. If we had not hired him, I am not sure whether I would have been able to send the suitcase at all. The dilemma for adoptive parents from abroad who are trying to negotiate Peru's adoption system without a lawyer to act as a go-between is that they do not know whether they risk insulting an official and losing their child by *not* giving a gift or risk losing their child and perhaps going to jail by *giving* a gift.

So during the visits from my social worker, I am terrified of making any misstep that could be used against me. I wait for her nervously, straightening up my little apartment, changing my children's clothes to make sure they look appropriately dressed, remembering to put baby socks on Michael, because Peruvian babies always wear socks, even in the sweltering heat of summer. I impress on Christopher the importance of being good when the social worker visits so that she won't take Michael away. I feel awful creating this particular kind of uncertainty in his three-year-old world, but I am grimly conscious of the priorities. After the social worker's visits, I curse myself for the mistakes I have made — for the fact that she noticed that Michael's diaper was wet before I did, or that I did not manage to get a burp out of him after his bottle. But I kiss her on both cheeks as she comes and goes, and as I come and go in her office at Inabif, and I thank her for her advice about how to hold and feed and clothe my child.

When I go to the various police agencies for the required medical exam, and my fingerprint check, and the baby's foot-print check, and my residence check, the experience is in ways comfortably familiar. I am now used to the sight of guards everywhere, with machine guns at the ready. But I talk with an adoptive parent who was forced by a group of armed policemen to remove her clothes in the process of what was supposed to be a residence check. She decided later that the problem must have been her failure to proffer a gift. So I approach my visits to the police longing for the protective presence of a lawyer like Yvonne. On my required visit to the police doctor, I sit humbly waiting on a bench with Michael in my arms for hours, in a hallway crowded with men in mana-cles who had been arrested the night before, and I avoid offending anyone by asking when I might be seen. When the doctor finally appears, I am frightened as I follow him into his empty office, sit as instructed in a chair facing him, with a bare bulb shining directly in my face, answer questions about the number of rooms in my house back in Cambridge, and stand up for the dreaded physical exam, which happily con-sists only of having my stomach and back poked through my clothes.

The psychiatric screening is a challenge. There are four interviews with the Inabif psychiatrist, who speaks only Spanish. I have been told that I cannot bring my own transla-tor to help me through the process; I am to use only the Inabif translator, presumably so that I will understand only what they choose to have me understand of what is going on. Their translator is an apparently sympathetic soul named Sylvie, but since she is the only translator, she is often off on other cases and unavailable to me. So I am left to get through my psychiatric interviews and tests on my own, with the benefit only of my Berlitz phrase book, my English-Spanish dictionary, and the few Spanish lessons I took back in Cambridge between adoption trips. I pray that I am right in assuming that this screening is essentially a charade.

In my second session I am asked to draw a "normal" person. I wonder whether the psychiatrist will think that this odd creature I produce is really my idea of a normal person or will understand that I simply can't draw. Then she asks me to draw a family. I am prepared for this, as another single parent told me that when she drew a mother with a child in her arms in response to this request, the psychiatrist told her that this would not do — she was to draw a real family. I draw a picture of a man, woman, and child, taking silent satisfaction in the fact that in my mind the man is my son Derek and not the requisite husband.

Then I am presented with a questionnaire, which, happily, has been translated into English. It contains a series of statements, each of which I am supposed to match with one of the following choices: "almost never," "a few times," "many times," and "continuously." Some of the statements have no obvious match, but getting the wrong answer doesn't seem too dangerous. "I eat as well as I used to." I figure that "many times" will do as the answer. "My life is too interesting." Here "continuously" seems clearly the correct answer for my current state, and not a dangerous choice in any event. I have great difficulty, however, in deciding on the right match for the statement "I still enjoy sex." "Almost never" or "a few times" would seem to imply that I don't enjoy sex, which must be considered an unhealthy thing. But for a single parent to say she still enjoys sex "continuously" seems obviously unwise. I compromise on "many times" and decide not to write an explanation of the healthy attitude about sex that I mean to convey, because I have already been criticized for messy drawing and I don't want to imply further disrespect.

When I get home, the adoptive parent who rents a room in the same large house where I have my tiny apartment, and who has completed this same psychiatric screening, tells me that my answer will mark me in this psychiatrist's eyes as a sex maniac. (This seems particularly unfair given the current circumstances of my life.) I take comfort in the fact that since the next psychiatric session will apparently focus largely on sex, I will have a chance to try to repair the damage. At the end of our final session, the psychiatrist pronounces me psychologically fit. She reads to me from her report, which notes that my answers revealed a certain amount of evasion. I find this insightful. The report also states that I used to like to lie in bed in the mornings but now that I have the baby I get up early. I have the sense of hearing my fortune told.

As the weeks go by in this adoption, I develop a sense of belonging. When then-president Alan García returns triumphant from a trip abroad, I rush home to my little apartment to watch the scene on television, sharing the excitement with my Peruvian nanny and in some odd way thinking of García as "our" president. Christopher and I settle in front of the television at five o'clock every afternoon to watch the Thundercats cartoon, understanding almost none of the Spanish but clinging to the routine as if it were our familiar *Sesame Street*. Christopher has quickly learned the sound of Lima's ice cream carts, and is an expert at waving down the gypsy cabs and assessing the relative degree of breakdown of one compared to the next.

I come to delight in my prowess in dealing with the challenges of the Peruvian adoption world. Two or three times a week I am off to Inabif or to court or to the police or to some other adoption-related destination. I have found a cabdriver to pick me and Christopher up on a regular basis in the mornings. We leave Michael behind with the nanny. The cab stops first at the nursery school I have found after two weeks of searching. We go in, greeting the teacher in our best Spanish. No one here speaks English, but Christopher is thrilled to have discovered this place with play equipment and other children (there are no playgrounds in Lima). I get back in the cab, where I start working with my Spanish-English dictionary to put together some sentences to deal with what I anticipate will be the problems of the day. When I'm done, I practice my Spanish with the driver.

On my regular visits to Inabif, I smile as I check in with the armed guards. I pass under the large clock downstairs, which is always set at the wrong time, and go upstairs to the offices, where another clock which is always set at a different wrong time hangs. I knock on my social worker's door and put my head in to let her know that I am there. This is the accepted form of announcing one's arrival and is not considered too pushy. I then return to the hallway waiting area. It is usually an hour or two before my social worker announces that we are off to court or some other destination, or that the plans have been canceled and I should come back tomorrow. I have learned to use this time. I talk to various Inabif workers as they pass by. I have managed to befriend a few of them, and have learned from one some details about Michael's birth parents that may be of interest to him in the future. Another has helped me make friends with one of the officials in the police agency that is housed in this building and that plays a variety of roles in the screening process. I knock on doors and kiss cheeks and say thank you and smile until my face aches. I talk to the adoptive parents who wait on the benches for their appointments and ask how their cases are going. I try to pick up useful information and warnings, and I try to help those whose cases seem to be in trouble figure out what has gone wrong and what they should do.

At the adoption court, I spend hours on the bench in the hallway outside my judge's chambers. I am on very friendly terms with the judge's clerk, Mario, and am intensely grateful that such an apparently goodhearted man is in this position. As clerk, he has enormous power to affect the course of my adoption proceedings. His good will proves crucial. He does his best to speed my case along, telling me after each legal step is completed what has to be done next and helping me think through how to push the Inabif authorities to do it. I strain to understand his Spanish and to put together from my limited vocabulary the words to convey my problems, my questions, and my appreciation. One day toward what should be the end of the process, I am due to make the vital appearance before my judge so that she can finalize the adoption and issue the long-awaited decree declaring me Michael's legal parent. The Inabif lawyer is supposed to meet me at court, but she doesn't show up at the appointed time. I am frantic, and appeal to Mario. He speaks to the judge and then ushers me in for the proceeding. I stumble through a few exchanges with the judge in Spanish, and emerge triumphant at having "represented myself" in adoption court in Peru!

But the triumphs are always short-lived, because every few days throughout the entire two months something happens to make me think that I might lose Michael. The worst legal crisis comes early in the process. He has been with me for six days, and we have lived through that first terrifying fever, the taxi drive to the hospital when I thought he might die in my arms, and the next night in our apartment, when I held him all night, afraid that I might fall off to sleep and afraid also that the killer fever might return and the medicine not work. He has recovered and we are supposed to go to court for the order that officially assigns him to me in provisional guardianship, pending the final adoption order. Inabif has twice before postponed this trip, and I am beginning to get nervous. Until we appear for the first time in court, Michael is entirely under Inabif's jurisdiction; I have no legal tie to him, and they can take him from me at will.

We arrive at Inabif, where I am to pick up my social worker for the trip to court. The moment I poke my head into her office I know that something has gone terribly wrong. She looks up without a smile, stares at me for a moment, and tells me to wait. Later I see her talking to the Inabif director, both of them looking at me and both seeming angry and agitated. An hour goes by and my social worker approaches me in the hallway to tell me that they think Michael should go back to the children's shelter. She talks vaguely about how things might go badly in court if the judge finds out that Inabif put Michael in my care without waiting for a court order. I know this is untrue and that something else is going on. I tell her how sick Michael was when he came to me from the shelter, and how the nurse there told me that he might die if he was returned — there were so many babies sick with the fever. She stares at me with eyes that are entirely cold and hard, and turns to go back into her office. I stand there knowing that I may be about to lose Michael. In a moment the social worker could reappear, and we could be off to leave him at the shelter. I am sure that if this happens I will never see him again.

By some happy miracle I have brought the nanny with me, and I decide to send Michael home with her. If the Inabif authorities are determined to take him from me, this will at least give me a day to figure out what to do to keep him. I hurry him and the nanny toward the steps and out of the building.

Sometime later I am called into the director's office, with my social worker and the translator. The director is icy but calm as she sends out a series of negative messages. It's a problem that I already have one adopted child. It's a problem that the judge has these negative feelings about North American adopters. This adoption is going to take many months — longer than they told me originally. I struggle desperately to decipher the real meaning of the messages. Suddenly she explodes with rage, screaming at me. The translator reluctantly tells me that the director has accused me of working with a private lawyer behind her back. Inabif hates the private adoption lawyers, as these lawyers sometimes take over cases involving Inabif babies. Unlike the salaried Inabif workers, the private lawyers make big money in Peruvian terms. During one of my first meetings with the Inabif director, I was required to sign a piece of paper on which I swore that I would not use a lawyer in connection with Michael's adoption. At that time the director was all smiles as we talked about the law (she was also a lawyer), and Harvard Law School (always my ticket to successful relations in Peruvian adoption matters). I rush to assure her now that I have not been seeing a lawyer and would of course not violate my pledge. I feel relieved to think that I finally have some idea as to what is going on. Since I have in fact not been seeing a lawyer, I am sure that I will be able to clear up the misunderstanding. But the director snarls something that is translated as "You can never tell they're lying until the end," and then talks about other North Americans who have left Inabif as soon as they have their babies in order to work with private lawyers. I plead my case desperately, and humbly, but seem to get nowhere. I shift topics, afraid that they will focus again on returning Michael to the shelter. They finally end the session, and I leave the Inabif offices as quickly as possible.

I go home in a state of real terror, and without even stopping in my apartment to see the children, I rush in to Sonia's quarters to consult with her. Sonia owns the villa, renting rooms out to adoptive parents to make ends meet. She prides herself on her knowledge of the adoption process. We talk for hours, trying to figure out what has gone wrong and how I can set things right before Michael is taken away. A phone call comes through for me. It is Carla, a lawyer I talked to early in my baby search. She has a baby for me. I tell her that I have a baby and get off the phone. Sonia is suddenly sure she knows what is going on. This lawyer, hungry for my case, must have been spreading the rumor that I had been working with her in the hope that I would then lose my Inabif baby and as a result would turn to her and the child that she has available. (Sonia later told me that she confirmed with her friends within the adoption system that this is exactly what had happened.)

That night I decide on what seems like a desperate strategy, suggested by a well-connected Peruvian lawyer who is a friend. He will take me in the morning to see an influential criminal court judge he knows. We will tell him my tale and see if he will come with us to the adoption court judge, to whom Inabif has so far refused to present me. The hope is that together we will be able to persuade her to accept my adoption application and to look favorably on my case. The danger is that Inabif will be further enraged at me for going around them and trying to present my own case in court. But since I am convinced that they have already decided to take Michael from me, I see no choice but to try the end run. I go to sleep feeling like one of Henry James's naive Americans, stunned at the complex machinations of the players in Lima's adoption world but grimly determined to get my wits together for what feels like the battle of my life.

The next day I hear my lawyer friend describe my case to the adoption judge as the criminal court judge sits watching. I have brought all my documents, pictures of Derek and my home in Cambridge, and a neatly dressed and combed Christopher as testimony to my fitness to parent Peruvian children. Suddenly the door to the judge's chambers opens and Carla, the private adoption lawyer, pokes her head in. Her face fixes in an expression of cold anger as she surveys the group. She and the adoption judge look at each other for one long moment and then Carla backs off, closing the door. My friend and I exchange a look; it seems that Carla's scheme somehow involved this judge as well. Later we will try to unravel the mystery, but for now what matters is that our strategy has apparently worked. The adoption judge asks me a few questions and then announces that she will open a file on my case. I am to tell Inabif that they should present it to her within the next few days. The adoption court now has jurisdiction over Michael. Inabif no longer has the power to remove him from me at will.

I go home to celebrate. I take Michael out to buy him some new clothes of his very own. I had held off on this symbolic "claiming" action out of superstitious fear that I might somehow jinx our chances of staying together. I think about how hard it would be for my friends to understand what it is like to have other people be in a position to take away for any or no reason the child you think of as your own. I realize that people who have not adopted might not even understand why I was so determined to hold on to this child anyway. It might all seem quite arbitrary. He had been in my life for only a week. Why him rather than some other child that I could have found the week before or could find next week? They would not understand why this child would feel uniquely mine.

Inabif does take me to court, as instructed, and the court issues the long-awaited order appointing me provisional guardian. But I never have a real sense of ease again until I am on the plane home. I worry to the end that someone at Inabif or elsewhere will sabotage my case, and every few days there seems some new cause for alarm — some hostile signal, or some indication that the process may have broken down — and the fear that Michael will be taken away seizes me and the ongoing tension begins to seem too much to bear.

In the meantime, I watch some of the adoptive parents around me begin to crack under the strain. On one of my early visits to Inabif I noticed a stunning-looking woman from Sweden, vibrant with energy and enthusiasm. I was impressed with her resilience: she had been coming to Inabif every day for three weeks when I met her, waiting for several hours each morning in the hope that they would eventually assign her a child, and she was still cheerful and positive. Finally they did give her a six-month-old girl. Two months later, on the eve of my departure for the United States, this woman comes to see me for advice, bringing the baby, whom she quite evidently adores. The once-vibrant face looks strained and tragic. Her case has been going badly for weeks — a series of unexplained delays. She has been living with the fear that they might take the child away but with no sense of why or of what she might do to turn things around. We talk. I give her some ideas. But I learn after my return to the United States that six weeks later Inabif removed the child, only to place her after a few more weeks with an adoptive mother from the United States. Now the Swedish woman comes every summer for a week to visit the child that once was hers.

The U.S. Visa

You cannot apply for the visa the child will need to leave Peru and enter the United States until the adoption is completed. But you may find at that point that you cannot satisfy the legal requirements for obtaining the visa, so although you are now the legal parent of a child with whom you have lived for some months, you are not free to take the child back to the United States. When I first arrived in Peru for Christopher's adoption, I heard of the case of an adoptive parent who had been in Peru for eight months and was still trying to get a visa for her child. Eventually Congress authorized a special emergency visa permitting her child to return with her. The problem was that the man named on the child's birth certificate as the father had signed the certificate, which meant that he had officially acknowledged paternity. U.S. law authorizes visas only for adoptees who satisfy a narrow definition of *orphan*, and this child did not qualify. No matter that the child's putative father had entirely disappeared from the scene and had demonstrated no interest in being a parent. No matter that notice to this man had duly gone out, as required under Peruvian law, informing him of the adoption proceedings and of his right to assert any interest he might have in the child. No matter that Peru, like other nations, allows children who have been abandoned or relinquished by their birth parents to be adopted whether or not they are orphans. The United States will not permit nonorphan adoptees to enter the country with their adoptive parents.

An adoptive parent I became friends with in Lima went to the American consulate for her visa at the end of a wracking three-month adoption process. She was desperate to go home. The adoption had been difficult from start to finish, her child had a possibly serious medical problem for which she could not get satisfactory treatment in Lima, her job leave was running out back in Boston — she was a single parent and needed this job — and she had long ago run through the money she had brought to Lima. She came back from the consulate that afternoon in despair. The INS fingerprint clearance she had obtained before coming to Peru had expired. The prints would have to be cleared again to ensure that she had not recently committed some crime that would disqualify her in the eyes of the U.S. authorities as a fit parent for the child who was already legally her child. The Massachusetts adoption agency, which had charged her some $5,000 for its part in arranging this adoption, had not advised her before she left home about the need to update her INS clearance, and it did not give her much help now, either. She sat with her bags packed for two more weeks in Lima, waiting for the new fingerprint clearance to come through so that her child could get the visa.

Getting Michael's visa goes relatively easily for me. Before turning my visa application papers over to the consulate officials, I read with care the letter Inabif has given me describing Michael's legal status. My Spanish is good enough by now for me to see that the letter's description is not entirely accurate and could cause problems. It is unnerving to think that I might have unwittingly turned this letter in, and also unnerving to be dependent still on the good graces of my friends at Inabif, but I go and knock on doors and kiss cheeks one more time and ask for a new letter, and they give it to me. A few days later I sit with Michael in the tiny interviewing cubicle at the American consulate, talking through bulletproof glass to an official who concludes that all my papers are in order. I will be able to pick up the visa later this week.

A Problem at the Airport

My final night in Lima I go out for a last pisco sour with my closest Peruvian friend. I am up at four the next morning to sort the money and documents I will need for the final adoption procedures and for the airport clearance. I stuff a few more items in our packed suitcases. (Christopher insisted that we start packing as soon as I dared to tell him that we would really be going home, and he has talked of little except our departure for three days. He has been so cheerfully enthusiastic about our life in Lima that I had not realized he was in fact desperately anxious to go home.)

We are off at seven to the superior court, where we need one more vital signature. We stop by on the way at the Peruvian passport agency, where I check in with the man who has been waiting in line for me since five and will continue to wait until I return. We are at the superior court from seven-thirty until noon, and I have just about given up on our prospects for returning home today when a man emerges with the document containing the essential signature of the president of the court. We race over to the passport agency, where we get Michael's passport in record time. Then we're off to the translator for official translations of the key documents and then on to the American consulate, just in time for my three o'clock appointment to pick up Michael's visa. It is all done in a mad rush, and the only reason it is possible is that Yvonne has stepped in to help me at the last minute. We tear around Lima with the cast of characters familiar from my first adoption: Bonnie driving the ancient orange Volkswagen, Roger tearing off with legal papers to be copied or legalized, and Yvonne disappearing without explanation in her maddening way but reappearing magically just in time to take us to the next place and, after all I have been through with Inabif, seeming to me at this moment the personification of gracious goodheartedness and lawyerly effectiveness.

Back home we have a quick dinner; then I put Michael in a frontpack to free my hands for our bags, and we are off to the airport. We make our way through the various checkpoints and at midnight are standing before the final Peruvian official. I produce my stack of documents: Michael's adoption papers, the judicial permit authorizing him to leave the country, his passport, his visa, and Christopher's U.S. passport, together with my own. The guard studies the documents and then looks up. "Just one problem." The world seems to stop. I stare at him, willing this not to be happening. He goes on. "Not with the little one, but with this one," pointing at Christopher. "He's a Peruvian; he needs a Peruvian passport."

I rush to explain: "But he's a United States citizen. I have his citizenship papers with me." (I pushed through Christopher's citizenship before I came down for this second adoption precisely because I feared that something like this might happen.) The guard shows absolutely no interest in Christopher's U.S. citizenship. "He was born in Peru, wasn't he? He's a Peruvian and he needs a Peruvian passport." My numb brain is struggling to cope. I updated Christopher's Peruvian passport and brought it with me as an extra piece of protection, and I start to reach for it in my carry-on bag. But I am thinking about the Peruvian law that requires the father's written permission or special judicial authorization for any minor to leave the country. I stand there wondering if we are all about to return to Lima for another stretch of time. But then the guard waves us on. "Just remember next time."

America the Beautiful

My head is screaming with pain the entire fifteen-hour trip home. Tension and lack of sleep have gotten to me. But I am still thrilled that we three are finally going home and that the adoption process is essentially over. It will take another two years to complete the U.S. adoption and to make Michael an American citizen, but I know that these steps will involve a relatively minimal amount of additional bureaucratic maneuvering. And at least we will be home.

I think back to the naturalization ceremony at Boston's historic Faneuil Hall, where Christopher became a citizen. The great room was filled with hundreds of new citizens who had come from all over the world. The judge had done a lot to make this a meaningful ceremony. He had brought his son, dressed in Boy Scout regalia, to lead the pledge of allegiance to the flag. He had arranged for a local high school band to play "The Star-Spangled Banner." He had also prepared a moving speech about the meaning of being a citizen of the United States. As he talked I looked at some of the faces around us: the tired face of an old woman wrapped in a peasant shawl who held tightly on to the arm of a man I took to be her son; the strong, determined face of a young man who seemed to be fighting back tears as he listened to the judge's words. I wondered about the stories that lay behind the decisions of all these people to make their way to this country. I thought of snatches of the story that had brought Christopher and me to this room. And for the first time in my life, I wept at the sound of our national anthem.

CURRENT SIGNIFICANCE AND FUTURE PROSPECTS[1]

International adoption plays an enormously important part in the total adoption picture. How the various nations of the world shape the rules governing international adoption will define to a great degree adoption's future role as a parenting alternative. This is because the world divides into essentially two parts for adoption purposes, one consisting of countries with low birth rates and small numbers of children in need of homes and the other consisting of countries with high birth rates and huge numbers of such children. In the United States and other industrialized Western countries, the number of children surrendered or abandoned by their birth parents has been limited in recent decades by contraception, abortion, and the increased tendency of single parents to keep their children. As a result there are very few children available for adoption, in comparison with the large numbers of people who are eager to adopt.[2] In the poorer countries of the world there are very few prospective adopters, in comparison with the vast numbers of children in need of homes.[3]

For the infertile who want to parent, finding a child in

another country is the major alternative to infertility treatment and to infertility "bypass" arrangements such as donor insemination and surrogacy arrangements. The oft-proclaimed notion that "there are no babies available for adoption" has some truth if the focus is limited to babies born in the United States, but there are many babies available for adoption elsewhere, and masses more in need of homes. For potential adopters ranked low on the agency fitness scales, international adoption significantly increases the range of parenting choices. Other countries have their own screening systems, but the criteria vary enormously, so the single person or the couple over forty will be able to find at least a few countries abroad where they can adopt.

For most of the homeless children of the world, international adoption represents the only realistic opportunity to have a permanent family of their own.

On a symbolic level, international adoption presents in extreme form the issues that are at the heart of all adoption. It can be understood as the ultimate form of the exploitation that some see at the heart of all adoption — the taking by the rich and powerful of the children born to the poor and powerless. In international adoption, the privileged classes in the industrialized nations adopt the children of the least privileged groups in the poorest nations. Whites adopt black- and brown-skinned children from various Third World nations. Children are separated not only from their birth parents but from their racial, cultural, and national communities.

But international adoption can also be understood as a particularly positive form of adoption, with prospective parents reaching out to children in need rather than fighting over the limited number of healthy white infants available for adoption in this country. The fact that these families are built across lines of racial and cultural difference can be understood as a good thing, both for the parents and children involved and for the larger community. These are families whose members must learn to appreciate one another's differences while experiencing their common humanity. The evidence indicates that they succeed in doing so.

The tensions between these different visions of international adoption are evident in recent developments. The past few decades have seen a vast increase in the number of children placed for adoption across national borders.[4] Roughly 10,000 children per year have come into the United States from abroad for adoption in recent years. They make up one fifth to one sixth of all nonrelative adoptions in this country and a somewhat larger percentage of all infant adoptions. Worldwide, there are an estimated 15,000 to 20,000 international adoptions per year.[5]

But this increasing openness to international adoption is colliding with a new hostility to it. The politics are similar to those involved in the debate about transracial adoption in this country. Children are said to belong with their "roots" and in their communities of origin. Political forces in the "sending" countries have been condemning in increasingly loud voices the practice of giving children to the imperialist North Americans and other foreigners. South Korea, which is responsible for sending more than half the children that have ever come to this country for adoption, is now eliminating its foreign adoption program in response to such pressures.[6] There is widespread acceptance of the notion that there is something shameful in sending homeless children abroad rather than taking care of them in their country of origin.

In today's international adoption world, many barriers stand between the children in need of homes and those eager to become their parents. A central issue for the future is whether these barriers should be reduced or made even more impregnable.

THE ROLE OF LAW

When the judge in Christopher's adoption case first heard my story in her crowded office above the dusty courtyard of

Lima's adoption court, she smiled kindly and seemed genuinely pleased that this four-month-old Peruvian would have a chance to go to the United States, the proverbial land of opportunity, to live with this woman who taught at the famous Harvard University. She looked at the photographs of Derek and of my house in Cambridge and seemed to approve of the life I would provide. Then, after I had sworn the appropriate oaths and waited for the necessary papers to be typed up by her secretary, who tapped out the words painstakingly as she stood over him, she told me to come back the next day so that I could reaffirm what I had just sworn to.

Six weeks later she was still smiling and apparently delighted that the adoption was proceeding, but she decided that one more notice should go out to possibly interested parties, just to make sure that no question could be raised about the proprieties in this adoption. Then my papers were mysteriously held up for a week by an official who was supposed to be the "people's representative" in the court proceedings. At the end of the week this official announced that some of the documents I had brought with me from the United States were inadequate. She produced a list of new documents that I would have to obtain. I panicked at the prospect of additional weeks of delay, but finally I discovered the problem: she thought that I had it in my power to get her a student visa to the United States and to get her admitted to Harvard. Once she realized that I couldn't do these things, she dropped the new demands and signed my papers.

The law poses as the protecter of children but in the end functions as their enemy. Most of those implementing it are as well-meaning as my kindly judge; they are simply playing their part, as caught up in the machinery of the system as I was and almost as helpless.

The problem is that the law focuses only on the *negative* potential of international adoption and ignores its *positive* potential. Regulations address the risks of removing children from their birth parents for adoption abroad but do nothing to ensure that children growing up on the streets or in institutions are provided with permanent homes. Few seem aware of the *cost* of law. Few recognize that legal procedures that are apparently designed to protect children against abuse often translate in the real world into barriers that deny them the loving homes that they need to escape a life of abuse.

We do of course need regulations that guarantee that children are not improperly taken from their birth parents or transferred to situations in which they will be mistreated or exploited. But the law should also guarantee children the fundamental right to grow up in a nurturing environment. They should not be living and dying on the streets or languishing in inadequate institutions, and the law should be designed to ensure that they do not. By focusing exclusively and excessively on the negative potential of international adoption, the law fails entirely in its overall obligation to serve children's best interests.

NATIONAL LAWS AND POLICIES

While there is great variety in the way nations deal with international adoption, few have designed their laws to facilitate the placement of children in need of homes. Some countries prohibit foreign adoption, and others place special restrictions on it. Islamic countries prohibit all adoption, whether foreign or domestic. Although today most countries apparently allow foreign adoption, their laws and policies are not designed to accommodate its unique features, and therefore often effectively prevent many prospective parents from adopting across borders. Thus most Latin American countries insist that adoptive parents from abroad go through essentially the same steps that domestic adopters do — steps that might not be unduly burdensome for someone who lives locally but that require the foreigner to leave home, family, and job to undertake the adoption.

South Korea stands out as the country that has made the

most significant effort on the governmental level to enable foreigners to adopt its homeless children. Of course, it is in large part because this effort has been so successful that the South Korean government came under pressure to close down its foreign adoption program.

Most of the countries that function primarily as "receiving" rather than "sending" countries have done little to adapt their adoption, immigration, and citizenship laws to accommodate the realities of international adoption. As a result, these laws pose unnecessary hurdles in the foreign adoptive process. Our own country's restrictive approach to immigration, together with the complications of our federal system, means that would-be parents face a particularly challenging series of hurdles in accomplishing a foreign adoption. They must satisfy the laws and policies of three different jurisdictions: their home state, the federal government, and the foreign government. Because these jurisdictions have not coordinated their systems, the parents and their future child are screened repetitively and are subject to overlapping and often inconsistent standards.

Prospective parents must initially satisfy their home state's requirements with respect to parental fitness and other matters. A satisfactory home study is a prerequisite under federal law for all international adoptions. The foreign country decides which children are available for adoption and frees specific children for placement, and it decides whether adoptive parents must go to the child's country to be screened and to process the adoption or whether the child can be sent to the United States for placement. A requirement that the adoption must take place in the child's country of origin adds significantly to the financial and other costs, particularly when lengthy or uncertain periods of time or multiple trips abroad are involved.

The U.S. government's immigration rules determine whether a child placed by a foreign country will be permitted to enter the United States with his or her adoptive parents.

These rules allow the issuance of "preferential visas," which permit the immediate entry of foreign-born adoptees, only when the adoptive parents can demonstrate that they satisfy federal criteria for parental fitness and that they have fulfilled all requirements under the applicable laws of their home state and of the child's country of origin.[7] This adds yet another level of significantly duplicative processing.

In addition, Congress has severely and irrationally limited the scope of foreign adoption by granting entry only to foreign adoptees who fit a narrow definition of *orphan*.[8] For an adoptee to qualify, both parents must have died or have abandoned the child, or there must be a demonstration that the "sole or surviving" parent is unable to care for the child. Excluded are children who in some technical sense have two parents — even if the child is born to an unwed mother and the father consists of nothing more than a signature on a birth certificate, even if those parents are demonstrably unable or unwilling to care for the child, and even if those parents want to surrender the child for adoption.[9] Even children who have been left in an orphanage or on the streets, whose parents want them to be adopted, may not qualify as "unconditionally abandoned" for U.S. immigration law purposes.[10] And children who have already been adopted in foreign countries are not permitted to enter the United States with their legal adoptive parents if U.S. officials decide that they do not meet the restrictive *orphan* definition.

This restriction is an anomaly. Virtually all jurisdictions within this country and throughout the world permit parents to surrender their children for adoption without regard to whether the child has one parent or two or whether the parents are able to provide care.[11] The restriction causes many problems. It prevents the adoption of children who are in need of homes and who are free for adoption under the laws of their own country. It means that birth parents may feel compelled to abandon their children rather than surrender them in an orderly way in the hope of making them eligible for adoption in the United States. And it can add significantly to the emotional difficulties of adopting abroad. The visa decision is not made until the parents have completed the adoption and are ready to return home. Since the facts that determine whether a child satisfies the definition often cannot be known until late in the adoption process, adopters must go through the entire process of becoming the child's emotional and legal parents without knowing for sure whether they will be permitted to bring the child home with them.

Even after adoptive parents have returned to the United States, they must undertake a variety of legal steps in order to protect their child and their own parental status fully. A U.S. adoption is required if the child has not been adopted abroad, and is in any event advisable. A foreign adoption decree is not entitled to the "full faith and credit" accorded a U.S. adoption decree by courts within the United States. In addition, the decree from this country is generally necessary to obtain a U.S. birth certificate. It can be very important as a practical matter for adoptees to have their key birth and adoption documents issued by U.S. agencies in a language and style that is familiar and to know that they will be able to obtain copies of these documents with relative ease in the future if the need arises. Although a second adoption in the United States is usually no more than a formality, state law requirements have to be satisfied. Only a few states have adapted their adoption laws to ease recognition of foreign adoption decrees.[12]

Enabling the child to become a U.S. citizen is generally the final step in the international adoption process. Foreign adoptees do not become citizens by virtue of their adoption by citizens of the United States. They must apply for citizenship, a process that ordinarily takes from six months to a year. This final bureaucratic hurdle appears to have no substantive meaning. My Christopher, at the age of two and a half, was asked to raise his right hand and swear to renounce all foreign potentates. But he was quite obviously not being seriously screened for current and future loyalty to the United States; it was simply another absurd moment in a long absurd process. Obviously, the goal is simply to provide citizenship status to all foreign-born adoptees who apply.

From start to finish, international adoption involves an enormous amount of process with very little substance. For prospective parents with sufficient resources and determination, it is doable. There are many who are able and willing to endure a lot for the opportunity to adopt. Many adoption agencies have established ongoing programs with foreign agencies, and for parents who are able to work through these programs, a foreign adoption may be no more difficult than a domestic one. But the bureaucratic hassle has very significant costs in financial and other terms. The expenses generally begin at $10,000 and run up, with many international adoptions costing $15,000 to $25,000, even when there are no major hitches. Prospective parents can easily devote years of their lives to efforts that turn out to be futile. The children who are eventually adopted have generally lived for long periods of their young lives in orphanages or other institutions, waiting for placement. Also, of course, huge numbers who could have been adopted will not be — the barriers are simply too great for most of those interested in adoptive parenting to surmount.

Yet at the same time, the process provides less protection than it should for the children who manage to get adopted. The lack of coordination between the different jurisdictions means that some children fall through the cracks and are denied full adoptive status as well as citizenship, and the difficulties of the process provide incentives to find ways around the legal system.

INTERNATIONAL LAW AND THE HAGUE CONVENTION

International law has been largely silent on the topic of adoption. The United Nations has in recent years taken some significant action, with the passage by the General Assembly of a 1986 declaration[13] and a 1989 convention[14] recognizing the legitimacy of international adoption. However, these documents relegate such adoptions to last resort status, the preferred options being adoption, foster care, or other "suitable" care in the child's country of origin.[15] They do nothing to establish standards and procedures that might facilitate adoption between nations.

The Hague Conference on private international law recently embarked on a project designed to produce a convention on international adoption that could be agreed to by the major sending and receiving countries of the world. This effort once seemed to present significant promise for increased cooperation among nations in making international adoption work. But conference proceedings have been largely dominated by the concerns of those who emphasize the negative rather than the positive potential of this kind of adoption. While there is still room for hope that the Hague Conference will produce some positive changes, it now seems clear that it will stop short of establishing the kind of new legal structure needed to make the process work effectively. It will be left to the various nations of the world to take the initiative, either under the aegis of a vague convention or, in the absence of an agreed-to convention, by developing country-to-country treaties or other arrangements.

OF REAL PROBLEMS AND MYTHICAL CONCERNS

The problems that should be seen as central to the international adoption debate have to do with the misery and deprivation that characterize the lives of huge numbers of the children in the world. Countless millions of children die of malnutrition and of diseases that should not kill, and millions more live in miserably inadequate institutions or on the streets.[16] Their situations vary: some institutions are worse than others, and some street children maintain a connection with a family, while others are entirely on their own. But there can be no doubt that overwhelming numbers of children in poor countries are living and dying in conditions involving extreme forms of deprivation, neglect, exploitation, and abuse.[17] These are the real problems of the children of the world.

International adoption should be seen as an opportunity to solve some of these problems for some children. It should be structured to maximize this positive potential — to facilitate the placement of children in need of nurturing homes with people in a position to provide those homes. International adoption can of course play only a very limited role. Long-term solutions lie in reallocating social and economic resources, both between countries and within countries, so that children can more generally be cared for by their birth families. But international adoption *can* play at least *some* role. Given the fact that cosmic reordering is not on the immediate horizon, such adoption clearly serves the interests of at least those children for whom parents can be found.

Some have suggested that international adoption might conflict with programs designed to improve the lot of the huge numbers of children now in need or with efforts to accomplish the kind of social reordering that might help the children of the future. For example, some argue that instead of promoting and pursuing adoption, governments and individuals in the well-off industrialized countries should devote increased resources to more cost-effective programs designed to promote the well-being of children in their native lands — programs that might range from individual fostering arrangements, to sponsoring orphanages abroad, to a wide variety of UNICEF projects. But there is simply no reason to believe that foreign adoption is inconsistent with such efforts. Indeed, quite the reverse: foreign adoption programs are likely to increase awareness in the United States and other receiving countries of the problems of children in the sending countries. These programs give those who adopt reason to identify, through their children, with the situations of those children not lucky enough to have found homes. Foreign adoption can help create a climate that is more sympathetic to wide-ranging forms of support for children everywhere. Indeed, there is evidence that it has functioned in just this way to date.

Another argument is that international adoption might relieve pressure within some sending countries to deal with social problems that need attention. But this argument too collapses upon analysis. Sending children abroad for adoption tends to highlight rather than hide the fact that there are problems at home. Indeed, opposition to foreign adoption is based in large part on embarrassment within the sending countries over having their domestic problems revealed by this public confession of inability to take care of their own children. Although speculative arguments can always be mounted, it is hard to believe that there is any real risk that providing some of the world's homeless children with adoptive parents would stand in the way of helping other children in this or even in some future world.

The nations of the world are in general agreement that the best interests of the child should be the paramount principle governing the placement of children outside their biologic families. Given the real problems confronting children, it should be clear that this principle requires laws and policies that are designed to facilitate the international placement of children in need of homes.

Obviously the law should guarantee that international adoption does not create new problems. Adoption should not be used to break up viable birth families. Those who want to adopt should not be allowed to use their financial advantage to induce impoverished birth parents to surrender their children. We need laws that prohibit baby-buying, and we need rules that ensure that birth parents have voluntarily surrendered their child for adoption or have had their parental rights terminated for good reason. Adoption should also not be used simply to transfer children from one miserable situation to another. We need rules to ensure that adoptees receive loving, nurturing adoptive homes — rules protecting the adopted against any form of exploitation.

But it makes no sense to focus solely on the problems that might be created by international adoption while ignoring the very real problems of abuse, neglect, and exploitation suffered by homeless children in the absence of such adoption. It is patently absurd to talk as if the real dangers for children were that they might be stolen or bought from their birth parents to be transferred to other adults for purposes of abuse and exploitation.

Nonetheless, public discourse about international adoption focuses overwhelmingly on its alleged risks and dangers. Some of the concerns that have been voiced have no basis whatsoever in fact. One notorious example is the "baby parts" rumor, prevalent in recent years in a number of sending countries, which involves the claim that people from the United States and other receiving countries are adopting foreign children in order to kill them for their organs, which are then used in organ transplants.[18] The claim is entirely unsubstantiated and has been repeatedly debunked, but it has received widespread circulation in the media of some fifty countries, has been taken seriously by a number of international human rights groups, and is apparently widely believed.

Other concerns about international adoption have some basis in reality but are enormously exaggerated. For example, critics both in this country and abroad focus on the danger that children will be kidnapped or bought from their birth parents for sale to rich North Americans who are desperate to parent. The media in this country give headline coverage to any stories of "kidnapping rings" or "baby trafficking." There are indeed some documented instances of kidnappings and of improper payments to birth parents, but there is no evidence that these practices are widespread or that they are significant in the larger picture. Moreover, it is quite unlikely that they are common.[19] Current law makes it extremely risky for would-be adopters and intermediaries to engage in baby-buying or kidnapping. Even if some people might be willing to undertake such activities if this were the only way or the easiest way to accomplish an adoption, the fact is that it is *not*. International adoption is unduly difficult to accomplish in a lawful manner, and the legal barriers do create pressures to cut corners, but the fact remains that even those who are willing to break the law in certain respects should feel no need to violate the fundamental rules that prohibit using money to induce birth parents to surrender their children or that prohibit kidnapping. Sadly, the world is all too full of birth parents who are desperately eager to find homes for the children they cannot care for and of children who have already been surrendered or abandoned. When you look beneath the surface of most media and other stories of "child trafficking," it becomes clear that the term *trafficking* is used very loosely. The stories sometimes involve claims that what is characterized as a bribe may have been paid to an official in a country in which small payments to officials are a part of how official business is traditionally done. Often the stories involve nothing more than allegations that the adoptive parents paid high fees to agencies or other intermediaries for services required to accomplish their adoption. This is entirely legitimate, and is made necessary by the complications of the current legal system. Evidence that birth parents have been paid or that children have been taken from birth parents who are capable of and interested in raising them is extremely rare.

My point here is not to justify everything that has been done in the name of international adoption. Children quite obviously should not be stolen, nor should they be bought and sold; birth parents should not be encouraged by the prospect of payment to give up children whom they are interested in and capable of raising. But if we really care about children, we should be prepared to see even these evils in perspective. They are by no means the worst things that are happening to children or their birth parents today, and they occur relatively rarely. They should not divert us from the basic problems that children face, or cause us to ignore their need for the homes that international adoption can and on a regular basis does provide without any improper payments to or pressures on birth parents.

Recent events involving Romanian adoptions illustrate my point. The foreign adoptions that followed the fall of the communist regime in Romania in 1989 became the source of the major adoption scandal story of the early 1990s. This story became a focal point for media discussions of international adoption and was used effectively by forces opposed to such adoption. It described would-be adopters from the United States and other countries wandering through Romanian villages offering money to baffled villagers to induce them to give up their children for adoption. There undoubtedly were more than a few cases involving illicit payments to Romanian birth parents, but the real story of the children in Romania, and the role of international adoption in their lives, is quite different from the scandal story, and it is one in which baby-buying deserves a limited amount of space.

The real story has to do with a country in which tens of thousands of children lived in orphanages and state hospitals, where thousands of them acquired AIDS.[20] A recent documentary film, *Lost and Found*, is a moving testament to some of the horrors. It shows children lying in the cribs where they have been virtually imprisoned all their lives. Some of these children have learned to bang their heads against the crib or rock their bodies back and forth throughout their waking days as a form of comfort in a life that provides none. The film shows children who look like three-year-olds but turn out to be ten- and twelve-year-olds who have "failed to thrive" — and failed to grow or learn to talk or walk — because of the absence of care. Seriously ill children lie in their own filth, waiting for death. The real story also has to do with the fact that once news of the situation in Romania got out, thousands of people who were eager to adopt some of the children they read about and saw on television came forward. Thousands of children were adopted, some from institutions and some directly from birth parents who were unable to care for them.[21]

International adoption was mishandled in Romania. But the real scandal is not that some abuses occurred; it is that when would-be adopters presented themselves, there was no system in place to handle adoptions in a way that would have eased placement while preventing abuses. And international adoption has not been a tragedy for the children of Romania or for their birth parents, although it has been described that way. The tragedy lies in the fact that Romanian women were forced to produce children they could not care for by the Ceausescu regime's policies, which denied them birth control and abortion rights. It lies in the conditions in which Romanian children were and are living and dying. And it lies in the current move to restrict international adoption in ways that may or may not eliminate abuses but will almost surely prevent huge numbers of Romanian children from escaping the desperate situations of their lives to live in loving adoptive homes.[22]

Critics of international adoption often voice concern that children will not receive appropriate care in their new families and countries. They argue that it is unfair to separate children from their racial, ethnic, cultural, and national groups of origin. Loss of the group link and sense of group heritage is said to be a deprivation in itself, and growing up in a foreign land is said to pose risks of discrimination. Those who raise these issues again ignore the reality of children's current situations.

International adoption clearly represents an extraordinarily positive option for the homeless children of the world, compared to all other realistic options. Most of these children will not be adopted otherwise. They will instead live or die in inadequate institutions or on the streets. To the limited degree that foster care is available in these countries, it is likely to be no better than foster care in our country and is often much worse, resulting in little more than indentured servitude. The critics of international adoption engage in a tremendous amount of false romanticization in talking about the dangers of tearing children from their ethnic and cultural roots and their communities. The children we are talking about do not live in richly supportive communities where they have an opportunity to appreciate their ethnic and cultural heritage; they live in states of near-total deprivation. Those who survive to grow up are apt to face virulent forms of racial and ethnic discrimination in their own countries, based on their racial or ethnic status or simply on the fact that they are illegitimate or orphaned. Similarly false romanticization is involved in much of the talk about the problems inherent in losing one's national identity. The fact is that the United States is seen as the land of opportunity for many, many adults in the countries that have large numbers of homeless children. Life is hard for most of those who live in places devastated by poverty, war, or natural disaster. Large numbers would emigrate to the United States if they could.

This is not to deny that international adoptees, many of whom are children of color and others of whom look "foreign," face a complex challenge in resolving issues of individual and group identity. How important will the parents think it is to affirm a connection to the child's various groups of origin? How will they go about the task, if they see it as important, given that they were not themselves born to those groups and may have limited knowledge of and access to the cultures involved? How *should* biracial, bicultural, binational families think about issues of group identity?

But it is not clear that there is anything intrinsically negative about growing up in a family whose members come from different racial, ethnic, or national groups. It is simply *different* in some ways that might be extremely positive. At the same time, it is not so very different from the upbringing that many children have. Many children in this country grow up with parents who have crossed various lines of racial, ethnic, and national difference. Throughout their lives, all children in all countries face issues as to which groups they choose to identify with and what importance they choose to place on their group identities.

The evidence provides no support for the critics of international adoption. The research shows that these children and their families function well and compare well on various measures of emotional adjustment with other adoptive families as well as with biologic families.[23] These are rather striking findings, since the vast majority of international adoptees have had problematic preadoptive histories which could be expected to cause difficulties in adjustment.[24] The studies show that adoption has for the most part been extraordinarily successful in enabling even those children who have suffered extremely severe forms of deprivation and abuse in their early lives to recover and flourish. For instance, one major study involved children who had been caught up in the Vietnam War and who arrived in Norway for adoption at ages ranging from two to five. "Many could not walk. They were passive, apathetic, retarded, and malnourished." At ages seventeen to twenty-two, these children were basically well adjusted and strongly attached to their families.[25]

Some of the studies hint at the complex issues involved in being part of a biracial, bicultural, binational family.[26] But there is no evidence that the challenge of establishing a satisfactory ethnic and cultural identity causes any actual harm to the international adoptee.[27] These findings are consistent with the transracial adoption studies discussed in Chapter 6. There is simply no basis for assuming that a multicultural identity is problematic from the perspective of the children involved.

In general, the research has not focused on determining

what special *positive* factors might be inherent in international adoption for the children, their adoptive families, or the larger society. But some studies hint at the rich quality of the experience of being part of an international adoptive family and the special perspective its members may develop on issues of community. One nationwide study found that half of the international adoptees involved felt that as a result of their status, "they may be bridge-builders between the nations."[28] Cheri Register's recent study of U.S. families with children adopted from abroad provides a powerful and moving description of the special qualities that parents and children find in living life as part of an international adoptive family. She writes, "We, like these children whom we claim so adamantly as our kids, have deeper roots than we knew, an enlarged sense of family, another place in the heart, and a rich and varied history of facing life issues we would never have encountered without them." Register concludes that a dual heritage can be seen "not as confusing, but as life-enhancing."[29]

In the end, it is clear that the debate over international adoption has little to do with genuine concerns about risks to children. There can be no doubt that children's interests are served by such adoption. If their interests were actually to govern, as they are supposed to govern, we would eliminate current barriers to international adoption so as to expedite placement of as many children in need of adoptive homes as possible.

The debate has instead to do with how national communities perceive their group interests. Children are the innocent victims, symbolic pawns sacrificed to notions of group pride and honor. "It is argued that the practice is a new form of colonialism, with wealthy Westerners robbing poor countries of their children, and thus their resources. National pride is involved. However poor the country, they find the implication that they cannot care for their own children to be undignified and unacceptable."[30] Thus poor countries feel pressure to hold on to what they term "their precious resources." Rich countries feel embarrassed to do anything that might look like colonialist exploitation.

However, there is no genuine clash here between the interests of the sending nations and those of the receiving nations. International adoption serves a *symbolic* function for those in power. Sending countries can talk of their homeless children as "precious resources," but it is entirely clear that the last thing they need is more children to care for. Clamping down on international adoption does constitute an easy, relatively cost-free way, though, to stand up to the United States and other industrialized nations. At the same time, the well-off countries of the world have no burning need for these children. These countries are not suffering from underpopulation. Their governments might be willing to permit the entry of adoptees from abroad to enable those struggling with infertility to parent, but international adoption is not seen as serving any significant national interest. So the homeless children end up as "resources" that the receiving countries are quite willing to give up to further the national interest in improved relations abroad.

DIRECTIONS FOR THE FUTURE

We should stop thinking of children as "resources" — as *belonging* in some fundamental way to their racial or ethnic or national communities of origin. We should take seriously the principles enshrined in international human rights documents that recognize children's rights to a loving, nurturing environment and that purport to make children's best interests determinative in matters relating to adoption.

Receiving countries need to take action to build trust. They must recognize that sending countries harbor deep resentment of the historic oppression and exploitation their peoples have been subjected to by imperialist powers, as well as genuine, even if misguided, fear that adoption abroad puts their children at risk of mistreatment. Receiving countries could demonstrate good faith and a genuine concern for children's interests by offering to develop and fund programs to benefit children's welfare within a sending country, in conjunction with any international adoption programs that are instituted. Mechanisms could be developed to provide sending countries with regular feedback on what has happened to the children who are sent abroad for adoption. Regular reports could help assure sending countries that their children are receiving good treatment and are thriving in their new homes.

Sending and receiving countries need to agree on a legal framework for international adoption that would facilitate placement. The model should be one in which each of the key decisions in the adoptive process is made carefully by a responsible agency and then deferred to by all others. All duplicative processes should be eliminated. Several agreements that already exist between particular sending and receiving countries provide examples of how two nations' laws can be coordinated so as to ease the adoption process. Receiving countries should revise their adoption, immigration, and nationalization laws to remove impediments to international adoption, and to ensure fully protected status to all foreign adoptees.

For the United States, this would mean development of specific agreements with other nations, either under the aegis of a new Hague Convention or apart from it. We should also move swiftly to eliminate the immigration law provisions that now restrict U.S. citizens to adopting only those children who satisfy the narrow *orphan* definition; all children found to be available for adoptive placement by appropriate authorities in foreign countries should qualify for entry into the United States. We should revise our laws to ensure that foreign agency decisions that free children for adoption and foreign adoption decrees are honored by our agencies and courts, so that foreign adoptees are expeditiously provided with the full rights of a child adopted within the United States, and so that adoptive parents are spared the necessity of duplicative adoption proceedings.[31] We should develop simple procedures to ensure that every foreign adoptee receives an English-language birth certificate from a U.S. agency upon submission of a foreign adoption decree. We should make U.S. citizenship automatic upon completion of adoption, just as it is now automatic upon birth of a child to U.S. citizens whether they are living here or abroad.

And we should build into the new agreements that we develop with other countries mandates that push everyone to streamline the adoption process in recognition of the fact that children deserve nurturing homes now and not simply at some distant point in the future. Delay hurts, and it may do permanent injury.

Powerful forces in today's world are aligned against international adoption. The current tendency to glorify group identity and to emphasize the importance of ethnic and cultural roots combines with nationalism to make international adoption newly suspect in this country, as well as in the world at large. But closing down international adoption does not put poor countries in a better economic position or a better power position with respect to foreign governments. It is simply a symbolic gesture "for" the nation and "against" the foreigners. It is a gesture that is easy and cheap to make because the children at issue have no political clout; their voices are not heard.

The nations of the world need to move beyond political hostilities and symbolic acts and focus on the real needs of children. If they did, they would accept international adoption as a good solution for at least some portion of the world's homeless children and could begin to restructure their laws and policies to make it work effectively. A side benefit would be that many more people who want to parent would be given the opportunity to do so through adoption. These people now feel under significant pressure to pursue parenthood through high-tech infertility treatment techniques or complicated surrogacy arrangements, things that make little sense in a world suffering in myriad ways from overpopulation. Another side benefit would be enrichment of our understanding of the meaning of family and of community.

EIGHT

Adoption and Stigma

Adoption has a very bad name. All characters in the adoption story are regularly described as victims, forced by circumstances to live out lives that are significantly diminished in quality. Birth parents and the children they relinquish are said to suffer from the loss of their primal connection. Adoptive parents who have not been able to bear children are said to suffer from the loss of the dream child of procreation.

The stigma surrounding adoption constitutes part of the social conditioning to which we are all subject from birth onward and thus helps shape reality. Birth mothers are conditioned to keep their children; no matter what the circumstances, it is considered "unnatural" to give your child away. Less than one percent of the children born in this society are relinquished for adoption at birth. Indeed, only two percent of the infants born to single mothers are relinquished.[1] The infertile are conditioned to experience their loss as devastation, and they pursue infertility treatment with ever-increasing enthusiasm. It is considered "natural" to want to have your "own" child, even at the cost of years of quite *un*natural treatment at the hands of the high-tech infertility specialists.

Adoptive parents and their children are regularly reminded that their families are inferior in important ways to regular families.

This stigma helps shape the priorities for those in charge of regulating adoption. Adoption is set up as a choice of last resort both for birth parents and for the infertile, largely because the regulators think badly of it. This regulatory structure then reinforces the stigma by helping to make adoption an unattractive option.

Despite this universal denigration, the available evidence shows that adoption works extremely well for all those immediately concerned. Why is the success story being suppressed? It may be too threatening. It means, among other things, that women can give away their children or lose their capacity for pregnancy and still function as full human beings. It means that children who are mistreated by their birth parents can be removed for parenting by others. It means that biology is *not* destiny. It raises questions about the goal of self-perpetuation and the value of promoting our own racial, cultural, and national groups. It forces us to think about the appropriate definition of family and community.

THE TRADITION:
BLOOD IS THICKER THAN WATER

The stigma surrounding adoption is so pervasive that most people are unaware of its existence; it is part of the air we breathe, part of the atmosphere of our daily existence. But with adoptive parenthood comes a new consciousness, and as time passes you feel successive jars of recognition. You see and hear and feel the stigma because you and your family have become the alien outsiders — the object of the stigma.

We are brought up on stories that illustrate the principle that blood ties are essential to parenting. Fairy tales teach us that stepparents exploit and abuse children, feed them poisoned apples, and cast them out into the forest to starve.[2]

Myths involving famous foundlings teach us that children cannot find "real" parents or permanent homes or a community to which they belong in adoption; our biologic origins are central to our destiny. The infant Oedipus, left by his father to die on the mountain, is rescued and adopted by the king of Corinth and grows up thinking, mistakenly, that his adoptive parents are his real parents. But he is compelled by destiny to return to his origins and to fulfill the prophecy that he will kill his father and marry his mother. Moses, saved from the slaughter of male Jewish children by being hidden in the bulrushes of the Nile, is found and brought up by one of Pharaoh's daughters. He fulfills his original destiny by leading "his people," the people of Israel, out of Egypt to the Promised Land.

In raising my adopted children, I am painfully conscious of the prevalence of negative adoption themes in the stories that help shape childhood. The popular *Are You My Mother?* features a baby bird that falls from its nest and then wanders through the world, rushing up to various nonbird creatures to ask eagerly whether they are the missing mother and being told each time that of course they are not. In the end the baby bird is deposited by one of these nonmothers in its original nest, and the mother, who has been off looking for food, reappears. Instant recognition! The absurdity of adoption by any of the nonbirds is patent, and the story turns on this humor and on the rightness of the fact that the bird belongs where he came from. Kipling's story of Mowgli the Jungle Boy is one of many classic children's stories about a child raised by "others," here the jungle animals, with whom he *thinks* he's happy and *feels* he belongs. But in the end Mowgli must go back to live with humankind, and the story teaches that that is where he most surely belongs.

The language surrounding adoption regularly reinforces the message that real parenting is blood-linked. Those struggling with infertility are told, "You should go ahead and adopt, and then you will relax and be able to have one of your own." Adoptive parents are regularly asked, "How much do you know about his *real* parents?" The adopted child's birth parents are described in legislation as well as casual conversation as the "natural" parents. Friends ask of my two adopted children, raised together since birth, "Are they brothers?" And they ask of my biologic child, "How does your *own* child feel about them?" Thus parenting is equated with procreation and kinship with the blood link. It is only genetically linked parents who are truly entitled to possess their children, and to whom children truly belong. Blood strangers who rear and nurture children are unreal, unnatural substitutes for the real thing.

The language surrounding adoption regularly conveys the additional message that adoptive parenting relationships are less powerful, less meaningful, less loving than blood relationships. Adoptive parents are commonly asked, "What made you decide to adopt?" and are commonly told, "What a good thing for you to have done." The clear implication is that people would not adopt for the same reasons that they would produce a child — they would not expect to enjoy the same pleasures or experience the same kind of giving-and-getting relationship. Therefore, some aberrational and perhaps altruistic motive must be involved.

Adoptive relationships are not seen as entitled to the same kind of privacy or respect as birth parenting relationships. Strangers in a supermarket who see me shopping with my children will come up to ask, "Where did you get them?" (Few are questioned in the supermarket about how they happened to get pregnant or whether their husband is of a different race.) When I first adopted, a number of acquaintances told me that they knew others who had adopted and "it had really worked out quite well." A man I had always thought of as a rather sweet and sensitive person launched into an extensive discussion of the troubles that a couple he knew had had with their several adopted children and the negative findings allegedly contained in the literature about adoptees. It was clear that these people assumed that my relationship with my adopted children was far more removed and impersonal than a "normal" parent-child relationship, and that I would therefore be able to discuss with cool detachment the prospects of my children's turning out well or badly.

Some people are quite ready to reveal that they see adoptive parenting as a debased form of parenting and adopted children as inherently inferior to those that you could have produced biologically. "Your children really are very cute, and they seem smart, too": the tone of voice shows how surprising the speaker finds the latter. He goes on. "You're really very lucky, aren't you, because you can't know what you'll get, can you?"

Many people believe they think well of adoption and resist the notion that it is stigmatized generally. "But I think adoption is a *wonderful* thing to do," they protest. They are unaware that when they heap praise on the noble adoptive parent, the implicit message is that adoptive parenting lacks the joyous quality that characterizes true parent-child relationships. They are unaware that when they talk of how lucky the child is to have been adopted, their well-meaning phrases are insulting to the child. Children's reactions are revealing. One study reports that when adoptees first tell their childhood friends of their adoptive status, the most common reaction is a sympathetic "I'm sorry." The friends then tend to avoid discussing the topic or respond to mention of it with embarrassed silence, conveying their sense that being adopted must be so awful that suppression is the best course.

Media coverage reinforces negative stereotypes about adoption. The improper removal of children from birth parents is a favorite topic, and headline status is accorded to stories about alleged kidnapping and baby-buying rings and those that show adoption agents and prospective parents otherwise breaking the law in their efforts to find and place children for adoption. A current hot topic involves the search and reunion theme, emphasizing the centrality of the biologic link. Stories about violent and shocking crimes committed by people who happen to have been adopted tend to highlight their adoptive status, implying that adoption is probably connected in some way to the commission of horrible crimes. "Baby swap" stories, about children who are switched by accident at birth and raised by the "wrong" parents until the accident is discovered, have generated intense media interest. These stories exude sympathy for the "adoptive" as well as the biologic parents, but their basic point is that the switch has created a situation of desperate tragedy for all involved.[3]

The basic vocabulary of families in our society reflects the degree to which we see blood as central to kinship. Family members are identified by terms designed to show who is related by blood and to what degree: mothers-in-law are distinguished from mothers and stepbrothers from half-brothers. The term *family* implies a group linked by blood ties: a married couple are not really a family until they produce the children who provide the blood link tying them all together; when people talk about "starting a family," they refer not to the creation of a marital relationship but to the production of children. Only our blood relationships are permanent: we speak of ex-husbands but not of ex-sisters. David Schneider's classic work *American Kinship* gives this account: "What is out there in nature, say the definitions of American culture, is what kinship is. Kinship is the blood relationship, the fact of shared biogenetic substance. Kinship is the mother's bond of flesh and blood with her child." Schneider points out that while American kinship is typical of modern Western societies, "it is different from the kinds of kinship systems found elsewhere in the world."[4]

The American conception of adoption is also different from that which appears in many other parts of the world. Adoption is both a common and a revered form of family in Pacific island cultures. A study of adoption in Tahiti reports societies in which from 25 to 40 percent of all children are adopted, and the majority of households are involved in either placing or receiving children in adoption.[5] The author speculates that in Polynesian and Micronesian societies, adoption may be at the top of the family hierarchy, and asserts that the goal seems to be to establish "between parents and natural children relationships which coincide as nearly as possible with those between parents and adopted children."[6]

In our society, the law has reflected and reinforced the degraded status of the adoptive family. Judges in earlier times refused to adapt the common law to give legal status to adoptive parenting relationships because blood ties were thought so central to the meaning of family. Legislation was necessary to validate adoptive arrangements in both this country and Great Britain, but even when it was introduced, which was not until the latter half of the nineteenth century, it was strictly construed. In 1891 the Supreme Court of California removed a child from its adoptive parents, ruling that "the right of adoption . . . was unknown to the common law, and as the right when acquired under our statute operates as a permanent transfer of the natural rights of the parent, it is repugnant to the principles of the common law, and one who claims that such a change has occurred must show that every requirement of the statute has been strictly complied with."[7] Legislation giving fully protected parent-child status to the adoptive relationship was not enacted in Europe and Great Britain until the middle of this century.

In formalizing the institution of adoption, the law gave parents and children some important protections. For example, for the first time adoptees had the same entitlement to care and support from their parents and the same inheritance rights as biologic children. But by structuring adoption in imitation of biology, the law reinforced the notion that the adoptive family was an inferior family form.

The sense of shame associated with adoption was intense. Sealed records were designed in part to enable the adoptive family and the birth family to keep their shameful secrets from the world. One goal of placing children with physically similar adoptive parents was to enable the adoptive family to pass as a biologic family. Parents were often advised not to tell anyone, even their children, about the adoption.

Modern adoption orthodoxy emphasizes the importance of acknowledging both the fact of adoption and some of the differences associated with this form of parenting, and today's parents are advised to tell children about their adoptive status as soon as they can understand what that means. But this change in philosophy appears to have occurred largely because it has proven difficult or impossible to keep adoption a secret, particularly when older children and children who look significantly different from their adoptive parents are involved. The secrecy that surrounds the practice of donor insemination reveals that the shame associated with infertility and with parenting that is not biologically linked is still a powerful force. Recent studies show that in families where the wife has become pregnant with sperm from a donor rather than her husband, the parents often keep the child's origins a secret from the outside world[8] and even from the children born of this process.[9]

NEW SOURCES OF STIGMA:
OF ROOTS AND THE TRAGIC TRIANGLE

Although some progress was made in the earlier part of this century in upgrading the status of adoptive parenting, powerful forces at work in recent years have revitalized the traditional stigma associated with parenting that is not biologically linked. The search movement, consisting of birth mothers and adoptees, the various advocacy and support groups they have formed, and professionals associated with their cause, represents one such force. The movement has grown apace in the past two decades and exerts a powerful influence. Its basic message is that children "belong" in some primal sense with their family of origin.

The immediate focus of the search movement's efforts is

the sealed record system. Movement members advocate opening records so that birth parents and adoptees can identify and connect with each other. The underlying rationale is that biologic links are of fundamental importance.

The long-term goal for many members of the search movement is to eliminate adoption altogether, or at least to limit it to situations of absolute necessity. A recent statement by two search movement leaders argues that the time has come to move beyond the demand for openness to address the "basic issues." It condemns adoption as a "flawed institution," one that "causes pain and lifelong suffering to all the parties involved," and calls for its transformation to a form of guardianship that would permit birth parents to retain some rights over their children even in those "last resort" situations in which it would be necessary physically to remove a child from the birth family.[10]

Search movement activists paint an overwhelmingly negative picture of the impact of adoptive arrangements on all the key parties. They describe a tragic triangle involving the birth parents, the adoptive parents, and the adoptees, with each set of characters doomed to a lifetime of grieving. The birth parents must forever suffer the pain associated with the loss of their child and, if they bear no other children, the loss of genetic continuity into the future. Adoptive parents who are infertile, as is commonly the case, must forever suffer the pain associated with their loss of genetic continuity into the future and of the genetic child of their dreams. Adoptees must forever suffer the loss of their birth parents and the related loss of genetic continuity with the past. In addition, they will suffer the pain of rejection as they become aware of the "original abandonment" involved in their birth parents' decision to give them up, and will struggle with the resulting injury to their sense of self. They will be prone to "genealogical bewilderment" as they struggle to live a life cut off from their genetic origins, in family structures characterized as inherently abusive.[11]

The movement has generated a significant body of literature in recent years whose fundamental message is that the institution of adoption is sick to its core and destructive of the human beings it affects. A news column by Betty Jean Lifton, a leading figure in the movement, gives a sense of the message that is being promoted. She writes about a fourteen-year-old child who killed his adoptive parents by setting fire to their home, allegedly so that he could search for his birth mother, and describes his actions as related to the so-called adopted child syndrome: "The syndrome includes conflict with authority, preoccupation with excessive fantasy, setting fires, pathological lying, stealing, running away from home, learning difficulties, lack of impulse control." Lifton claims that while most adoptees "adjust" to their unfortunate condition, others "cannot control the inchoate rage caused by their feelings of powerlessness and of rejection by the birth parents."[12] Elsewhere she writes that the adoptee, "by being excluded from his own biological clan, forced out of the natural flow of generational continuity, feels as if he or she has been forced out of nature itself. He feels an alien, an outsider, . . . outside the natural realm of being."[13]

Other forces at work in the society at large have helped to make adoption newly suspect in today's world. There has been a new emphasis in recent decades on the importance of "roots" and of group identity. People are supposed to go back to their roots and derive strength from their racial, ethnic, and national communities of origin. This thinking provides fertile ground for theories that children belong with their birth families and that they will suffer a grievous loss if cut off from their prebirth history and their genetic group. And, of course, it helps make transracial and international adoption particularly problematic.

Egalitarian politics have also contributed to the new stigmatization, with critics attacking adoption as one of the ultimate forms of exploitation of the poor by the rich, the black by the white, the Third World by the capitalist West, the struggling single mother by the economically privileged couple. The fact that adoption functions to improve the economic situation of birth mother and child is ignored.

Finally, the current emphasis on the importance of genetic heritage has revived certain classic fears about the viability of adoption — fears rooted in an assumption that parent-child relationships are likely to work only to the degree that parent and child are significantly alike. In the ongoing nature-nurture debate, the voices of genetics theorists have prevailed lately.[14] Their new studies do not show that environment is an unimportant influence. They simply show that biologic heritage is also important and that children do not start life as blank slates on which adoptive parents can write what they will.[15] But those who think that parent-child relationships are threatened by differences in intellect and personality will find it troubling to think that genetic heritage plays a significant part in the child's development. And those who believe that children belong with their birth parents will find confirmation in the evidence of genetic influence.

The last couple of decades have been bad ones for adoption. Its advocates can easily get the sense that they are fighting the tide of history.

THE STUDIES:
OF MODERN-DAY MYTHS AND REALITIES

The professional literature on the adoption experience constitutes yet another source of stigma. Much of this literature describes adoptive relationships as inherently problematic, presenting a high risk of damage to all parties involved.[16] But the negative claims are not grounded in evidence that anything actually does go wrong as a result of severing the genetic link between parent and child. The empirical studies discussed at the end of this chapter indicate in fact that as far as anyone can tell, adoption works extremely well from the perspective of everyone involved. It certainly works far better than existing alternatives, such as keeping children with birth parents who are not actually interested in or prepared for parenting. Adoption enables children who have suffered severe neglect and abuse to recover and lead essentially normal lives. Interestingly, when children are placed in adoptive homes in infancy, they apparently do just as well as children raised in birth families.

The negative claims with which the professional literature is filled are based largely on negative *assumptions* about what will happen when birth parents turn their children over for others to raise. Thus the professional literature reflects as it reinforces the adoption stigma.

Much of the literature consists of theoretical work from a psychological perspective. Often it is based on case studies of adoptees referred for treatment and consists of conclusions drawn by clinicians seeking explanations for their patients' pathology. The underlying theory was, of course, developed in a society in which adoption is considered abnormal. This literature conveys an extremely negative message about the nature of adoption. The focus is on identity formation, and the basic argument is that adoptees are necessarily, by virtue of their transfer to an adoptive family, especially susceptible to identity conflicts and especially prone to problems in personality development.[17] Their sense of security is said to be fundamentally damaged by the loss of the original parenting relationship. The theory holds that their ability to resolve developmental conflicts appropriately is complicated because of the existence of two sets of parents, and their identity formation is additionally impaired by the break in genetic and historical connections with the past and the resulting "genealogical bewilderment."[18] One theorist asserts that "the creation of families based on psychological, not blood, ties contains inherent identity problems that practice and law seek to mitigate, but can never eliminate."[19] Another contends, in an article on the "adoption trauma," that adoption puts children at risk for "an 'adopted child' pathology, which can flower into narcissistic character disorder, psychotic episodes, delinquency, homosexuality, fantasied or attempted suicide, incest, homicide, fratricide, murder of one or both adoptive parents, and to patricide or matricide."[20]

While adoption research has generally focused on adoptees, some attention has been devoted more recently to birth and adoptive parents. Again, most of the theoretical literature paints an extremely negative picture, purporting to show birth mothers traumatized by the experience of surrender and adoptive parents traumatized by the experience of infertility.[21]

Search movement advocates have contributed significantly to the negative reports on all parties to the adoption experience. An influential early work is *The Adoption Triangle*, first published in 1978. Since then, books and articles that describe adoptees, birth parents, and adoptive parents as suffering lifelong pain as a result of problems attributed to adoption have poured forth. This literature casts particular blame on the closed and secret nature of the adoption system, but conveys the general impression that opening the system would at best alleviate the pain and suffering caused by separating children from their birth parents. While this literature contributes to the adoption stigma, it provides no sound basis for drawing negative conclusions about adoption. It is written by people who have a powerful bias in demonstrating that adoption is a flawed institution — people whose goal is to eliminate adoption in any form that we know today. It consists largely of anecdotes and speculation. The "studies" that purport to describe characteristics of birth mothers, adoptive parents, and adoptees rely on extremely skewed and misleading samples of these populations. Typically, volunteers are solicited by means of a notice in a search movement newsletter, a method that is quite obviously likely to produce birth mothers and adoptees who are particularly hostile to the institution of adoption or troubled by its effect on their own lives. In addition, no effort is made to compare sampled members of the adoption triangle with appropriate control groups. So, for example, the studies depict birth mothers who testify to the pain they have experienced as a result of having surrendered their children, but provide no basis of comparison with the experience of women in similar circumstances who kept their children and who might have something to say about how they felt about lost opportunities for education or employment or the difficulties of being a single parent without an adequate income.

Much of the negative literature focuses on the entire group of adoptees or on undifferentiated or particularly problematic subgroups. For example, claims about the risks allegedly inherent in adoption are often bolstered by reference to the evidence that adoptees are overrepresented in various clinical populations, such as mental health clinics for troubled children. Also, empirical studies showing that some subgroups of adoptees have adjustment difficulties are used to generalize about the inherently risky nature of adoptive parenting. The fact that some number of adoptions "disrupt," or fall apart, is similarly used.

A major problem with these studies is that they tend to ignore the fact that the adoptee population contains many subgroups whose members are likely to have adjustment difficulties for reasons that have nothing to do with their adoptive status. The literature does not adequately differentiate between those adopted in early infancy and those adopted at older ages, and it does not adequately control for a wide variety of factors likely to influence adjustment, such as preadoptive abuse and neglect. By definition, any child placed after infancy will have suffered abuse, neglect, or the disruption of a significant bond with a primary caretaker; many will have suffered all of these.[22] A significant proportion of all adoptees are placed only after many years of what is often severely damaging treatment.[23] Many of these children have significant physical and mental disabilities relating either to their prebirth histories or to their postbirth experiences. As a consequence, studies that focus on undifferentiated groups of adoptees are of essentially no relevance to one of the issues at the heart of the adoption stigma, namely, whether the mere fact of transferring a child from a birth to an adoptive family poses any risk to the child or to the quality of the parent-child relationship. Yet such studies are systematically used to illustrate the alleged problems inherent in the adoptive relationship.

What *is* telling about the studies of undifferentiated groups of adoptees is that these children do so well once adopted, despite the fact that so many of them have suffered very negative preadoptive experiences. There is no evidence that by the time adoptees reach adulthood they are overrepresented in clinical populations.[24] Also, there is reason to think that their apparent overrepresentation in child clinical populations is largely explained by adoptive parents' greater readiness to refer their children for treatment. The vast majority of all adoptive relationships are deemed successful,[25] and the empirical studies reveal that the vast majority of all adoptees function normally in terms of various adjustment measures.[26] Even the studies of children adopted after infancy, including those adopted at older ages and those with traumatic preadoptive histories, show that on the whole the children do very well, and that relatively few of the adoptive relationships disrupt.[27] These studies provide persuasive evidence that many children are able to recover from the adverse effect of disastrous starts in life when placed in nurturing adoptive homes.[28]

The negative claims made in the body of literature described above make a powerful contribution to the adoption stigma. They convey the impression that all sorts of things are likely to go seriously wrong when a child is transferred to a nonbiologic parent for raising. They thereby provide support for the attitudes and policies that give adoption its status as a last resort in our society. Yet when analyzed in any depth, this literature clearly provides no evidence that anything actually *does* go wrong for any of the parties to an adoptive arrangement.

One question that is central in assessing the real effects of adoption has to do with how it compares to existing alternatives for the various parties involved. The available evidence indicates that it compares extremely well. Studies that compare single birth mothers who place their children for adoption with single mothers who keep their children to raise themselves indicate that the decision to place for adoption is likely to have a positive impact on socioeconomic status and is not likely to have any negative psychological effects compared with the decision to keep and parent the child.[29] For the infertile, adoption provides the opportunity to parent; almost all those who choose to pursue this form of parenting find it enormously satisfying. By contrast, roughly half of those who pursue infertility treatment will be unable to become parents by this route.[30] Finally, studies show that children placed in adoptive homes do far better in terms of standard measures of adjustment and self-esteem than children raised in institutional situations or in foster care,[31] or children returned from foster care to their birth families,[32] or children raised by birth mothers who once considered adoption but decided against it.[33] And the evidence that older children have more trouble adjusting in adoptive homes constitutes a powerful argument against maintaining adoption's status as a last resort — an argument for moving more quickly to remove children from inadequate biologic and foster care situations to permanent adoptive homes. This evidence demonstrates the risks for children in a system that places such a priority on biologic parenting, because it is this priority that is responsible for the reluctance to remove children from damaging homes and legally sever the birth ties so as to free them for adoption.

Another central question has to do with how adoptive parenting compares with biologic parenting when the children are placed at or near birth. This analysis should provide some insight into the question of whether any problems are in fact associated with parenting that is not biologically linked. Only recently have empirical studies focused on nonclinical groups of early-adopted children and compared them with carefully selected control groups of children raised in their birth families. *These studies fail to confirm the negative claims made in the great body of adoption literature. They reveal no significant disadvantages of adoptive as opposed to biologic parenting, and some significant advantages.*

Some of these studies have looked at the quality of "attachment relationships" between adoptive and nonadoptive mother-infant pairs. They have found that adoptive parents and their infants develop warm and secure attachment relationships, which effectively rebuts the claims made in the negative theoretical literature that adoptive bonding is necessarily problematic.[34]

Other studies have looked at the early-adopted children at later stages of development and have found either few or no differences; the general view is that any differences in adjustment that may exist disappear by adolescence.[35] For example, Stein and Hoopes studied a group of adolescents placed in adoptive homes before the age of two and compared them with a closely matched group of adolescents raised in biologic families that were similar in socioeconomic terms. The adopted adolescents looked comparable in terms of various classic measures of identity formation and adjustment.[36] Marquis and Detweiler looked at children aged thirteen to twenty-one who had been placed in adoption during their first year, comparing them to a control group of nonadopted children. In a study designed to test empirically the classic claims in the theoretical literature, they found "not a shred of evidence . . . that indicates any of the previously reported negative characteristics."[37]

The only interesting differences found in the early-adopted adolescents relate to apparent *advantages* in adoptive relationships. Marquis and Detweiler found that adoptees saw themselves as more in control of their lives, had more confidence in their own judgment, and viewed others more positively than did those in the control group. They also rated their parents significantly more favorably, describing them as more nurturing, comforting, and helpful, with more predictable standards and more protective concern. Of course, the research has not generally been designed to assess potentially positive aspects of adoption. The bias has been overwhelmingly in the negative direction. The working assumption of virtually all theoretical and empirical work is that adoptive relationships are somewhere on the spectrum between disastrously and modestly inferior to biologic relationships.

My point is not that adoption is the same as biologic parenting but that it should be recognized as a positive form of family, not ranked as a poor imitation of the real thing on some parenting hierarchy. My attack on the adoption stigma should be understood as an argument for adoption but not against biology. I do not think we should jettison the biologic model of parenting and insist on a universal baby swap at the moment of birth. But I would like to put biology in its place and give appropriate value to nurturing and other social aspects of the parenting relationship.

In my view, there are many good reasons for having some presumption in favor of biologically linked parenthood. Birth parents no doubt do generally feel significant pain at the prospect of severing their relationship to the child they have created and in some sense "known" during pregnancy, and in my view they should; our world would be sadly diminished if relinquishment were a nonevent. I am prepared to think that there are other good things to be said for biologic parenting, and even that there may be some risks inherent in adoptive parenting. The sense that a child is your genetic product, the experience of pregnancy and childbirth, the experience of parenting and nursing a child during its first moments of life — all these things may help create a healthy bond between parent and child, and their absence may create a greater potential for problems. Genetic heritage is an important influence on intellect and personality, and it may be that for many parents some level of likeness is important and too much difference is problematic. Adoption may require parents who are more open to difference, more flexible, and more imaginative than the norm. For these among other reasons, the rule giving biologic parents presumptive parenting rights and the rule forbidding payments to induce birth parents to surrender their children seem to me good rules. But we can recognize the validity of the biology-based family without denigrating adoption.

The adoption stigma helps shape reality in problematic ways. Saying that adoption is a bad thing helps make it a bad thing. In a world in which adoptive status is degraded, it will not feel good to be adopted. While it might feel perfectly all right in some world we can imagine, it will feel problematic in a world in which you and all those around you are conditioned to think that good mothers don't "abandon" their children for others to raise, a world in which others react to the nature of your family situation by saying, "I'm sorry." Thus the adoption stigma necessarily shapes the experience of birth parents who surrender children, of adoptive parents, and of adoptees. Birth parents are conditioned to think that they *should* feel lifelong pain as the result of their "unnatural" act of giving up their "own" child for another to raise. The infertile are conditioned to think that they *should* forever grieve over their inability to reproduce biologically.[38] Adoptive parents and children are conditioned to think that their family relationships are significantly inferior to those enjoyed by "real" families.[39] In fact, they are instructed by the new adoption dogma that they should experience and "acknowledge" the problematic differences between their families and normal families. Claims to normalcy are often treated as evidence of pathology.[40]

The stigma also affects the vision of those doing research

on adoption. Conditioned to believe that children "belong" in some essential sense with their birth parents, they are predisposed to look for problems in adoptive parenting situations and to see in such situations the explanation for problematic behavior.[41] It is worth speculating about what they would see if they thought more positively about adoption and designed studies to look for the positive. What if they started with the assumption that the norm and the ideal was the adoptive family, and the question was whether biologic parents should be allowed to raise the children they produce? What might the studies "find" if their starting assumption was that biologic parenting had inherent risks?

Stigma shapes reality in another way, helping to form the policies that in turn help to define the adoption experience. Social regulators translate their suspicion of adoption into screening rules that make the process of becoming an adoptive parent seriously frustrating and unpleasant, so that the infertile have all the more reason to see adoption as a last resort. And the policies designed to protect the biologic tie create the foster care limbo, which in turn produces the damaged children who may well have adjustment difficulties in adoption.

Given the predictable impact of the negative myths about adoption, it is a wonder that the evidence about the actual experience of those involved looks so positive. Given the power of those myths, it is hard to imagine thinking differently. But we should try to free ourselves from the forces that condition us to equate procreation with parenting. We should try to imagine living in a society in which adoption is revered rather than denigrated. We should focus on what might be the unique benefits of parenting relationships built entirely on social rather than genetic ties. We should come to understand adoption as a uniquely positive form of family — not necessarily better than the biologic family, but not inherently inferior, either. We should make this imaginative leap because adoption is quite obviously a good solution for existing human beings in this world, most particularly the millions of children in need of nurturing homes. But we should also do it because we have a lot to learn about parenting and family and community from adoptive relationships.

Adoption involves the provision of homes to children in need, and thinking well of adoption should involve placing a higher value than we now do on the nurturing aspects of parenting and a lower value on the self-perpetuating and proprietary aspects. Adoption also involves the exercise of conscious choice in matters related to parenting. Thinking well of adoption should be liberating for birth parents and the infertile, giving them far more choice and control over their lives.

The fact that conscious choice is a defining feature of this form of parenting is unnerving for those conditioned to think of biologic inevitability as a part of what parenting is all about, but it can be seen as an enormously positive feature of this form of family. Adoption critics scorn the tradition of referring to the adoptee as a "chosen child," but adoptees *are* chosen children. Adoptive parents may initially have wanted to produce a biologic child, and they are of course limited in the choice of which particular child they will adopt. But all of them consciously choose to become parents, and most of them devote a great deal of effort to becoming adoptive parents. By contrast, it is doubtful that as many as half of all biologic parents initially conceive out of a conscious desire to parent. Many conceive by accident, and many consider abortion or adoptive placement and reject these options not because they actually want to parent but because keeping their child seems the least bad of the various bad options available. The fact that a person has consciously chosen to parent seems as important an indicator of the likely success of the parenting relationship as any factor could be.[42] And indeed, controlled studies comparing wanted with unwanted children have shown a stark contrast; the unwanted do very badly.[43]

Virtually all the aspects of adoptive parenting that are generally understood to be "risk factors" can as easily be understood as opportunities for the development of a particularly good parenting relationship. They can also give us insight into possible problems in our current biologic parenting models. We could view the absence of a genetic connection as liberating. Adoptive parents might, for example, be more able to avoid neurotic forms of overidentification with their children, be more able to let their children develop their own personalities and interests, and feel less driven to relive their own lives through their children. Because of the existence of another set of parents, adoptive parents might have a lessened sense of entitlement to complete control and possession, and this could empower children in healthy ways.

Parents and children could experience a range of special satisfactions in family relationships that cross the various lines of difference involved in adoption. As a parent, I revel in the brown skin and thick black hair and dark eyes and Peruvian features that I could not have produced. I have also felt the shock of seeing myself — my intensity, my gestures, my expressions — as I watch these children. I am enchanted by the tempestuous moods of one child and the laid-back good nature of the other. I am intrigued by the mystery of who they are and will be and what part I will play in this. I am ever conscious of the miracle that these children who possess me to the core of my being are mine and also not mine. I am aware of myriad ways in which my consciousness has been expanded and my life enhanced by these adoptions, and I think of people who have known only biologic parenting as people who are missing a special experience. It is likely that adoptive parents and their children would testify to a wide range of special qualities in their family life if there was an audience for such evidence.

Adoptive parenting may produce parents and children who are unusually open to and tolerant of a wide variety of differences. There is evidence that children raised in transracial adoptive families or by gay or lesbian adoptive parents exhibit these traits. There is also evidence that parents who are initially interested only in adopting a healthy same-race infant, and who in fact adopt such a child are significantly more open at the time of their second adoption to considering an older, handicapped child of a different race.

Adoption creates a family that in important ways is not "nuclear." It creates a family that is *connected* to another family, the birth family, and often to different cultures and to different racial, ethnic, and national groups as well. Adoptive families might teach us something about the value for families of connection with the larger community.

NINE

High-Tech Reproduction: In Vitro Fertilization and Its Progeny

A WOMAN OBSESSED

An advertisement featuring a life-size photograph of a newborn infant's face announces the opening of a new in vitro fertilization clinic with the following come-on:

BEFORE YOU LET GO OF THE DREAM, TALK TO US

There's no other perfume like it, the smell of a newborn: a milk scent, warm-scent, cuddle essence.

Her skin, a kind of new velvet. Toes more wrinkled than cabbage, yet roselike. Tender, soft, totally trusting; a blessing all your own.

That dream might still come true for you. New techniques can resolve many infertility problems, including some that were previously considered hopeless . . .

Many formerly childless couples have become parents or parents-to-be by letting the experience of our staff enrich their lives, rather than giving up the dream of childbirth.[1]

There is, of course, no mention of the fact that the chances for a couple to achieve a successful pregnancy at a new in vitro fertilization center such as this are *zero*. It takes even experienced IVF practitioners many months of working together as a team to be able to achieve a pregnancy. It generally takes several years for new IVF clinics to equal the success rates of established clinics. Even then the success rates are very modest. The vast majority of IVF patients will never give birth to a child. What the clinics are selling *is* a dream.

The powerful message such ads convey is that the only alternatives are to pursue the dream or to let go of it — to give up. The dream child featured in the advertisement is the child of procreation. Procreation is equated with parenthood. The goal is childbirth.

I was sold on IVF long before the existence of this kind of advertisement. Like most IVF consumers, I pursued the dream child of procreation for years before I gave any serious thought to adoption.

I took my fertility for granted in my youth, and put off childbearing for the first five years of my marriage. Although I always knew that someday I would want this experience, I was astounded at the power of the feelings that came with my first pregnancy. I was fascinated by the creature growing within me and took enormous and to me surprising pleasure in the experiences of pregnancy, childbirth, and nursing. I assumed that I was responding entirely on an instinctive level to the physicality of these experiences. I had no idea that anything else was going on; I had not experienced myself as socially programmed for procreation (indeed, quite to the contrary). I loved the idea that my body had taken control of my life. I immersed myself in the primal pleasures of the early months of my child's life, reveling in the simplicity and satisfaction of my role as I hurtled out of bed at night in response to the sudden screams of terrifying hunger and as I sat for hours during the day, nursing peacefully and gazing on the contented face. All these experiences merged in my mind with the experience of raising this child. It seemed natural to think of parenting as an integrated whole that included pregnancy and childbirth. In fact, it seemed there was no other way to think of parenting.

When, years later, I discovered that I had developed a fertility problem, I did not have to be persuaded by the specialists that what I needed was a fertility fix. I *knew* that I needed such a fix, and that nothing else would do. I had no sense that I had been socially conditioned to experience infertility as inadequacy, as something I had to overcome if I wanted to feel good about myself again as a woman and as a person. And during my years of infertility treatment I gained no sense that I was being unfairly "sold." I was a desperately eager consumer of infertility treatment services, grateful that these services were available to help me solve "my problem." It wasn't until years after I decided to quit IVF and move on to adoption that I began to think that the problem lay not in my body's inability to conceive but in the forces that conspired to make conception seem necessary.

I give birth to my first child when I am twenty-seven, divorce a couple of years later, and am in my mid-thirties before I focus on my desire to have another child. The decision to pursue parenting as a single person is an easy one. Parenting is a primary goal for me. I would be happy to share this experience with a man, but only if I find one who seems right, and I am not going to wait for this to happen. I will find boyfriends who are willing to help me in my efforts to get pregnant, but I will be the parent, and decisions about whether there will be any other parent can be deferred until later.

For the next several years I try to become pregnant — casually at first, since I assume that once I stop using contraceptives the body that got pregnant so easily before will do it again. When it doesn't, I begin to see a series of infertility specialists, and eventually learn that my fertility has been impaired, if not destroyed, by a birth control device known as an IUD (intrauterine device). I had used an IUD for a brief period some years back, and it had triggered an infection which, unbeknown to me at the time, had seriously damaged my fallopian tubes. After this discovery I move on to another series of infertility specialists and spend the next few years in a classic treatment regimen that is supposed to discover the nature of the damage to my tubes and overcome the problem.

During all this time it never occurs to me that there might be any solution to my problem other than medical treatment. The thought of permanent infertility is so devastating that the only thing to do is push it away and pursue the medical fix. So I take fertility drugs and keep track of my temperature each day so that I can time sex to maximize the chances of pregnancy. I go through mini-operations designed to assess the nature of my fertility problem and to remove scar tissue from my damaged tubes. I endure painful tests designed to determine whether the tubes have been successfully cleared of obstructions. Every month I will myself to get pregnant, counting the days with growing tension, alert to each sign from my body that it might be or not be pregnant, and I am newly devastated each time as the beginning of my period announces another failed attempt.

All this culminates in a relatively major operation undertaken to reconstruct my fallopian tubes. My doctor has told me that this is the end of the treatment road; there is nothing else he can do if this operation fails. He has also told me that it has a small chance of success, but I push that information aside as not being to the point. The point, obviously, is to do everything that can be done. I spend a few days in the hospital and another week at home recovering. I then spend the next several months attempting to get pregnant. Then I have a test to see whether the reconstructed tubes are open so that sperm and egg are able to pass through. I am on a highway outside of Boston when the test results are supposed to be available. I stop my car at a roadside telephone booth at the precise hour and call in. I am told that my tubes are blocked, as they were before the operation. My last hope for fertility is gone. To this day I can see the scene — the telephone booth by the road and the woman holding the phone with tears pouring down her face.

The next months are bad ones. For the first time I let myself think about my infertile state as permanent. Until now I have not let myself focus on anything except the struggle to overcome the problem. Now I experience my infertility as the overwhelming tragedy of my life. Overnight I feel unsexed. Relationships with men seem fraudulent and pointless. I know that the men who have been part of my life during this struggle have shown no apparent interest in my capacity to get pregnant or produce children, but *their* feelings about me seem irrelevant to *my* feelings about me. It is as if a large part of who I am has been destroyed, and the rest is of little value. Sadness permeates my life.

But I do not relish the victim role, and I am not ready to give up on life. I begin to pull myself together and move on. I know that I want to parent, and I start in a preliminary way to explore adoption. The initial signals are off-putting. It seems that there are few children available for adoption and many people fighting over them, and that it is very difficult for singles to adopt. (I am struck with the contrast to the treatment world, where to date no doctor has shown any particular concern with my marital status.) Another problem is that the current man in my life, who has cooperated with the pregnancy quest, is resistant to adoption. He thinks that adopted kids have lots of problems, and that if I really want to have a child we should consider pursuing a surrogate mother arrangement, so that we would at least have control over half the child's genetic heritage. I am not interested in surrogacy, but I am not yet ready to throw myself into adoption efforts, either. I start a file of news clippings on adoption and make lists of things I should do to find out more.

By now it is 1983. Suddenly IVF clinics are opening up all around the country. The birth of the first IVF baby in Great Britain in 1978 had seemed so miraculous that I had assumed it would be many years before the doctors figured out what they were doing; I was sure that by the time treatment programs opened in this country, I would be too old to take advantage of them. But I have been avidly following the media accounts of new clinics and new miracle births. The IVF process bypasses the woman's fallopian tubes: her eggs are surgically removed from the ovaries and fertilized in a petri dish, and then the resulting embryos are inserted in the uterus. IVF means that women like me can become pregnant. So, just as I have begun to accept the finality of my infertile state and to move on with my life, I find that I am in fact not necessarily infertile, because of the new availability of this magical baby-making process. I am now forty-three, and on some level I am aware that my age will probably reduce my chances for success with a form of treatment that is highly unlikely to succeed in any case (IVF is in the early, wildly experimental stage of development). But I choose to hear the positive messages and to believe in the dream of the miracle baby. I am still ready and indeed eager to fight the odds for the chance to give birth.

One day in the spring of 1983 I pick up the phone and place calls to some twenty IVF clinics — every clinic in the country that I can imagine being willing to go to, on the basis of where it is and what I have been able to find out about its reputation. I ask my chosen twenty about waiting lists and eligibility criteria. By the end of my telephone survey, I have found only three that have reasonable waiting lists and that indicate any willingness to take a woman over forty. Each of these limits its services to married couples, as do the other clinics I have contacted. But I am determined to pursue this new last chance at pregnancy, and at this point a marriage requirement seems simply an obstacle to be surmounted. I decide that if possible I will simply finesse the issue; if that is not possible, then I will get married. I "propose" to the man I will call my IVF husband, a former boyfriend, and am thrilled and touched when he accepts. He agrees to cooperate in trying to father a child for me to parent and to pose as my husband for IVF program purposes. It seems the perfect arrangement. We still care about each other deeply, and it feels good to be doing this together.

I move on to apply to my first IVF program and renew my pursuit of pregnancy. When the program I select decides to admit me, I am overwhelmed with gratitude. But I still remember the way the doctor who seemed key to that decision looked at me when she said, "I have to wonder whether we're doing these women any favor in admitting them," referring to women over forty, like myself. It is only much, much later that I learn that the chances of an IVF patient over forty getting pregnant and keeping the pregnancy are near zero.

The next two years are largely consumed by the IVF pursuit. My life takes on a lunatic character. I have told almost no one about my infertility problems, and I continue in this secretive mode, but with IVF my secret life takes over and dominates the rest of my life in a new way. This has to do with both the constancy of the program demands and the power of the emotions involved.

I buy myself a wedding ring, which I wear on my right ring finger so that it is always at the ready for me to place it on my left when I walk through the IVF clinic doors. I nearly get married the night before one egg-removal operation, out of fear that some proof of marriage might be demanded at this crucial step in the process. I have the marriage license, the hour set for the justice of the peace to arrive at my house, a friend ready to witness the event, and the contract declaring that my spouse-to-be and I agree that this marriage will not have any of the normal consequences. We decide to call off the wedding two hours before the justice of the peace is due to arrive, realizing that we will probably be able to talk our way through any challenge.

My first IVF attempt takes place at a program in New Haven, Connecticut, selected in part because it is close to home. When that attempt fails, I am told that because of the program's long waiting list I will have to wait several months to try again. I decide that I can't afford to wait, so I sign up with a clinic in southern California that seems reputable and admits over-forties. I fly out there with my IVF husband, studying a little card on which I have listed facts about his family that a wife should know and afraid that the truth will come out under anesthesia. We spend the requisite ten days in a lovely small hotel, trying to read books and make casual conversation with the other hotel residents and otherwise figure out how to pass the endless hours between the daily clinic visits, when they draw my blood and give me hormone shots and look at my growing egg follicles with their ultrasound machines.

IVF is my only life for these ten days. The tension mounts as I watch the egg follicles grow, and then go in for the operation in which they will remove the eggs for fertilization in the petri dish. I wake slowly from the anesthesia, and as I emerge into consciousness I begin to wonder how many eggs they retrieved. I hear a voice saying something about not being able to locate any eggs. I push this disembodied voice away and open my eyes to look for my doctor and hear his news. But my doctor is looking right at me, and it is his voice, and he keeps repeating that there are no eggs until finally I have to let it sink in. I start to scream, "I don't believe it, I don't believe it, I don't believe it!" Then I try desperately to dive back into unconsciousness, hoping that if I can somehow do that, I can awake to a different reality.

This California clinic is a brand-new clinic and I am one of its first patients. Many years later, I learn that no one, not even a younger person, has any real chance of becoming pregnant during the early months of a clinic's operation. I also learn later that the IVF attempt that left me in despair on a California hospital bed was not counted as a failure when the IVF practitioners calculated their success rates. I was given the impression when I entered IVF treatment that I had roughly a 15 percent chance of success in any given IVF cycle; this was the standard line at the time. But this statistic was based on the number of women who became pregnant out of the women whose eggs had been successfully removed and fertilized and whose resulting embryos had been successfully placed in the uterus. If, like me, you didn't get as far as this "embryo transfer," you didn't count as a failure. And if you got pregnant but then lost the baby, as occurs in roughly one quarter of all IVF pregnancies, you didn't count as a failure either. This method of calculating made the rates look artificially high by ignoring the very real heartbreak of all those women whose IVF pregnancy attempts failed at either the early or the later stages. For women entering IVF, the goal is not the pleasure of the treatment or the opportunity to lose a pregnancy; the goal is to give birth to a live baby. The success rate of real relevance involves a calculation based on the number of women who give birth to a live baby out of all those who undertake an IVF treatment cycle. When I was being told that IVF had a 15 percent success rate, the relevant success rate was in the 5 percent range.

After my return from California, I finally persuade a Boston-area IVF clinic to admit me despite my age, and the craziness continues. It is a struggle to arrange my treatment sessions so that I won't have to miss the classes I teach, even though a law school teaching schedule entails an extraordinarily limited number of classroom hours per week. During the first two weeks of an IVF treatment cycle, I go to the hospital nearly every day. I wake to an alarm clock, which tells me it is time to pour eight glasses of water down my throat to fill my bladder for the ultrasound. I line up at the hospital with the other women to have my blood drawn. We chat about our absent husbands so regularly that I begin to feel as if I actually have one. I lie on my back while the ultrasound machine looks through me, throwing a picture of my ovaries up on the screen. I look at the fuzzy black-and-white shapes, trying desperately to make out, with the technician's help, which might be egg follicles and how big they are. It is important for me to have several, growing at the same rate. If one springs out ahead, or if there are only a couple, then the treatment cycle will be canceled. The doctors want to "harvest" several ripe eggs for fertilization so that they can transfer three or four embryos into my uterus. This is thought to maximize the chances for a successful pregnancy.

Each day I get a telephone call at work telling me whether the cycle will be canceled or go forward, and if it is to go forward what hormone dosage I should take in my shot that night. The tension is enormous, because if a cycle is called off, several thousand dollars are down the drain and my chance of becoming pregnant is put off for another two or three months. I am under orders not to do the things I might do to relax, such as jogging or playing tennis or drinking a glass of wine, and I live in fear of jolting myself and bursting an egg follicle. I am furious with myself one summer night at an outdoor concert because I succumb for a few minutes to the temptation to dance to some lively music and then am consumed with worry about whether I have destroyed a precious follicle by making some vigorous movement.

In a few IVF cycles I manage to get to the egg-removal stage and go in for the mini-operation called a laparoscopy. During the immediate preoperative period, I travel back and forth several times between the IVF clinic and my work each day, shifting the wedding ring back and forth as I go. Then in the evening I go to the local health services office, where I have been getting my nightly hormone shot. I am thrilled when I get as far as the operation, but I always wake from anesthesia worried: have they recovered any eggs, how many, how do they look, are they ragged or healthy-looking? Then the eggs are mixed with sperm and I wait for reports on their progress: have they fertilized, are the embryos developing as they should, do they look healthy, how many do I have? I am generally a very resilient patient, but the aftereffects of the anesthesia and the pain from the operation bother me more than I had expected. My body aches inside from the gas blown into me so that the doctors can visualize my organs and find the egg follicles.

I go back to the hospital for the embryo transfer. I am awake for this procedure, lying in the appropriate knee-to-chest position as the doctor inserts a device designed to deposit my precious embryos at exactly the right place in my carefully premeasured uterus. I gently flatten my body on the bed and then lie as absolutely still as possible for the next six hours. These are the orders, and I am afraid that the slightest motion will dislodge an embryo that otherwise just might attach itself to my uterus, so I lie there trying not to turn my head or shift the position of my arms. It is surprisingly hard and even painful to lie absolutely still for six hours.

Then I go home, with instructions for three days of bed rest. And then I try to go about my life again, making sure that I step ever so gently as I walk and being frightened when I step off a curb unexpectedly or when I sneeze. I am depressed; after the escalating excitement of the period leading up to the embryo transfer, I feel suddenly down, with no new IVF activity to concentrate on. I find myself thinking mainly about how unlikely it is that this latest attempt at pregnancy will succeed. I know from the statistics that there is very little chance that those embryos will attach. It is hard to treat myself for two weeks as the guardian of sacred embryos that must be protected against any harm from jostling when I don't believe that there are any embryos growing inside me.

During this period I go in for shots of a new kind of hormone that is designed to maximize the chances for implantation to take, and then for pregnancy tests. The negative results come back just about the time my period starts.

For all the horrors of the process, I am generally upbeat and enthusiastic throughout my IVF pursuit. I know it's an uphill battle, but I feel thrilled to have the chance to fight. I don't resent the obviously experimental quality of the treatment I am receiving, but take pleasure in thinking of myself as a sort of astronaut on some extraordinary trip in the outer space of medical understanding. I see myself as pursuing something that I really want, and as having chosen this course. Indeed, years later, when I am first exposed to a feminist critique of IVF, I am appalled at what I see as insensitivity to the feelings of the infertile women who choose to pursue this treatment because of their desperate desire to become pregnant. I still have little sense of how women are conditioned to make this "choice."

In the end, I began some eight IVF treatment cycles and got as far as embryo transfer in three or four. In the early spring of 1985 I finally quit. I had by this time spent ten years trying to get pregnant, and I had spent a good deal of the past eight years in the hands of infertility specialists. In deciding to cancel the IVF session scheduled for March 1985 and to withdraw from the program, I felt constrained by my limited funds and the fact that there was then no insurance coverage for IVF. If I could have gone on, I might well have "chosen" to do so.

Looking back years later, I realize that what I experienced as constraint actually helped me to escape from this particular obsession. But at the time I knew simply that I wanted to parent and not just to spend my life trying to procreate. I realized that I had to stop IVF if I was to have enough money to adopt. The decision to move on brought immediate relief.

AN ABBREVIATED PICTURE OF THE IVF TREATMENT PROCESS

IVF technology has thrust on us a plethora of important social issues, which have so far been left almost entirely to the doctors to resolve. We can now split parenting into its component parts, taking sperm and eggs from one man and one woman, transferring any resulting embryos to another woman to carry, and giving any resulting child to others to raise. The doctors are now institutionalizing contracts for the sale of eggs, embryos, and gestational services and arranging on a systematic basis "IVF adoptions," in which one couple's embryos are transferred to another. We can now freeze IVF embryos without destroying their capacity for life; they can be thawed later for transfer or other purposes. Embryo freezing is now offered as a standard option at the better IVF clinics. Thousands of frozen embryos are being stockpiled around the country, though there has been no societal resolution of such issues as whether they should be considered life or property or something in between, who "owns" them (if anyone), or whether they can be destroyed at will or have a "right to life" through embryo transfer.[2] We can also keep IVF embryos alive for long periods of time in their petri dish and subject them to genetic manipulation and various forms of research and experimentation.

The IVF doctors are making all the decisions as to what kind of embryo experimentation is appropriate, just as they have made the decisions from the beginning about discarding or destroying "excess" embryos — embryos that have been produced but are not needed for transfer into the patient's uterus. In leaving these doctors free to conduct the extraordinary social experiments that new technologies make possible, with no guidance from the larger society as to what ethical or other rules should govern, this country stands in stark contrast to the rest of the world. Other countries have created more than a hundred national commissions to struggle with and try to resolve the social issues involved.

My focus in this book is solely on those aspects of IVF practice that relate to parenting issues. In this chapter I discuss IVF as a form of infertility treatment, designed to enable women and their male partners to give birth to children that are the product of their own sperm and eggs.[3] The next chapter considers the use of IVF to separate genetic from social parenting.

In 1978 the attempt to produce "test-tube babies" seemed a wild and improbable experiment, but in little more than a decade IVF has become a standard part of the infertility treatment regimen. Initially it was reserved almost entirely for situations in which damage to the woman's fallopian tubes was the apparent cause of infertility. However, it is increasingly used today in other situations, including cases involving unexplained infertility and male fertility problems such as low sperm count. While virtually all clinics at first limited their services to married couples, in recent years a number have begun quietly to open their doors to singles. In 1990, roughly 240 IVF clinics were operating in the United States; 180 of them reported performing some 26,000 treatment cycles.[4] There are now about 270 clinics in operation.

The essentials of the classic treatment process in a typical IVF program are as follows. The IVF cycle is timed to coincide with the menstrual cycle. During the first part of this cycle, the woman is treated with hormones to induce her to "superovulate," with the goal of overcoming the natural ovulation process, which would ordinarily produce a single egg follicle. She is monitored on a daily or near-daily basis by means of blood tests and ultrasound examinations. The results are used to determine whether to continue with the treatment cycle, and if so, what hormone dosage is appropriate. The goal is to obtain as many mature eggs at the egg-removal stage as possible. Egg removal used to be accomplished by laparoscopy, under general anesthesia, but today's methodology generally involves procedures that are somewhat less intrusive and that require only a local anesthetic. The eggs are then placed in a special medium with the male partner's sperm. In the next two days fertilization usually occurs and the embryos begin to divide. Most programs allow the embryos to develop to the two- to eight-cell stage, at which point the doctors transfer three or four to the woman's uterus. (Transferring several is thought to increase the likelihood that one will implant, but transferring more than this is thought to unduly increase the likelihood of a problematic multiple pregnancy.) Any embryos not transferred will generally be frozen, if the program has the capacity to freeze and the couple choose this option. Frozen embryos can be thawed for use in a future IVF cycle, so that the woman can avoid the superovulation and egg-removal process in any such cycle.

The woman is subject to strict rules of conduct during IVF treatment: no drinking, no smoking, no exercise that might unduly jostle the egg follicles or risk dislodging any embryo that might miraculously be clinging to the uterine wall — and, for related reasons, no sex, an interesting example of the degree to which sex is separated from procreation in this process.

A single IVF cycle generally costs between $5,000 and $10,000. A cycle that is canceled before egg removal is less expensive than a completed cycle; one that involves the use of frozen embryos should also be less expensive, but embryo freezing and storage involves separate charges on an ongoing basis. IVF patients are generally advised to pursue several treatment cycles to increase their chances of achieving a successful pregnancy. Treatment costs have so far been largely excluded from health insurance coverage.

IVF has produced a variety of initialed relatives, such as GIFT and ZIFT, that involve essentially the same treatment regimen, including superovulation and egg removal.[5] I am using IVF as a shorthand reference to all these procedures, since they involve the same kinds of risks and burdens for the patients and quite similar chances of achieving a successful pregnancy.

A ROUGH COST-BENEFIT CALCULATION

IVF has obviously given many women suffering from infertility the opportunity to get pregnant and bear children. There are thousands of IVF babies alive today to prove the point. But it has also increased the likelihood that more of the infertile will spend more of their lives in infertility treatment. IVF is generally not a substitute for but a supplement to other forms of treatment. Typically, a woman who realizes that she is having trouble getting pregnant will start with an infertility workup, proceed through a series of increasingly intrusive treatment methods, and arrive at the IVF door at the end of an already long road. In many cases she will begin IVF treatment at the same point that, in the pre-IVF world, she would have been forced to accept her infertility and move on with her life.

Any serious attempt at an IVF pregnancy is likely to consume several more years. It takes some time to look into the factors relevant to selecting an appropriate program — track record, quality of staff, waiting list, location. It makes little sense to go through one IVF cycle without being willing to go through several more, since the chances of success in any given cycle are very low. Even if there is no waiting list, patients are usually advised or required to wait a minimum of one or two months after one treatment cycle before starting another. Often the wait is much longer, as the programs with the best success rates are often in heavy demand. Therefore, it can easily take several years to complete several treatment cycles.

Although most patients do stop after a few tries, one of the insidious things about IVF is that there is often no logical stopping point. Most failures occur after embryo transfer, and the reason for failure at this stage is almost always a mystery. As IVF practitioners are fond of pointing out, most attempts by fertile couples to conceive fail also.[6] For unknown reasons, most embryos that get as far as the uterus, whether naturally or by the IVF process, are unable to attach successfully so that a pregnancy is achieved or maintained beyond the early days or weeks. For the IVF patient, the mystery is dangerous. Failure provides no reason to think that you won't succeed the next time. IVF is a numbers game: the chances of succeeding are always low on any attempt, so it is easy to experience any given failure not as a reason to stop but as a reason to keep going. When you have invested so much, it can seem silly to stop, since next time could be the time your number comes up. Some IVF practitioners exercise responsibility in helping their patients decide when to stop, but many do not. And even those who do often encourage patients whose prospects for success seem good, based on age and other factors, to continue through four to six cycles, at which point the repeated failures are thought to signal a reduced likelihood that the patient will ever be able to achieve an IVF pregnancy. It is not uncommon for patients to undergo ten cycles, and there are many stories of patients who have kept going beyond that.

My experience with IVF had some unusual features. I went through it as a single person in an era when singles were officially excluded, and that undoubtedly added some stress. My chances for success were near zero as a result of my age and the experimental state of the IVF art at the time. But only a small percent of all patients have ever produced an IVF baby, and the chances for doing so today remain quite low. Other patients' reports indicate that my own experience is more typical than unusual. The literature is replete with descriptions of the "emotional roller coaster" that an IVF cycle represents, of the discomfort and pain and indignities of the process, of the tension throughout, and of the devastation at the usual end, when yet another pregnancy attempt fails. In many ways I had it easy. I was through in something less than two years. I was able to keep my job throughout, which probably helped me maintain relative sanity, and I was able to do most of my cycles in a first-rate program near my home. Most important, I was able to move on to become a parent, which IVF patients think of as their goal but are generally unable to achieve.

A quick assessment of the costs and benefits involved in

IVF treatment raises serious questions about whether this new methodology for dealing with infertility should be seen as a net plus for women, for children, or for the larger society. On the cost side of the ledger we must list the immediate burden of the process on women, and to a lesser degree on their male partners — the time, energy, and pain, both physical and emotional, for those who seek treatment. In addition there is the strain on a couple's relationship.

Health risks must be added to this list. Women's bodies are bombarded with hormones throughout the treatment cycle, first to stimulate egg follicle growth and later to encourage implantation. Hormone treatment has proven dangerous in the past, and although IVF patients are assured that hormones are being prescribed in safe dosages, the truth is that we do not yet know what risks may be involved. (When I asked one of my IVF doctors to give me a few days' worth of similar hormone treatment so that I could nurse my adopted child, his response was "I couldn't do that. These drugs are dangerous." He may have meant this partly as a joke — I never did respond to his form of humor — but he was serious about not giving me the drugs.) Knowledgeable critics of IVF treatment have expressed concerns that these hormones may cause cancer at some future time. Other aspects of this highly intrusive, technological method of producing human beings pose health risks as well, for both the women patients and the children they may conceive. The various manipulations to which eggs, sperm, and embryos are subject, the extensive use of ultrasound, and the interventionist medical procedures used to monitor IVF pregnancies all involve risks that are cause for concern.

IVF practitioners have assured the world and their patients that there are no real dangers beyond the minimal ones involved in other kinds of minor operations, and it is true that dramatic and obvious problems have not surfaced to any significant degree. But we have no way of knowing what the nonobvious or long-term health risks for women and children might be, and no one has been doing the kind of research that could tell us. We found out about the dangers of thalidomide only because babies were born with such obvious deformities. We found out about the dangers of DES only after doctors had been prescribing it to pregnant women for many years, and then only because the daughters of those women developed a very unusual form of cancer. There is no way for us to know whether the IVF treatment process creates a serious risk of health problems that are not obvious unless systematic research is done to examine appropriate samples of patients and babies in comparison to control groups and track their health in future years. Attempts at this kind of research have just gotten off the ground.

Even in the absence of such research, we know that IVF creates some real problems.[7] Some IVF patients suffer from ovarian hyperstimulation and other difficulties associated with the drug regimen. The treatment produces a high incidence of ectopic pregnancies, with all their attendant risks. It also produces a high incidence of multiple and of preterm births, and such births are inherently problematic for the babies involved.[8] There is also evidence of a somewhat higher incidence of chromosomal abnormalities and congenital malformations in IVF babies than in the general population.[9]

Financial resources are an obvious item on the cost list. For individual patients and their families, the cost of $5,000 to $10,000 per cycle must be multiplied by the number of attempts. Health insurance will provide at least partial reimbursement for some, but for the vast majority, huge out-of-pocket costs are involved in any given treatment cycle.[10]

For the society at large, it is irrelevant whether the individual patient or an insurance company pays a particular bill; it is the total cost of IVF that is relevant. Estimates indicate that over $100 million was spent for IVF treatment in this country in 1990.[11] These resources could be devoted to serving some of the most basic health care needs of women and children, which now go unmet; they could, for example, be allocated to prenatal and preventative health services, enabling poor women to give birth to healthy babies and poor children to grow up healthy. Escalating demands for health care reform in this country testify to the widespread sense that we already devote far too many resources to fancy medical services for the relatively privileged while providing far too little in the way of basic health care for the nation as a whole.

Another important item on the cost list is the pain involved in prolonging the struggle with infertility. A large body of literature documents the intense suffering associated with the discovery of infertility and with efforts to overcome it.[12] The loss of fertility — the loss of the fantasy child — is described as feeling like a major amputation or a death. Each failed attempt at pregnancy renews the sense of loss. The infertile are advised to grieve over their loss as they would over the death of a beloved person, so that they can achieve some sense of resolution that will enable them to pick up their lives and move on. But it is not possible to get beyond the sense of loss and the suffering if you are still fixated on *undoing* the loss.

A related cost is exacerbation of the stigma associated with infertility and adoptive parenting. As discussed in Chapter 8, this stigma helps push the infertile into increasingly intrusive forms of treatment like IVF. But it is simultaneously true that this form of treatment reinforces the stigma and increases the tendency to equate procreation with parenting. The literature demonstrates that the shame attached to infertility in this society is already intense.[13] The infertile describe in poignant terms their feelings of inadequacy and the ways in which they feel demeaned and degraded in others' eyes. People commonly hide infertility problems from all but a spouse or a very few intimates. Indeed, researchers have found it difficult to study the infertile population because so few people are willing to identify themselves, even in the context of confidential surveys. For the individual IVF patient, prolonging the struggle increases the sense of failure and inadequacy associated with infertility and makes the goal of achieving pregnancy ever more important. For the larger society, the proliferation of infertility treatment methods and the sight of IVF patients sacrificing years of their lives in the pursuit of pregnancy help demonstrate how important it must be to overcome infertility with a medical fix.

Finally, the list of costs must include, for the infertile, lost opportunities to parent, and for children, lost opportunities to receive nurturing homes. A major part of what infertility patients think they want is the opportunity to parent. Despite the related stigmas surrounding adoption and infertility, many infertile people express an interest in adoption. Years spent in the IVF pursuit obviously defer prospects for adoptive parenting, and for many, IVF is likely to eliminate such prospects altogether. Age is one problem. Many women are in their mid- to late thirties when they start IVF treatment. Several years later they will discover, if they look into adoption, that they are considered too old to rate as prime parental material; they will be low on the various priority lists and extremely limited in their adoption choices as a result. Battle fatigue is another problem. After years of struggling to overcome infertility, they may feel too tired and too discouraged to take on the world of adoption.

The benefits list for IVF is limited to one significant item: some of the infertile will experience pregnancy, childbirth, and biologically linked parenting. But *not that many* of those who engage in the process will reap this benefit. IVF practitioners have put out wildly exaggerated claims of success, and have worked together systematically to mislead the public and their patients. They have conveyed the impression — one picked up and reinforced by the media — that any given IVF cycle has a 25 to 50 percent chance of success. Even higher success rates have sometimes been claimed. But these claims have at best been based on a highly misleading set of statistics, and have at worst been entirely fraudulent.[14] It is only because of pressure by federal officials and agencies that in the past few years it has been possible to learn something about the *real* IVF success rates, those based on the number of live births per IVF cycle initiated.[15] These ranged from *6 to 9 percent* during the 1986–1988 period, and reached 12 percent in more recent years, with somewhat higher success rates reported for GIFT and ZIFT.[16] The success rate for women aged thirty-five to thirty-nine was 10 percent, and for women forty and over was only 3 percent.[17] These rates cannot simply be multiplied by the number of IVF attempts a woman is willing to endure. Although the chances of success will be greater if she tries five or ten times, they will not be anything like five or ten times greater.

Moreover, it is not clear how much better these success rates will ever look. IVF practitioners claim that they are already doing almost as well as nature, arguing that the main reason for failure has to do with the same phenomenon that results in failure in most natural attempts at conception: a high percentage of embryos fail to implant, for reasons that are as yet unclear. There is no reason to think that we will soon unravel the mystery, or that if we do, we will be able to coerce embryos into implanting and developing into healthy babies. In any event, while success rates rose during the early period of IVF development, they have leveled off in recent years.[18]

There is also no way of knowing how many of those who become pregnant through the use of IVF would have been able to become pregnant if they had not resorted to IVF. Studies of some IVF program populations demonstrate that patients who dropped out of the programs and pursued less intrusive methods of becoming pregnant achieved comparable success rates to those who remained in the programs.

For the infertile population, the addition of IVF to the arsenal of treatment methods contributes only marginally to opportunities to become pregnant and give birth. This benefit must be weighed against the enormous costs involved both for those who succeed in achieving childbirth and for those who don't, as well as for the larger society.

For that larger society, it is not clear that IVF's marginal contribution to the overall fertility rate should count as a benefit at all. There is no burning need for more children on the earth. We are fast destroying the earth's capacity to support its current population, and we have barely begun to contemplate the actions that will be necessary to save the environment so that the earth will be habitable in the future. We have many millions more children than we are currently capable of caring for. Even if we in the United States were to concentrate only on the needs of our own country, expanding the population is not a social priority. In today's world it makes little sense for society to condition its members to see procreation as central to their being. More births simply mean more mouths to feed, more pressure on the environment, and fewer homes for the children in need.

IVF'S REGULATORY STATUS: VARIATIONS ON A FREE MARKET THEME

IVF operates on a free market basis in this country. The state makes essentially no effort to restrict parenting options or provide protection to affected parties, as it does in adoption. The operating assumption seems to be that IVF is an essential good that should be allowed to flourish, in contrast to the operating assumption governing in the adoption area, where the creation of new parenting relationships is treated as inherently suspect and risky.

The state imposes no parental screening rules. IVF is part of the privileged world of biologic parenting, so anyone is allowed to call on the technicians for help in becoming a parent. And the doctors generally see it as their job to serve all those who have the arguable capacity to become pregnant, so long as they can pay the bill. Doctors do not see themselves

:gulators. Furthermore, there are obvious financial
for them to expand rather than restrict the patient
IVF doctors have imposed maximum age rules not
:hey are concerned that older people will prove less
fit for parenting but because older women's prospects for
procreating are so limited. As IVF resources have expanded,
the age limits have gone up. Singles have been excluded primarily for political reasons; it seemed important in the early
years of the industry's development to limit the controversy
surrounding the "test-tube baby" clinics and reduce any risk
that they might be shut down. As IVF has become more
established and as the increase in clinic numbers has reduced
waiting lists, many clinics have begun to admit singles, and
the trend seems sure to continue.

In today's clinics, IVF doctors struggle over the issue of
whether they should exclude *any* group from access to their
services solely on the grounds of parental fitness, even in
cases raising the most serious concerns. Special IVF ethics
committees discuss the issue of whether they should help a
couple with AIDS produce a baby before they die. The doctors wonder whether they should concern themselves with
whether the orphaned child will have a home and with the
risk that the child will be born HIV-infected, or whether these
issues are none of their business. They discuss the question
of whether they should help a seriously deranged woman
produce a child that she seems entirely incapable of taking
care of. They wonder whether it is morally responsible to help
these people become parents, but they are not sure that it is
their business, as doctors, to decide who should have access
to their services.

The government has done almost nothing to protect the
interests of IVF patients. Doctors, unlike adoption agencies,
have been largely trusted to regulate themselves, subject to
only the most general legal mandates prohibiting outright
fraud and medical malpractice. So it is the doctors who have
written almost the only IVF-specific guidelines that exist.

These are suggested rather than mandatory and provide little real protection.[19] The states have passed no significant protective legislation, nor have they moved on the administrative level to license IVF clinics or establish mandatory standards governing any aspect of IVF practice. The federal government has been largely inactive as well. However, in recent years it has taken a few steps to deal with some of the most obvious abuses. The Federal Trade Commission has acted to curb extreme forms of fraudulent IVF advertising. Congressional hearings on consumer protection issues highlighted the misleading nature of the information that IVF practitioners were disseminating on a systematic basis, as well as problems of fraudulent advertising and substandard medical practice. The resulting congressional report, published in March 1989, focused on the need to provide the public with success rate information specific to named individual clinics, and to include the live-baby-per-treatment cycle rate.[20] This helped push the IVF practitioners into finally agreeing to solicit such information on a voluntary basis.[21] However, the doctors' "IVF-ET Registry" is still published in a form that omits clinic names and that calculates success rates on the basis of egg retrievals rather than stimulation cycles initiated, omitting early failures.[22] In late 1992, Congress finally passed a bill designed to provide IVF consumers with at least some minimal protection with respect to success rate information and program quality. Entitled the Fertility Clinic Success Rate and Certification Act, it establishes new incentives for maintaining and disseminating meaningful success rates, including the live-baby-per-cycle rate, and promises a yearly report on such information to the public. The act also encourages certification of embryo laboratories as a method of maintaining certain minimum standards.[23]

These constitute important first steps in the right direction, but they are extremely limited in scope. The thrust of governmental intervention so far has been in quite the opposite direction. The significant IVF-related regulatory move has been to mandate insurance coverage so that treatment will be financially cost-free for patients. This is a major green light for the industry, since the high financial cost of IVF now functions as a major deterrent for those struggling with infertility. As of 1992, some ten states had passed laws mandating insurance coverage for IVF. The trend seems likely to continue unless something changes in the political forces at work. Such legislation clearly serves the interests of the IVF industry, and the infertile tend to see opportunities for more treatment, and for free treatment, as in their interest.

IVF has its critics. Those most adamantly opposed see it as inherently abusive. They include an interesting combination of radical feminist, religious, and politically conservative groups, which share a concern over the ways in which IVF interferes with "nature," although their perspectives as to why this is a bad thing differ enormously. They are interested in curtailing the practice, some calling for an outright ban and others focusing on education and socialization efforts.[24] Other critics see IVF as abusive in the form in which it is practiced, and are interested in reforming the practice so that consumers get more meaningful information, a higher standard of medical care, and better protection against health and safety risks.[25] Thus far the critics have not mobilized to become a powerful force for any significant change in IVF practice. Feminists have been divided on the issue. Some see IVF as expanding reproductive choice for women, and many feminists who are critical of IVF have been reluctant to call for a ban, or even to question the spread of mandated insurance coverage, because of concern with the danger of placing any limits on women's choice in reproductive matters.[26] Those calling for a halt, or even for a slowdown in the IVF industry's expansion, have been limited in number, and their voices have gone largely unheard.

DIRECTIONS FOR THE FUTURE

We are moving in exactly the wrong regulatory direction. Mandated insurance will give an extraordinary energy boost to the already burgeoning IVF industry. What we need to do is put on the brakes. And we need to do this *now*, because if we wait, it may be too late.

A legislative ban on IVF seems neither feasible nor appropriate. What we can and should do is call a halt to the mandated insurance movement, develop appropriate protective regulation, and begin the vital process of restructuring the way people think about issues of infertility and parenting.

The arguments for insurance coverage are based on appealing notions of fairness and freedom to choose: IVF shouldn't be reserved for the wealthy; the infertile shouldn't be limited in their parenting choices but should be free to pursue treatment and biologic parenting if they want. But these arguments assume that IVF treatment is a benefit and that the infertile are in a position to exercise free choice in opting for it. If you conclude, as I do, that IVF imposes very heavy costs on the infertile and that the "choice" of IVF is conditioned in myriad ways, then things look very different.[27] The fact that IVF treatment *is* costly then represents, as a practical matter, an essential restraint on the industry and an important counter to the other forces that condition choice. Providing third-party reimbursement for IVF expenses would simply add to the coercive pressures pushing the infertile to seek a medical fix for their infertility.

These pressures already shape parenting options in a way that makes little sense for the infertile and even less for the larger society. We drive people away from adoption by surrounding it with burdensome regulations, by artificially limiting the number of children available out of all those desperately in need of homes, and by characterizing it as a grossly inferior form of parenting. We lure people into infertility treatment by encouraging them to believe that their efforts to pursue the dream of childbirth will be worth it, and by glorifying procreation. We subsidize procreation by using our health insurance, free medical care, and tax systems to reimburse the costs of childbirth as well as the costs of most infertility treatment. At the same time we make those who choose adoption pay every step of the way to parenthood. Making it cost-free to engage in yet another form of infertility treatment would simply stack the deck even more in favor of procreation.

What we need is a very different kind of regulation — regulation that would ensure that IVF consumers are provided with meaningful information about the likely costs and benefits of the process and adequate protection against the risk of harm. Leaders in the IVF world have themselves testified to a variety of problems that go beyond the misinformation problems discussed above, alleging that in many clinics medical personnel are inadequately trained, patients for whom IVF should not be considered the treatment of choice are admitted, and appropriate standards of practice are otherwise violated. These leaders have also argued that there are dangers inherent in the situation, given the huge profits to be made, the desperation of infertile patients, the relative ease with which private clinics can be opened, and the absence of any real safeguards to ensure minimal standards of practice in clinics operating independently of established hospitals.[28]

Protective intervention should be designed to ensure the following kinds of action:

- the establishment of mandatory standards governing IVF clinics, with respect to such matters as staff credentials, lab facilities, and the creation of systems for providing meaningful information on the costs and benefits of pursuing treatment;[29]

- the creation of licensing and other agencies to monitor clinics and the IVF industry on an ongoing basis, to ensure that appropriate standards are complied with and to consider new issues and assess the need for additional forms of intervention;

- the conduct of appropriate research to assess health and other risks related to the IVF process;
- the systematic dissemination of meaningful information on IVF risks, success rates, and related matters, so that the infertile can make better-informed choices among parenting options, and so that policymakers can make appropriate regulatory decisions.

The new federal legislation noted above represents a useful first step in the right direction.

But this kind of intervention, although sorely needed, will not begin to solve the most basic problems. Conditioned to feel that they must deal with infertility by undoing it, people will continue to plunge eagerly into IVF and other forms of treatment if they can find the money to pay for it, *even if* they have access to appropriate information about the risks and about the limited prospects for success. We need to begin to change the conditioning process itself. We need to address the stigma issues discussed in Chapter 8 and rethink the meaning of fertility and infertility, of parenting and family.

Although this kind of restructuring is an enormous project, we could take some concrete steps now that would help those struggling with infertility exercise more meaningful choices in the immediate future. To begin with, we could create agencies designed to provide counseling when infertility is first suspected or discovered, to help people work through their feelings about procreation and parenting and about the various options open to them *before* they commit themselves to any particular course of action. Infertility counseling exists in today's world, but if the infertile resort to it at all, it is usually only at the end of a long road of medical treatment. We need to promote the provision of such counseling, on a widespread basis, and to encourage the infertile to take advantage of it early.

In addition, we could make infertility counseling a precondition to undertaking IVF and other burdensome forms of infertility treatment. The only counseling typically afforded now in connection with IVF is provided by the clinics themselves, and is at best likely to help patients understand the nature of the treatment process and get some sense of the chances for success.[30] Many reform proposals urge improvement of these IVF counseling procedures to ensure that patients receive a more accurate assessment of the probable costs and benefits of pursuing treatment. This kind of medically oriented counseling is important, and would be required by the kind of protective regulation I have proposed above. But it serves a very different function from the infertility counseling I am proposing here, which would be designed to help the infertile come to terms with their infertility, think about the conditioning to which they have been subject, and explore nonmedical options such as child-free living and adoptive parenting.

Counseling can, of course, accomplish only so much. Its effectiveness will be limited by the quality and biases of those doing the counseling. Doctors must be educated to think of infertility as a social rather than a purely medical problem, so that they can help their patients consider nonmedical options. However, doctors are unlikely ever to be capable of providing the kind of counseling needed. It is hard to imagine any educational reform that would eliminate the medical propensity to analyze problems in terms of their susceptibility to medical treatment. New organizations should be created to provide the necessary counseling, staffed by professionals committed to undoing what I have characterized as the adoption stigma. IVF clinics are quite obviously not suited to the task. The major infertility counseling organization that exists today, Resolve, has to date been significantly treatment-oriented in its approach.[31]

Even the best counseling can only hope to counter the negative *attitudes* that push the infertile away from adoption and toward treatment as a route to parenthood. It cannot eliminate the *realities* of the adoption world that help make adoption a last resort even for those who would like to pursue it. To give the infertile truly meaningful choice among parenting options, we need to restructure adoption, by removing the regulatory barriers and developing a range of policies designed to facilitate rather than impede the placement of children in need of homes with those eager to parent.

TEN

Modern Child Production: The Marketing of Genes, Wombs, Embryos, and Babies

Adoption regulation rests on the premise that biologic parenting relationships are sacrosanct. These relationships are to be disrupted only as a last resort, and the regulation is designed to ensure that they are not unnecessarily disrupted. The universal rules against baby-buying reflect and affirm the value placed on these relationships, for if birth parents could be paid for agreeing to give up their children, it would both encourage such action and risk devaluing such relationships more generally.

Although this premise continues to govern the traditional adoption world, technology has ushered in a new world of adoptive arrangements where entirely different rules apply. Technology facilitates the separation of biologic from social parenting. It means that a child can have as many as five parents: an egg mother, a sperm father, a gestational mother, a social mother, and a social father. Technology is increasingly being used to produce children for the specific purpose of separating them from their genetic and birth parents. While in the traditional adoption world parenting rights and babies are not supposed to be for sale, in this new technological adoption world *everything* is for sale. The raw materials for producing babies are being marketed with increasing aggression and sophistication.

Our new technological capacities enable a wide range of parenting experiments. We can remove sperm from a man and eggs from a woman for fertilization in a laboratory dish or in another woman. We can insert an IVF embryo produced with one woman's egg in the womb of another woman for pregnancy and childbirth. We can flush an early-stage embryo out of one woman's womb and place it in another's. We can freeze sperm and embryos and thaw them for reproductive use at a later time. We are learning how to do the same with eggs.

We have been making increasing use of technology to divide parenting into its component parts and to separate children from one or more of their genetic and gestational parents. Donor insemination, which has been popular for decades, has traditionally been used to bypass a husband's fertility problem and is increasingly used by women without male partners. So-called surrogacy or contract pregnancy arrangements have become increasingly common in the past decade, as surrogacy brokers and IVF clinics have promoted contracts under which women provide pregnancy and childbirth services and turn the resulting children over to others.[1] In what can already be called traditional surrogacy, the woman is artificially inseminated and the child is her genetic product. In gestational surrogacy, the woman providing pregnancy services receives embryos created by using another woman's eggs in the IVF process. IVF clinics have become more and more involved in recent years in arrangements involving the donation or sale of sperm, eggs, embryos, and pregnancy services.[2]

Technological adoptions come in basically two forms. In the first, which I will refer to as partial adoption, one of the social parents has a biologic link to the child, and the arrangement looks in genetic terms like a traditional stepparent adoption. In the second, which I will refer to as full adoption, neither of the social parents has such a relationship, and the arrangement looks in genetic terms like a traditional nonrelated adoption. I use "adoption" here to characterize the *social* as opposed to the *legal* nature of these new parenting arrangements. Part of what is so interesting about them is that although they result in the social equivalent of adoption, they are generally not subject to any of the legal requirements involved in traditional adoption.

Donor insemination and surrogacy arrangements are regularly used to facilitate partial adoptions for traditional husband-wife couples, with donor insemination enabling the wife to bear her own genetic product and surrogacy enabling the husband to father his own. The IVF process is increasingly used to facilitate full adoptions, whereby one couple's embryos are donated or sold to another for implantation. The advent of embryo freezing can be expected to encourage such arrangements on a large scale. Tens of thousands of frozen embryos are now being stored for future reproductive use; most of them will probably not be used by the contributing couples. Proper IVF protocol now requires that patients be asked when they sign up for treatment whether they are willing to transfer embryos that they do not use to other couples.

In our rush to embrace these new forms of adoption, it is not entirely clear whether we are trying to get away from or hold on to traditional notions of parenting. Both things seem to be going on simultaneously. Technological adoptions are being pursued in large part in order to give husband-wife couples as much as possible of the procreation experience. For example, one member of the couple may get the experience of genetically linked parenting, or of carrying and giving birth to a child in the case of embryo donation. But at the same time, these adoptions are based on the premise that there is nothing fundamentally problematic in separating procreation from parenting. In addition, technological adoptions are opening new opportunities for singles, gay and lesbian couples, and others who don't fit the traditional parent profile. Single women and lesbian couples now use artificial insemination on a widespread basis, and gay men see the burgeoning surrogacy industry as providing them with an equivalent opportunity for parenting.

Such conflicts characterize particular arrangements as well as the general picture. The classic surrogacy arrangement is largely motivated by a man's desire to parent his own genetic product, yet it can be justified only if we conclude that genetically linked parenting is *not* important for the woman who serves as birth mother, for the child who will be cut off from that mother, or for the man's wife, who will serve as an adoptive parent.

Like IVF, technological adoption operates in a free market. Money is systematically used to induce genetic and birth parents to turn over their sperm, eggs, embryos, and, in surrogacy arrangements, their live babies. Sperm "donation" has generally involved sale: although the men who provide sperm are not paid large sums of money, they are paid what it takes to induce them to engage in a process that involves little trouble on their part. Money is an increasing part of the picture in IVF clinic arrangements that involve the transfer of eggs and embryos. The going price for "egg donation" is now $1,500 to $2,000. Some clinics place commercial advertisements for women who are willing to go through the IVF process so their eggs can be harvested for sale to others, and other clinics encourage patients to solicit egg vendors on their own. Patients in some programs pay for part of their treatment by agreeing to surrender some of the eggs or embryos that they produce for use by others. Surrogacy arrangements have typically involved payment of at least $10,000 to the birth mother for her agreement to bear a child and to surrender it after birth.[3] The payment methods and amounts vary, but the goal is the same: to pay what it takes to persuade people to provide what is needed to produce a child for others to raise. The contrast to the traditional adoption world is stunning. There adoption is a grudging last resort for already existing children, and baby-buying is strictly forbidden. Here we are using money to encourage the creation of adoptees.

Almost no protective regulation has been initiated in this country to govern these new arrangements — no regulation that focuses on the risks that are arguably involved, as regulation in the traditional adoption area does. Nor has there been any significant action on the national level to consider the need for such regulation. This is in stark contrast to the situation in most other developed countries, where many commissions have been formed and much regulation has been proposed to deal with what are generally seen as issues raising profound moral and ethical questions. Some countries ban the sale of sperm, eggs, and embryos, and most countries that have considered the issue of commercial surrogacy have taken a strong position against it.

Commercial surrogacy is the only issue that has triggered concern with the need for protective regulation here, and some states have ruled it illegal by either legislative or judicial decree.[4] Many proposals regarding surrogacy have been introduced in legislatures across the nation, some designed to ban or otherwise discourage the practice, others designed to regulate it so that the interests of those involved are better protected. Some proposals would require parental screening for the future social parents, as in a traditional adoption arrangement. But there is no consensus on how to deal with surrogacy. Some states have acted to legally validate it, and most have taken no action. Influential groups like the American Bar Association and the Uniform Law Commissioners have been ambivalent.[5]

Significant regulation governing donor insemination does exist, but almost all of it is designed simply to validate the parenting arrangements sought by the private parties involved.[6] Thus, roughly half the states now have legislation that automatically cuts off any legal parenting relationship between the sperm donor and his genetic child, and makes the husband of the woman who is impregnated the legal father. This legislation eliminates the need for the new father to adopt the child legally, thus ensuring that the state will *not* engage in the parental screening or other inquiries that it insists on in the traditional adoption context. In the other states, the same result is achieved by court-made law, in combination with traditional paternity legislation that presumes the husband to be the father of any child born to his wife. Only recently have a few states passed legislation designed to ensure that donor insemination is governed by minimal medical standards relating to health and safety issues — action triggered by the AIDS crisis. The fact that surveys have long revealed a shocking level of incompetent and ethically questionable practice among the doctors involved in donor insemination has produced no call for comprehensive regulation in this area.[7]

IVF embryo adoptions and egg transactions are entirely unregulated.

A rapidly expanding industry is engaged in producing children for these new forms of adoption. Thousands of donor insemination children have been born every year for decades, and thousands of surrogacy babies have been born and delivered to the intended rearing couples in the past fifteen years.[8] We stand on the edge of a probable explosion in IVF embryo adoptions and other IVF involvement in the splitting of biologic from social parenting. The time to figure out whether we want to continue in this direction is now. If we take no regulatory action, we will discover in another five or ten years that surrogacy brokers and IVF clinics have arranged for the production of huge numbers of new adoptees, and that a vast array of new enterprises has developed to market genetic material, gestational services, embryos, and babies. This will not be easy to undo.

There are many reasons for concern with these new adoptive arrangements — many reasons to question the direction in which we are moving. A growing body of literature catalogues the problems that some of these arrangements pose for women. Feminist and other critics argue that such practices as egg and embryo sale and surrogacy should be understood as inherently oppressive and exploitative.[9] Egg vending practices mean that women subject themselves to the rigors of the major part of an IVF treatment cycle not for the pleasures of parenting but for a fee. Gestational surrogacy means that two women share an IVF treatment cycle, then one of them carries and gives birth to a child in order to surrender it to a man who is seeking genetically linked parenting and to his wife, who will usually end up doing the bulk of the social parenting. Critics of these arrangements also argue that by commercializing reproduction and putting a price on parenting rights and on children, we are turning people into property and devaluing parenting relationships in ways that are likely to erode the quality of all our lives.[10] Surrogacy has raised this specter most vividly; many find an apt analogy in slavery, pointing out that "American slavery had the effect of causing black women to become surrogate mothers on behalf of slave owners," with "no legal claim of right or ownership over their natural children."[11]

For me, these concerns are compelling. But my focus here is on issues that have been almost entirely ignored in the general debate — issues that have to do with the discrepancy between the way we treat traditional adoption and the way we treat these technological forms of adoption. The debate goes on as if traditional adoption existed only in an earlier age or on another planet and had no real bearing on these modern methods of constructing families. My thesis is that we have something to learn from our experience with traditional adoption.

The traditional adoption world espouses the principle that the best interests of the child should govern. Debate on the issues involved in the new adoptive arrangements has focused to date largely on the *adult* interests involved, with proponents and opponents fighting over whether women should be seen as empowered or oppressed by these arrangements and over how to resolve conflicts between one adult's right to parent and another's.

Taking children's interests seriously would require us to think about the children we are creating with these new arrangements and about the children who already exist in this world. It would require us to ask whether it is good for children to be deliberately created so they can be spun off from their biologic parents and raised by others. It would require us to ask whether encouraging adults who might provide adoptive homes to produce their own adoptees is good for the existing children in need of such homes.

The traditional adoption world makes the claim that biologically linked parenting serves children's interests, as well as the interests of birth parents, in important ways. My contention is that society has enormously overvalued the biologic family and undervalued adoptive arrangements. But it is quite a different thing to say that biologically linked parenting is *without* value. I argue that for children in need of nurturing homes, adoption is a great solution that simultaneously serves the needs of infertile adults. But it is quite different to say that we should promote the removal of children from biologically linked parents so that they can be raised by others, or promote the creation of children for this very purpose. I argue that we should recognize adoptive families as having some uniquely positive features. But this does not necessarily mean that we should see biologic family bonds as shackles to be cast off or as simply irrelevant.

Surrogacy, embryo adoption, and the other new methods of child production force us to consider these more radical arguments. *Should* we hold on to the biologic model of parenting? Should we instead view it as a positive good for people to give away or sell their genetic products for others to raise? Would this produce families that make more sense than traditional families? Would it be a better world if babies were systematically scrambled in the hospital nurseries, so as to ensure that no parent goes home with a genetically linked child?

The possibilities are intriguing. And the new adoptive arrangements are in fact already breaking open traditional understandings of the family. Donor insemination has enabled large numbers of single women and lesbian couples to establish families. The doctors have discovered that IVF embryos obtained with donor eggs can be successfully transferred into postmenopausal women, so that significantly older women can experience pregnancy and childbirth.[12] Couples can now contemplate producing embryos during their fertile years and freezing them for use when child-rearing seems more convenient. Many soldiers banked frozen sperm before going off to war in Iraq, so that if they died, their wives could give birth to their children. The new methods have opened up the possibilities for experimentation with the family on a grand scale, in ways that will be seen as positive by some and as deeply troubling by others.

What should be clear is that it makes no sense to rush to experiment with the family by creating these new adoptive arrangements without first rethinking and significantly revamping the way we structure traditional adoption. If we genuinely cared about children's interests, we would focus on finding adoptive homes for existing children in need rather than on creating new made-to-order adoptees for adults in need. We would eliminate the barriers to traditional adoption before encouraging people to sell their genetic material and products to facilitate new adoptions. We would enable singles, gays and lesbians, older people, and other nontraditional parent types to give homes to existing children rather than insisting that they parent children whose production they have arranged. At present, we drive such people away from traditional adoption by parental screening and other policies, at the same time that we lure them into the new child production world with promises that they can purchase whatever combination of genetic material and gestational services it takes to produce their baby of choice.

We should call a halt to these new methods of child production while we move forward with the business of reforming the traditional adoption system. We would then have some time to think about the hard questions involved in deciding whether we want actually to *promote* the separation of children from their genetic and gestating parents on a systematic basis. Do we want to permit payments of the kind now forbidden — payments to already pregnant women to surrender their children upon birth? Do we want to permit payments of the kind now generally allowed — payments to enable the *creation* of children to be raised by biologic others?

My sense is that the answer to both questions should be the same, and that it should be no. Biologically linked parenting may be overvalued, but we should not simply jettison it as having no value. If we allow people to buy and sell parenting rights, we put the quality of all parenting relationships at risk, because that quality has to do with an understanding that parenting is or should be about relationship, about holding on to and nurturing those to whom we are connected rather than letting go and spinning off. Surrogacy expresses "an inferior conception of human flourishing."[13] Treating people as disposable procreators seems likely to do injury to them, to their children, and to the quality of our parenting relationships more generally.

Adults in today's world obviously feel a powerful need to procreate and to have a relationship with any resulting children. Children apparently feel a somewhat reciprocal need to have a relationship with the people who brought them into being. The evidence from the traditional adoption world indicates that large numbers of birth mothers and adoptees suffer when biologic links are severed and generational continuity is destroyed. Sperm donors, their offspring, and birth mothers in surrogacy arrangements increasingly voice complaints of the pain they suffer from being cut off from genetic forebears or descendants.[14] I think that search movement descriptions of this kind of pain are wildly exaggerated and that the stigma associated with adoptive arrangements contributes unnecessarily, but I am convinced that some level of real pain exists, and I do not think that it all results from something we can call socialization. Nor does it seem to me that socializing people to feel that they should maintain a parenting relationship with their biologic offspring is a bad thing. Indeed, it seems a good thing for a child to be conceived in the context of a loving relationship between two people, to be carried in pregnancy by someone who begins to develop a loving parenting relationship during those nine months, and to be born to a person who wants to continue the relationship. It is chilling to read how Mary Beth Whitehead, the birth mother in the famous Baby M. case, which involved a custody battle over the child produced as a result of a classic surrogacy arrangement, promised in her surrogacy contract *not* to develop a loving relationship with the child that she would bear. And it is troubling to find the trial judge castigating her for undue emotionalism because despite her promises, she actually *did* develop a relationship that made the child's surrender enormously painful.

Adults are very ready to disparage children's needs for generational continuity while at the same time asserting their own. In the Baby M. case, the genetic and intended social father, Mr. Stern, talked of how his need for the daughter he achieved through a surrogacy arrangement related to his own tragic loss of all living relatives from earlier generations and his resulting sense of isolation at being cut off from his connections to the past. He argued for the legality of his surrogacy agreement, and for his related right to enjoy with his wife exclusive custody of his daughter, on the basis of his felt need for generational continuity, both backward and forward in time. Because he had lost the connection backward in time, he was, he argued, particularly entitled to a connection forward in time. This argument struck a sympathetic chord in many. Yet from his *daughter's* perspective, the surrogacy arrangement was designed to destroy generational continuity, cutting her off from a major piece of her historic past — her link to and through her mother.

These new forms of parenting are largely fueled by the adult obsession with procreation and with generational continuity. They are largely about giving adults as much as possible of what they want. Adults who want to parent and can contribute eggs, sperm, or gestational services are enabled to do so. Adults who can't can at least get a newborn who will have genetic material from their partner and therefore be somewhat like the child they might otherwise have had. And so on. It seems more than a little unfair in a world in which adults are so obsessed with procreation to ignore any interests the child might have in connecting with forebears.

If we really care about children, we should question why there is so much talk of the adult's right to procreate, right to control his or her body, and right to parent, but so little talk of the child's right to anything. We should focus on existing children and their most vital needs, and begin to talk not about a vacuous "best interest principle" but about a *right* to a nurturing home. We should concentrate on reforming the world of traditional adoption, and decide in that context how far we want to venture into the brave new world of child production.

AFTERWORD

The "flight into the unknown" that landed me in Lima, Peru, in the summer of 1985 was part of a long journey, one that started much earlier and is still going on. The child born to me in 1968 will be married next month. I wonder about what it means to be a parent to a grown child. The two children that I adopted are now aged four and seven. I puzzle over how to survive the sibling battles, how to structure a Peruvian American upbringing, how to manage the details of it all, how to have it be more fun than crazy-making.

I have arrived at a place where many things seem clear to me. I feel that I have learned a lot from my travels through the infertility treatment and adoption worlds, and I am convinced that if others could take this journey, literally or figuratively, they would also learn a lot. My current vision seems to me so clearly right that I find myself impatient with the society that apparently sees things so differently. Adoption works, and works well, both for children in need of homes and for the infertile who want to parent. Why structure it in ways that drive prospective parents away from the existing children in need? Why structure the new worlds of infertility treatment and child production in ways that encourage the infertile and others interested in parenting to produce new children, or to spend their lives trying? There may be some inborn need to procreate, but there are also inborn needs to nurture. Why does organized society seem to want to encourage its members to obsess over the former at the expense of the latter?[1] With my postadoption eyes I find it so obvious that we have it all backward now, so obvious that we should instead be encouraging the nurturing instinct so as to favor the care of existing children over the production of new ones. The directions for change seem similarly obvious.

We need to *deregulate* adoption. The current regulatory framework creates obstacles on both a pragmatic and a psychological level: it makes the adoption process costly and unpleasant, and it simultaneously degrades and demeans this form of family. Indeed, it is clear that the essential *point* of the current framework is to maintain barriers to adoption so as to ensure that this form of family arrangement can be kept in its place as a last resort. We need, therefore, to deregulate in all the ways discussed in this book. We need new policies that focus on the positive rather than the negative potential of adoption. For example, we need meaningful guarantees that children will receive nurturing homes and will not be held in limbo for longer than absolutely necessary. We need new systems providing financial reimbursement for some of the costs involved in adoption, so that more of those who are interested in this form of parenting are able to pursue it. Deregulation would make adoption less costly, but expenses would still be involved. At present we make adoptive parents pay all such expenses, except in the case of certain special-needs adoptions. By contrast, as noted in Chapter 2, we provide significant subsidies to those who pursue procreation. We should revise our state and federal tax systems to provide credits for the costs of all adoptions, and we should revise insurance plans and employer benefit plans so that those who parent through adoption receive at least the same benefits as those who parent through procreation.[2]

At the same time, we need to *regulate* infertility treatment and the new child production methods. The goal should be not simply to protect the rights of parties engaged in these arrangements but to discourage certain practices, such as egg and embryo sale and commercial surrogacy, altogether.

Most of all, we need to think about how to begin to *rethink* the meaning of fertility, parenting, and family.

In my postadoption state, I find all this so obvious that I am left with a genuine sense of puzzlement as to why society is now organizing things the way it is, why it is such an uphill battle to argue the case for adoption. Maybe it is too threatening to think what might happen to the family if it was *not* defined and confined by biology and marriage. Maybe it is too threatening to think what might happen if people were *not* understood to belong to their racial, ethnic, national, or other groups of origin, if they were free to merge across group lines, if they were free *not* to reproduce more of the group's "own."

Living life as an adoptive parent forces a person to think about these issues. It provides no easy answers. It represents freedom from some constraining concepts of family, but it hardly brings instant liberation. Single women and infertile women may see adoption as opening up new opportunities for parenting, without men and free of the ministrations of the high-tech fertility doctors. But this society does not make single parenting, whether adoptive or biologic, an easy ride. Until and unless such parenting becomes financially viable, it will be oppressive both for the women involved and for their children. Adoptive families can be models for the families of the future or they can be poor imitations of the families of the past. Adoptive parents and children have to figure out whether to break the old molds, and if so, what to salvage.

In my family we are making it up as we go along. It began

with the names. I wanted my adopted children's names to signify that they had become part of my family in the sense that my forebears were theirs. I gave each of them Wetherill as a middle name in part because a Wetherill ancestor is supposed to have discovered Mesa Verde, the fabulous ruins inhabited long ago by native peoples of this country, whom I think of as distant relatives of my boys' birth ancestors. I have talked to Christopher and Michael from the beginning about adoption and about the fact that they have birth parents in Peru. I don't know what meaning these connections will have for them as the years go by.

I have found myself thinking a lot about some of our assumptions about difference. A friend asked me when I first returned to this country with Christopher if his baby babble sounded the same as Derek's baby babble. It did sound the same, of course, but I had to confess that this was somehow surprising to me, and that on some level I must actually have expected that the four-month-old gurgles would have a particularly Peruvian ring to them. When Chris went back to Peru with me for Michael's adoption, our friends there were stunned to hear him speak English and immediately declared that he must be brilliant to have mastered it so. Although they knew he had grown up since babyhood in North America, on some level they didn't quite believe that he would learn the things that other North Americans learn.

On a daily basis I find myself experiencing the ways in which this parenting is the same as and different from the parenting of a child born to me. And on a daily basis I find myself choosing to emphasize the sameness and then the difference. In each of the past two school years Christopher and I have worked together on a presentation about Peru for his class, gathering from our home llama bells and ponchos and other mementos from our time in Lima, looking through our books to select pictures of Incan footbridges across huge mountain chasms, of the amazing Machu Picchu ruins, and of the extraordinary textiles and other artifacts from early civilizations. I can see him now, standing proudly behind a table strewn with our Peruvian treasures, describing them one by one and then handing them to an eager friend to be passed around the class; telling his classmates about how the Spanish invaded and how they stole the golden artworks of the Incan rulers and boiled them down; calling upon the outstretched hands, summoning up all his limited knowledge to answer their questions. This year our Peruvian flag hung over the entrance to his first-grade building and the Peruvian collection from our living room decorated the classroom walls for eight weeks while the class used Peru as the focal point for their learning.

Each spring we drive to a park in western Massachusetts to get together with other Peruvian adoptive families for a picnic. And last month we celebrated the Inti Raymi, the Incan Sun Festival, in a local park here in Cambridge. Inti Raymi originated in pre-Columbian times, was outlawed by the Spanish conquerors in the 1500s, and was then revived early this century. It is today celebrated with great enthusiasm in Cuzco, the "belly button of the universe," the capital of the Inca empire. Our Inti Raymi was attended by some forty Peruvian adoptive families; it featured a Peruvian band and home-cooked Peruvian food. We sang songs about a kind of love that knows no colors and no borders and we raised money for the Peruvian Children's Food Fund, a community food kitchen in one of the poor shantytowns in the outskirts of Lima. We recited the words from an Incan prophecy: "When the eagle of the North flies with the condor of the South, the spirit of the land she will awaken." You had to wonder what people in Peru would think to see this group of North Americans with their Peruvian-born children dancing and singing on the top of a hill in Danehy Park in Cambridge, paying tribute to the Incan god of creation.

All this has felt right, but it is also a small part of our lives, wedged in between the play dates with school friends, the tennis and soccer day camps, the Little League games, and the Norman Rockwell beach scenes of our summers. We are feeling our way to what it means to us to be a Peruvian American family. Chris's teacher showed me one morning this year a picture he had drawn of himself the day before. The children were supposed to use only pencil for this picture, but he had insisted on adding some color. He needed to make his face brown and his rollerblades neon orange and green. Right now Christopher's favorite flag is the Peruvian, while Michael's is the American. I don't know exactly how they will identify themselves, who they will be, or where they will seem to belong in the future. My hope is that they will experience a rich sense of choice and connection.

Cambridge, Massachusetts
July 1992

NOTES

2. PARENTING OPTIONS FOR THE INFERTILE: THE BIOLOGIC BIAS

1. Some of the material in this chapter appears in somewhat different form in Elizabeth Bartholet, "Parenting Options for the Infertile," in Mary Joe Frug, *Women and the Law* (Mineola, N.Y.: Foundation Press, 1992), and in Elizabeth Bartholet, "In Vitro Fertilization: The Construction of Infertility and of Parenting," in Helen Holmes, ed., *Issues in Reproductive Technology I: An Anthology* (New York: Garland, 1992).
2. Sociobiology teaches that we are genetically programmed for reproduction. See Richard Dawkins, *The Selfish Gene* (New York: Oxford University Press, 1976).
3. U.S. Congress, Office of Technology Assessment, *Infertility: Medical and Social Choices* (Washington, D.C.: Government Printing Office, May 1988), pp. 4–5; also William D. Mosher and William F. Pratt, "Fecundity and Infertility in the United States, 1965–1988," Advance Data No. 192. Dec. 4, 1990, National Center for Disease Statistics, Hyattsville, Md. Infertility rates have increased for certain subgroups in the population, such as women who postpone efforts to get pregnant until later in life; see Mosher and Pratt.

4. Mosher and Pratt, pp. 1–2; U.S. Congress, *Infertility*, pp. 3–5 (one in seven estimate, based on a population that excludes the surgically sterile).

5. E.g., Patricia Conway and Deborah Valentine, "Reproductive Losses and Grieving," *Journal of Social Work and Human Sexuality* 6 (1987): 46–64; for a review of the literature, Sarah Eaton, "Adoption *v.* Reproductive Technologies: The Biological Link Reexamined," unpublished manuscript, Harvard Law School, 1990, pp. 13–16.

6. Only 50,000 nonrelative adoptions take place per year. A recent survey indicates that only 200,000 women are currently taking steps to pursue adoption, while 2 million have investigated it at some time. See C. Bachrach, K. London, and P. Maza, "On the Path to Adoption: Adoption Seeking in the U.S.," *Journal of Marriage and the Family* 53 (August 1991): 705–18; "New Study Challenges Estimates on Odds of Adopting a Child," *New York Times*, Dec. 10, 1990, p. B-10.

7. See Kevin O'Flaherty, "Financial Support for Adoption: Programs, Issues, and Proposals," unpublished manuscript, Harvard Law School, 1992.

8. See U.S. Congress, *Infertility*, pp. 149–52.

9. O'Flaherty, "Financial Support for Adoption"; also Elizabeth Bartholet, "Where Do Black Children Belong? The Politics of Race Matching in Adoption," *Pennsylvania Law Review* 139 (1991): 1163, 1198–99.

10. U.S. Congress, *Infertility*, p. 143.

3. ADOPTION: TALES OF LOSS AND VISIONS OF CONNECTION

1. See Robert I. Levy, "Tahitian Adoption as a Psychological Message," in Vern Carroll, ed., *Adoption in Eastern Oceania* (Honolulu: University of Hawaii Press, 1970), pp. 70, 81–86.

2. Ibid., p. 77.

3. See Carol B. Stack, *All Our Kin: Strategies for Survival in a Black Community* (New York: Harper & Row, 1975).

4. ADOPTION AND THE SEALED RECORD SYSTEM

1. On the issues discussed in this chapter, see Joan Hollinger, "Aftermath of Adoption," in Joan Hollinger, ed., *Adoption Law and Practice* (New York: Matthew Bender, 1988; supplement 1992); Lincoln Caplan, "Open Adoption," parts I and II, *New Yorker*, May 21 and 28, 1990.
2. See Carroll, *Adoption in Eastern Oceania.*
3. See Stack, *All Our Kin.*
4. Classic search movement texts include Arthur D. Sorosky, et al., *The Adoption Triangle: Sealed or Opened Records: How They Affect Adoptees, Birthparents, and Adoptive Parents* (Garden City, N.Y.: Anchor, 1984); Florence Fisher, *The Search for Anna Fisher* (New York: Fawcett Crest, 1974); Betty J. Lifton, *Twice Born: Memoirs of an Adopted Daughter* (New York: McGraw-Hill, 1975), and *Lost and Found: The Adoption Experience* (New York: Harper & Row, 1988); H. David Kirk, *Shared Fate* (New York: Free Press, 1964); and Ruthena H. Kittson (pseud.), *Orphan Voyage* (self-published, 1981).
5. See Annette Baran and Reuben Pannor, "It's Time for Sweeping Change," *American Adoption Congress Newsletter*, Summer 1990, p. 5.

5. ADOPTION AND THE PARENTAL SCREENING SYSTEM

1. See Alfred Kadushin and Judith A. Martin, *Child Welfare Services*, 3rd ed. (New York: Macmillan, 1980), and Cynthia Martin, *Beating the Adoption Game*, rev. ed. (New York: Harcourt Brace Jovanovich, 1988).
2. See Joan Hollinger, "Reflections on Independent Adoptions," in *Legal Advocacy for Children and Youth* (Washington, D.C.: National Legal Resource Center, 1986), pp. 366–92; Joan Hollinger, "Introduction to Adoption Law and Practice," in Hollinger, ed., *Adoption Law and Practice*, section 1.05; Jacqueline H. Plumez, *Successful Adoption: A Guide to Finding a Child and Raising a Family* (New York: Crown, 1982), pp. 69–79.
3. On issues involving gay and lesbian adoptive parenting, see Wendell Ricketts and Roberta Achtenberg, "The Adoptive and Foster Gay and Lesbian Parent," in Frederick W. Bozett, ed., *Gay and Lesbian Parents* (New York: Greenwood, 1987), pp. 89–111;

Jonathan Crawford, "Agency Adoptions by Homosexuals in New York State," unpublished ms., Harvard Law School, 1990; Joseph Evall, "Sexual Orientation and Adoptive Matching," unpublished ms., Harvard Law School, 1990.

4. William Feigelman and Arnold R. Silverman, *Chosen Children: New Patterns of Adoptive Relationships* (New York: Greenwood, 1983), p. 177.

5. Alfred Kadushin, "Single-Parent Adoptions: An Overview and Some Relevant Research," *Social Service Review* 44 (1970): 263.

6. One study indicates that more than one third of the children born between 1960 and 1980 spent part of their childhood in a single-parent family because of birth out of wedlock, divorce, or death; the figure went up to roughly half of those born in the 1970–1984 period. See Larry Bumpass and James Sweet, "Children's Experience in Single-Parent Families: Implications of Cohabitation and Marital Transitions," *Family Planning Perspectives* 21 (Nov./Dec. 1989): 256.

7. Some recent court-made law prohibits use of such factors as race, age, religion, marital status, and sexual orientation to absolutely preclude an adoptive applicant from consideration or prevent a child's placement. But these rulings are of limited significance given the enormous discretion that adoption agencies have to consider these and other factors in arriving at a final determination of parental fitness.

8. See e.g., National Conference of Commissioners on Uniform State Laws, "Proposed Uniform Adoption Act," draft of Nov. 25, 1991, article 3, section 21.

9. Ibid., article 2 and comments.

10. Ibid., sections 23(e) and (g), providing that adoptive applicants must be found suitable unless an investigator makes written findings as to the reasons that adoptive placement would pose a risk to the physical or psychological well-being of a child. See also Martin, *Beating the Adoption Game*, pp. 282–83, which advocates issuing parenting "licenses" to all adoptive applicants who are not demonstrably unfit.

11. The U.S. Supreme Court indicated significant respect for the foster parenting relationship but refused to establish any meaningful legal right to protect such a relationship, in *Smith* v. *Organization of Foster Families*, 431 U.S. 816 (1977).

12. For examples of proposals for licensing schemes in the area of biologic parenting, see Roger W. McIntire, "Parenthood Training or Mandatory Birth Control: Take Your Choice," *Psychology Today* 9, no. 5 (Oct. 1973): 34–39, 132–33, 143, and Claudia Mangel, "Licensing Parents: How Feasible?" *Family Law Quarterly* 22 (1988): 17.

13. The Supreme Court has accorded the right to procreate near-absolute protection against government intervention. See *Skinner* v. *Oklahoma*, 316 U.S. 535 (1942), and Lawrence H. Tribe, *American Constitutional Law*, 2nd ed. (Westbury, N.Y.: Foundation Press, 1988), p. 1340.

14. See "A Plan to Pay Welfare Mothers for Birth Control," *New York Times*, Feb. 9, 1991, p. A-9, and "Judge Is Firm on Forced Contraception, But Welcomes an Appeal," *New York Times*, Jan. 11, 1991, p. A-17.

15. For 1990 figures, see *VCIS [Voluntary Cooperative Information Systems] Research Notes*, no. 3 (Washington, D.C.: American Public Welfare Association, May 1991); see also Bartholet, "Where Do Black Children Belong?" pp. 1163, 1173–74, note 10; note 2, Chapter 6 (below).

16. Reports indicate that roughly one third of the children born to married parents experience the disruption of that marriage before the age of sixteen. See Bumpass and Sweet, "Children's Experience in Single-Parent Families."

17. See Judith Wallerstein and Sandra Blakeslee, *Second Chances: Men, Women, and Children a Decade after Divorce* (New York: Ticknor & Fields, 1989), which documents the ongoing pain and trauma suffered by the children of divorce.

18. See Alfred Kadushin, "Factors Associated with Adoptive Outcome," in Kadushin and Martin, *Child Welfare Services*, pp. 530–31.

19. See Hollinger, "Reflections on Independent Adoptions"; James B. Boskey, "Placing Children for Adoption," in Hollinger, ed., *Adoption Law and Practice*, section 3.04, pp. 3–35, 3–36; W. Meezan, S. Katz, and A. M. Russo, *Adoptions Without Agencies* (New York: Child Welfare League of America, 1978), p. 232.

20. On single-parent adoption, see Feigelman and Silverman, *Chosen Children*, pp. 173–92; Vic Groze, "Adoption and Single Parents: A Review," *Child Welfare* 50, no. 3 (May-June 1991): 321; Joan

Shireman and Penny Johnson, "A Longitudinal Study of Black Adoptions: Single Parent, Transracial, and Traditional," *Social Work* (May-June 1986): 172, 175; and Joan Shireman, "Growing Up Adopted," Chicago Child Care Society, 1988, pp. 5, 36.

On gay and lesbian parenting, see Daniel Goleman, "Studies Find No Disadvantage in Growing Up in a Gay Home," *New York Times*, Dec. 12, 1992, p. c-14; *Opinion of the Justices*, 530 A.2nd 21, 28 (N.H. 1987) (Batcheldor, J., dissenting); D. Hutchens and M. Kirkpatrick, "Lesbian Mothers/Gay Fathers," in Diane H. Schetky and Elissa P. Benedek, *Emerging Issues in Child Psychiatry and the Law* (New York: Brunner-Mazel, 1985), pp. 115–26; David J. Kleber, Robert J. Howell, and Alta Lura Tibbits-Kleber, "The Impact of Parental Homosexuality in Child Custody Cases: A Review of the Literature," *Bulletin of the American Academy of Psychiatry and the Law* 14, no. 1 (1986): 81–87.

On age as a screening criterion, see H. Witmer, E. Herzog, E. Weinstein, and M. Sullivan, *Independent Adoptions: A Follow-up Study* (New York: Russell Sage Foundation, 1963), pp. 349–50.

6. ADOPTION AND RACE

1. This chapter is drawn in substantial part from material that first appeared in Bartholet, "Where Do Black Children Belong?" which contains a more detailed treatment of the issues and includes extensive documentation of my sources. An edited version of that article, together with comments from adoption experts, appears in *Reconstruction* 1, no. 4 (1992): 22–55.

2. The number of children in "out-of-home" placement increased from a total of 262,000 in 1982, to 280,000 in 1986, to 379,000 in 1989, to 407,000 in 1990. The number of these children who are black rose from 34.2 percent in 1982, to 34.9 percent in 1986, to 37.1 percent in 1987. In 1987 only 46.1 percent were white. These figures are drawn from a telephone interview with Dr. Toshio Tatara, director of the Research and Demonstration Department, American Public Welfare Association, Jan. 29, 1991, and *VCIS Research Notes*, p. 1. Other estimates generally show that roughly half the children in out-of-home placement are children of color, and more than one third are black. See House Select Committee on Children, Youth, and Families, *No Place to Call Home: Discarded*

Children in America, 101st Cong., 2d sess., 1990, H.R. Report 395, pp. 5, 38; J. Munns and J. Copenhaver, "The State of Adoption in America," Child Welfare League of America, 1989, pp. 3–4.

Most adoption professionals believe that the enormous increase in the number of children entering foster care in the past few years will continue, with young minority children representing a large part of the increase. Estimates indicate that if current trends continue, the population of children in out-of-home placement will increase 68 percent by 1995, rising from 500,000 to 840,000; see Select Committee, *No Place to Call Home*, p. 5. (These figures include children under the jurisdiction of juvenile correctional and mental health authorities, who are not included in Dr. Tatara's statistics, noted above.)

3. *VCIS Research Notes*, p. 3.
4. National Association of Black Social Workers, position paper, April 1972, in Rita J. Simon and Howard Altstein, *Transracial Adoption* (New York: Wiley, 1977), pp. 50–52.
5. There is, to be sure, a lot of variation among agencies. Some of the private ones are quite open to transracial adoption, and as a group private agencies are generally more open to such adoption than the public agencies are. But public matching policies control private agencies to a significant degree, either through the regulatory process or through contracts for services. Public agencies also have under their jurisdiction a disproportionate share of the minority children available for adoption.

In the independent adoption world, where birth parents and private intermediaries make the placement decisions with limited intervention by the state, race may or may not play a major role in placement decisions, depending on the view of the individuals and organizations involved.
6. See note 2, above. By contrast to their numbers in the foster care population, blacks make up only 12.3 percent of the general population. See U.S. Department of Commerce, *Statistical Abstract of the United States* (Washington, D.C.: Government Printing Office, 1990), p. 12.
7. Memorandum to staff from C. Johnson, director of the National Adoption Center, March 28, 1991, and memorandum to E. Bartholet from C. Johnson, April 16, 1991. The Massachusetts Adoption Resource Exchange figures for December 1990 show that 121

of the children registered there were of color and 198 were white, whereas 41 of the families registered were of color and 281 were white; telephone interview with Carolyn Smith, Massachusetts Adoption Resource Exchange, Jan. 24, 1991. A study done for the Child Welfare League provides additional documentation for the mismatch; see Munns and Copenhaver, *The State of Adoption in America*, p. 8.

8. See James Breay, "Who Are the Waiting Children?" internal report of the Massachusetts Department of Social Services, Office of Field Support Services, Table 3.1.

9. See National Association of Black Social Workers, "Preserving Black Families: Research and Action Beyond the Rhetoric," February 1986, p. 31, and NABSW, unpublished paper on transracial placements, 1986.

10. North American Council on Adoptable Children, "Barriers to Same-Race Placement," 1991, pp. 17, 21, 27. Seventy-six percent of the state agencies and 44 percent of the private agencies surveyed had such policies.

11. See Westat, Inc., "Adoptive Services for Waiting Minority and Nonminority Children," April 15, 1986, pp. x–xi, 3–7 to 3–8, 3–17 to 3–44, 6–1; Jeffrey Rosenberg, "Despite Advances, Minority Children Lack Permanence," *National Adoption Report*, National Committee for Adoption, Jan.-Feb. 1987, p. 3; Janet Mason and Carol Williams, "The Adoption of Minority Children," in *Adoption of Children with Special Needs: Issues in Law and Policy* (Washington, D.C.: National Legal Resource Center, 1985), pp. 83–126, noting that minority children are disproportionately represented and spend longer in foster care than white children; and House Select Committee on Children, Youth, and Families, *No Place to Call Home*, pp. 38–39.

The VCIS statistics for 1987 indicate that blacks leave out-of-home care at a lower rate than whites. Black children made up 37.1 percent of the children in care and 34.1 percent of those legally free for adoption at the end of fiscal year 1987 (and 34.9 percent of those in care and 42.4 percent of those free for adoption at the end of fiscal 1986). However, they made up only 26.5 percent of the children who left care and 27.7 percent of those whose adoptions were finalized in fiscal 1987. See Tatara interview.

12. See Breay, "Who Are the Waiting Children?" pp. 9, 13.

13. Ibid., Tables 1.0, 1.6, 3.1.

14. Ibid., Tables 1.6 and 3.3 reveal that one third of the waiting white adoptive families in Massachusetts said they would consider a child with severe physical, emotional, or mental disabilities.

15. See Bartholet, "Where Do Black Children Belong?" pp. 1207–26, for a detailed description of the studies and documentation of sources.

16. Rita J. Simon and Howard Altstein, *Transracial Adoptees and Their Families: A Study of Identity and Commitment* (New York: Praeger, 1987), pp. 82, 10.

17. Joan Shireman, "Growing Up Adopted: An Examination of Major Issues," Regional Research Institute for Human Services, Portland State University, Aug. 1988, pp. 36–37.

18. William E. Cross, *Shades of Black: Diversity in African-American Identity* (Philadelphia: Temple University Press, 1991), p. 113.

19. *National Association of Black Social Workers Newsletter*, Spring 1988, president's message, pp. 1–2.

20. Bartholet, "Where Do Black Children Belong?" pp. 1220–21; Cross, *Shades of Black*, pp. 108–14. Cross notes that studies of transracial adoptees reveal significant variety in the group in terms of "group identity" measures but consistently high scores on "personal identity" measures, which assess basic self-esteem and adjustment. He concludes that these studies make sense when we recognize that there is not necessarily a connection between measures of personal and group identity. Noting that almost all studies of black identity issues have proceeded on the assumption that there *is* such a relationship (p. 50), Cross finds no basis for this assumption, and points out that studies that have looked at both personal identity measures and group identity measures have found no linear relationship (p. 108). He argues that opposition to transracial adoption was grounded on this erroneous but commonplace assumption, and concludes: "It must be recognized that the theoretical basis for . . . opposition [to transracial adoption] has been tested and found wanting. . . . As the evidence continues to build, there seems to be no scientific basis for opposing transracial adoptions" (pp. 113–14).

21. Bartholet, "Where Do Black Children Belong?" p. 1236, note 206.

22. Cross, *Shades of Black*, pp. 189–225, discusses the rich variety of

ways in which black people today choose their group affiliations and emphasizes the benefits inherent in this variety: "I, along with other nigrescence theorists and researchers, have tried to offer a way of looking at . . . the development of various black identities — nationalist, bicultural, and multicultural — including Afrocentricity. We have sought to clarify and expand the discourse on blackness by paying attention to the variability and diversity in blackness" (p. 223).

23. See, e.g., North American Council on Adoptable Children, *Barriers to Same-Race Placement*, p. 27, which indicates that the main impact of adoption cases that have limited the use of race in decision-making has been to change the *language* of written policies to make it more open-ended and less restrictive.

7. ADOPTION AMONG NATIONS

1. Some of the material in this chapter appears in different form in Elizabeth Bartholet, "International Adoption," *The Future of Children* 5 (Spring 1992; issued by the Center for the Future of Children, Los Altos, California). See also Elizabeth Bartholet, "International Adoption: Overview," in Hollinger, ed., *Adoption Law and Practice*, and Bartholet, review of *Are Those Kids Yours?* by Cheri Register, *Harvard International Law Journal* 33 (Spring 1992): 649–53. For an excellent discussion of the history and current nature of international adoption, see the Hague Conference on Private International Law, *Report on Intercountry Adoption*, Preliminary Document No. 1, April 1990.

2. It has been estimated that more than a million families in the United States are interested in adoption, although only about 200,000 are currently taking steps to pursue it. See Bartholet, "Where Do Black Children Belong?" pp. 1163, 1166, note 5; ch. 2, note 6.

3. See Bartholet, "International Adoption: Overview," pp. 10–35 to 10–36.

4. Ibid., pp. 10–6 to 10–7,

5. National Committee for Adoption, *1989 Factbook* (Washington, D.C.: NCA, 1989), pp. 61, 71–72; Hague Conference, *Report*, p. 62, note 96.

6. This has resulted in a dramatic decrease in the total number of international adoptions, with only 6,500 in the U.S. in FY 1992.

7. Without the preferential visa, the foreign-born adoptee is subject to the normal quota restrictions on immigration.

8. Less restrictive requirements are applicable when the adoptee has lived abroad with the adoptive parents for two years; there is then no home study requirement and no orphan restriction.

9. Children whose birth father's paternity has been established (in countries that have procedures for legitimating such children, as most countries do) cannot qualify as orphans even if the parents have never married or lived together, and even if the father has never known or has abandoned the child. See Immigration and Naturalization Service, *The Immigration of Adopted and Prospective Adoptive Children*, Form M-249Y (1990), pp. 18–19.

10. Ibid., pp. 19–20.

11. See Harry D. Krause, "Creation of Relationships of Kinship," in *International Encyclopedia of Comparative Law*, vol. 4 (New York: Oceana, 1973), ch. 6, pp. 85–86.

12. See Richard R. Carlson, "Transnational Adoption of Children," *Tulsa Law Journal* 23 (1988): 317, 366–70.

13. "Declaration on Social and Legal Principles Relating to Adoption and Foster Placement of Children Nationally and Internationally," U.N. General Assembly Resolution 41/85, Dec. 3, 1986, in Hague Conference, *Report*, annex H.

14. "Convention on the Rights of the Child," adopted Nov. 20, 1989, in Hague Conference, *Report*, annex I. Articles 20, 21, and 35 deal with the protection of children without families, adoption nationally and internationally, and trafficking in and abduction of children.

15. "Declaration on Social and Legal Principles Relating to Adoption," article 17 ("If a child cannot be placed in a foster or an adoptive family or cannot in any suitable manner be cared for in the country of origin, intercountry adoption may be considered as an alternative means of providing the child with a family"); "Convention on the Rights of the Child," article 21(b) (Governments that recognize adoption shall "recognize that intercountry adoption may be considered as an alternative means of child's care, if the child cannot be placed in a foster or an adoptive family

or cannot in any suitable manner be cared for in the child's country of origin").

16. Institutionalization is far more common than foster care in the poor nations of the world as well as in South Korea. The Hague Conference report notes that these institutions, "often poorly staffed, managed and supervised, are a major, perhaps the major, 'source' of children being adopted abroad" (p. 64).

    Estimates of the number of street children — children who essentially live in the streets — vary from 31 to 80 million, about half of whom live in Latin America. While most of these children are thought to have "continuous" contact with their biologic families, it is estimated that some 25 percent have only "occasional" contact or no contact whatsoever. See Hague Conference, *Report*, annex B (UNICEF Executive Board, *Exploitation of Working Children and Street Children*, U.N. Document E ICEF/1986/CRP.3), p. 16. Others have estimated the number of street children at 100 million, and project that this total will double in the next decade; see Edward Epstein, "Children on the Streets," *San Francisco Chronicle*, Oct. 12, 1989, p. A-25. The number of street children in Brazil alone is estimated between 10 million and 36 million; see Hollinger, ed., *Adoption Law and Practice*, and *Boston Herald*, Nov. 26, 1989. In addition, there are said to be more than 10 million children who are refugees.

17. General economic, health, and related conditions for children in Africa and Latin America have been getting worse in recent years, and this trend is likely to continue. See UNICEF, "Summary: The State of the World's Children, 1989."

18. See U.S. Information Agency, "Misinformation and Disinformation: The So-Called 'Baby Parts' Rumor Spreads Worldwide," report dated June 1, 1990; Hague Conference, *Report*, p. 90.

19. A publication put out by Defense for Children International, an organization that has focused on the negative aspects of international adoption, concedes that trafficking cases are extremely limited in number: "The vast majority [of birth parents] do not part with their child for money, but out of despair or with the hope to ensure the child's welfare or survival. . . . [Trafficking] cases are reported from time to time but not well documented. No doubt they constitute only a tiny proportion of the displacements of children for adoption purposes." See Marie-Françoise

Lucker-Bubel, *Inter-Country Adoption and Trafficking in Children: An Initial Assessment of the Adequacy of the International Protection of Children and Their Rights* (Geneva: Defense for Children International, 1990), p. 2.

20. Jeanine Pollitt, "Intercountry Adoption: Serving the Welfare of Children," unpublished ms., Harvard Law School, 1992; Nigel Cantwell, "Who Said 'Best Interests'?" *International Children's Rights Monitor* 7, no. 1/2 (1990): 4.

21. Pollitt, "Intercountry Adoption," pp. 49–50. Five thousand were adopted from December 1989 until July 1991; of these, 1,500 were adopted by people from the United States, and roughly half of those were adopted from institutions.

22. For a description of legal "reform" action in Romania, see ibid., pp. 58–63; Nigel Cantwell and Paulo David, "Romania: Is the Adoption Jungle a Thing of the Past?" *International Children's Rights Monitor* 8, special issue (1991): 29–30; Moira Farrow, "Romanian Orphans Suffer by New Rules, Supporter Says," *Vancouver Sun*, Aug. 9, 1991, p. A-11, and "Romania's Children Continue to Struggle," *Vancouver Sun*, Dec. 4, 1991, p. B-2 (notes a 20 percent increase in the number of children in Romanian orphanages in the brief period since the government halted adoptions in the summer of 1991 with a view toward imposing new restrictions).

23. See Barbara Tizard, "Intercountry Adoption: A Review of the Evidence," *Journal of Child Psychology and Psychiatry* 32, no. 5 (1991): 743–56, a review of studies on outcomes of international adoption that concludes that "results [are] similar to those found in studies of incountry adoption"; Jan Linowitz and Neil Boothby, "Cross-Cultural Placements," in Everett M. Ressler et al., *Unaccompanied Children: Care and Protection in Wars, Natural Disasters, and Refugee Movements* (New York: Oxford University Press, 1988), pp. 181–85, a review that finds that all the major follow-up studies "stress the successful adaptations of most adoptees"; Howard Altstein and Rita J. Simon, eds., *Intercountry Adoption: A Multinational Perspective* (New York: Greenwood, 1991), p. 184, which concludes that "studies of intercountry adoptees in the United States suggest that children who are adopted as infants make positive adjustments to their new environments."

Feigelman and Silverman's study of Korean adoptees in the

United States (*Chosen Children*, pp. 159–62) dealt with adoptees in their adolescent and young adult years, and found extremely successful adjustment; in fact, the Korean adoptees scored higher on adjustment measures than their white American counterparts. Earlier studies of Korean adoptees also showed consistently high success rates. See Bartholet, "International Adoption: Overview," pp. 10–20 to 10–21, notes 23 and 25; Hague Conference, *Report*, p. 76, note 118.

A major study undertaken in Denmark is similarly positive. See M. Rorbech, *Mit land er Danmark* (Copenhagen: Social Forsknings Instituttet, 1989; English abstract *Denmark — My Country*, 1990), described in Hague Conference, *Report*, pp. 76–78. See also Torben Melchior, "Adoption in Denmark," in R. A. C. Hoksbergen, ed., *Adoption in Worldwide Perspective* (Berwyn, Ill.: Swets North America, 1986), pp. 218–19, and Gunilla Andersson, "The Adopting and Adopted Swedes and Their Contemporary Society," in Hoksbergen, ed., *Adoption in Worldwide Perspective*, p. 27.

24. Tizard, "Intercountry Adoption," pp. 747–51. Feigelman and Silverman found that Colombian children who had medical problems requiring extensive treatment at the time of adoption adjusted "remarkably well," better overall than adoptees born in the United States; *Chosen Children*, pp. 140–42, 144–45.

25. M. Dalen and B. Saetersdal, "Transracial Adoption in Norway," *Adoption and Fostering* 11 (1987): 41–46. Ian J. Harvey, "Adoption of Vietnamese Children: An Australian Study," *Australian Journal of Social Issues* 18, no. 1 (1983): 55, 59–61, 65–68, finds high rates of success among Vietnamese adoptees who arrived in Australia suffering from malnutrition, deprivation, and other traumatic early experiences. The research generally indicates that age at placement and preadoption trauma are the most powerful indicators for problems in adjustment; see Altstein and Simon, *Intercountry Adoption*, p. 190, and Hague Conference, *Report*, p. 78, notes 122–24. The studies nonetheless tend to show that after some time of adjustment, the adoptees and their families function very well; see Linowitz and Boothby, "Cross-Cultural Placements," pp. 183, 185, and Juliet Harper, "Inter-Country Adoption of Older Children in Australia," *Adoption and Fostering* 10, no. 2 (1986): 27–28, 30–31.

26. See Tizard, "Intercountry Adoption," pp. 52–54; Feigelman and Silverman, *Chosen Children*, pp. 141–43, 145, 154–62 (indicating that Colombian and Korean adoptees had developed a limited sense of identity with their culture of origin).
27. See Tizard, "Intercountry Adoption," p. 755. The only study Tizard cites as providing evidence of such harm is inapposite, since it deals with the *in*-country adoption of Native children in Canada. In any event, this study suffers from serious methodological problems that undercut the significance of its findings. It is reported in Christopher Bagley, "Adoption of Native Children in Canada: A Policy Analysis and a Research Report," in Altstein and Simon, *Intercountry Adoption*, pp. 55–79. The Feigelman and Silverman study found that the Korean and Colombian adoptees involved had high rates of adoptive success.
28. Rorbech, *Mit land er Danmark*, p. 20.
29. Cheri Register, *Are Those Kids Yours? American Families with Children Adopted from Other Countries* (New York: Free Press, 1991), pp. 207, 205.
30. Tizard, "Intercountry Adoption," p. 746.
31. A variety of proposed and existing laws dealing with the registration, recognition, and enforcement of judgments entered by foreign jurisdictions could be used as models. New Hampshire has legislation that specifically provides for recognition of a "foreign decree affecting adoption" (N.H. RSA Public Safety and Welfare sec. 170-B:23 (1973)). See also the Uniform Adoption Act (1969 Revised Act), sec. 17, "Recognition of Foreign Decree Affecting Adoption"; Uniform Enforcement of Foreign Judgments Act (1964 Revised Act), providing for the filing and enforcement of judgments entered by other courts within the United States; Uniform Foreign Money Judgments Recognition Act, providing for the recognition and enforcement of judgments entered by non-U.S. courts.

8. ADOPTION AND STIGMA

1. Christine Bachrach, et al., "Relinquishment of Premarital Births: Evidence from National Survey Data," *Family Planning Perspectives* 24 (Jan.-Feb. 1992): 27, 29. A recent study showed that only 13 percent of birth mothers who wanted but were denied abor-

tion gave up their babies for adoption. While the author of the study found this figure startlingly low, another researcher commented, "Society frowns terribly on a woman who gives up her own child. . . . The opprobrium is enormous." See "Study Says Anger Troubles Women Denied Abortion," *New York Times*, May 29, 1991, p. C-10.

2. See Renee Pruitt, "The Fairy Tale as Indicator of Societal Views Toward Non-Traditional Families," unpublished ms., Harvard Law School, 1991: "A recurring theme is that whenever a child is taken from its birth parents, bad things happen to them until they either escape or are rescued by the 'real' parents. Rapunzel, Hansel and Gretel, Snow White, and most obviously Cinderella all have as a central theme the evil that is done to them by a social (non-blood-linked) parent." Pruitt notes that fairy tales both reflect a society's most basic beliefs and play an important role in shaping those beliefs.

3. Adoptive parents have long been aware of the media bias, but a recent survey provides powerful confirmation of their impressions. It shows that the largest category of adoption-related news concerns courts and crimes, and features adoption rackets and other abusive practices. One third of all adoption news stories deal with birth parents who are searching for or reclaiming their children. Television and screen dramas are similarly dominated by themes of the corruption and abuse involved in adoptive arrangements and of the search for birth parents and children. See George Gerbner, "Adoption in the Mass Media," unpublished paper for the Catholic Adoptive Parents Association, Inc., New York, Nov. 21, 1988.

4. David M. Schneider, *American Kinship: A Cultural Account* (Chicago: University of Chicago Press, 1980), pp. 107, vii.

5. See Levy, "Tahitian Adoption," pp. 75–76, note 5.

6. Ibid., p. 83.

7. *Ex parte Clark*, 87 Cal. 638, 641 (1891).

8. See Annette Baran and Reuben Pannor, *Lethal Secrets: The Shocking Consequences and Unsolved Problems of Artificial Insemination* (New York: Warner, 1989).

9. See Elizabeth Gibson, "Artificial Insemination by Donor," unpublished ms., Harvard Law School, 1991, p. 7, note 12.

10. Baran and Pannor, "It's Time for a Sweeping Change," p. 5.

11. See also Carole Anderson, "Child Abuse and Adoption," unpublished ms. for Concerned United Birthparents, Inc., Des Moines, Iowa, 1991. This paper by the president of the leading birth parent organization argues that issues of infertility and the lack of a genetic connection between parent and child contribute to a great risk for child abuse in adoptive families. See generally ch. 4, note 4.

12. "How the Adoption System Ignites a Fire," *New York Times*, March 1, 1986, p. 27.

13. Betty J. Lifton, "Brave New Baby in the Brave New World," *Woman and Health Magazine* 13, no. 1–2 (November 1987): 149–53.

14. See Remi J. Cadoret, "Biologic Perspectives on Adoptee Adjustment," in David M. Brodzinsky and Marshall D. Schechter, *The Psychology of Adoption* (New York: Oxford University Press, 1990), pp. 25–41.

15. See John C. Loehlin, Lee Willerman, and Joseph M. Horn, "Personality Resemblances Between Unwed Mothers and Their Adopted-Away Offspring," *Journal of Personality and Social Psychology* 42 (1982): 1089.

16. A helpful review of the literature, including the limited body of empirical evidence discussed below, is contained in Colette Sartor, "The Biological Link and Its Effect on Adoption as a Viable Family Alternative," unpublished ms., Harvard Law School, 1990.

17. For a summary of this literature, see Janet Hoopes, "Adoption and Identity Formation," in Brodzinsky and Schechter, *The Psychology of Adoption*, pp. 144, 149–53. See also Paul M. Brinich, "Some Potential Effects of Adoption on Self and Object Relations," in Albert J. Solnit, et al., eds., *The Psychoanalytic Study of the Child*, vol. 35 (New Haven: Yale University Press, 1980), pp. 107–33.

18. Early support for the claim that adoptees are at risk for permanent psychological impairment appeared in H. J. Sants, "Genealogical Bewilderment in Children with Substitute Parents," *British Journal of Medical Psychology* 37 (1964): 133.

19. Carl Schoenberg, "On Adoption and Identity," *Journal of the Child Welfare League of America* 53 (1974): 549.

20. Luis Feder, "Adoption Trauma: Oedipus Myth/Clinical Reality," *International Journal of Psychoanalysis* 55 (1974): 491.

21. See the review of the literature in Paul M. Brinich, "Adoption from the Inside Out: A Psychoanalytic Perspective," in Brodzinsky and Schechter, *The Psychology of Adoption*, pp. 42, 52–59. This literature consists of clinical case studies, reports on people in psychiatric treatment, and other studies based on obviously skewed and distorted samples of the relevant population. Rarely has there been even an attempt to use control groups or other research methods designed to test the validity of the theoretical assumptions at issue. See Anne B. Brodzinsky, "Surrendering an Infant for Adoption: The Birthmother Experience," in Brodzinsky and Schechter, *The Psychology of Adoption*, pp. 295–315.

22. About half of all nonrelative adoptive placements involve children over the age of one year; National Committee for Adoption, *1989 Factbook*, pp. 61, 72. There is a fair amount of evidence of the importance of developing attachment relationships in the first six to eight months of life. Children who fail to develop such relationships, or who suffer from the disruption of such relationships, are thought to be at risk for developmental difficulties. See Harold Grotevant and Ruth McRoy, "Adopted Adolescents in Residential Treatment: The Role of the Family," in Brodzinsky and Schechter, *The Psychology of Adoption*, pp. 167, 170–71.

23. Adoption studies show repeatedly that the older a child is at placement, the less likely the chances for successful adjustment. See Feigelman and Silverman, *Chosen Children*, pp. 92–93, and Richard D. Barth, et al., "Predicting Adoption Disruptions," *Social Work* 33 (1988): 227.

24. Brinich, "Adoption from the Inside Out," pp. 49, 52; Paul M. Brinich and Evelin B. Brinich, "Adoption and Adaptation," *Journal of Nervous and Mental Diseases* 170 (1982): 489.

25. Hoopes, "Adoption and Identity Formation," p. 153.

26. Empirical studies comparing generalized groups of adoptees to nonadopted children have yielded mixed results, with some reporting significant differences between the two groups in terms of such factors as emotional and school adjustment and others reporting no such differences. See, e.g., Melissa Norvell and Rebecca Guy, "A Comparison of Self-Concept in Adopted and Non-Adopted Adolescents," *Adolescence* 11 (1977): 443, in which the generalized group of adoptees revealed no greater self-

esteem problems than the nonadopted group; age of the adoptee at placement was found to be a key variable in self-esteem. Studies that do find differences nonetheless report that adopted children fall within normal ranges on personality and behavioral tests. See, e.g., Hoopes, "Adoption and Identity Formation, p. 154, and Byron W. Lindholm and John Touliatos, "Psychological Adjustment of Adopted and Non-Adopted Children," *Psychological Reports* 46 (1980): 307–10, in which research on an undifferentiated sample of adoptees revealed a small number with behavioral problems and indicated that the adoption factor was of little value as a predictor.

27. See Barth and Berry, "A Decade Later: Outcomes of Permanency Planning," in *The Adoption Assistance and Child Welfare Act of 1980: The First Ten Years* (St. Paul, Minn.: North American Council on Adoptable Children, 1990), p. 22, finding that existing evidence on outcomes of older children adoptions is generally favorable. The more recent adoption disruption studies tend to focus on this population. Richard P. Barth and Marianne Berry, *Adoption and Disruption: Rates, Risks, and Responses* (New York: Aldine de Gruyter, 1988), one of the most significant, shows a disruption rate of 10 to 11 percent (pp. 90–91, 99–100), and other such studies have shown comparable rates. They reveal that the probability of disruption is directly related to preadoptive experience; adoptions involving the oldest children and those with the most problematic backgrounds are most likely to disrupt. See also Trudy Festinger, "Adoption Disruption: Rates and Correlates," in Brodzinsky and Schechter, *The Psychology of Adoption*, pp. 201–18.

28. See, e.g., John Triseliotis and Malcolm Hill, "Contrasting Adoption, Foster Care, and Residential Rearing," in Brodzinsky and Schechter, *The Psychology of Adoption*, pp. 107, 115–16.

29. See Christine Bachrach, "Adoption Plans, Adopted Children, and Adoptive Mothers," *Journal of Marriage and the Family* 48 (May 1986): 243; Steven D. McLaughlin, et al., "To Parent or Relinquish: Consequences for Adolescent Mothers," *Social Work* (July-Aug. 1988): 320–25; Richard Barth, "Adolescent Mothers' Beliefs About Open Adoption," *Social Casework* (June 1987): 330–31.

30. Barbara Menning, "The Psychology of Infertility," in James Aiman, ed., *Infertility: Diagnosis and Management* (New York: Springer-Verlag, 1984), p. 17.

31. See, e.g., Barth and Berry, *Adoption and Disruption*, pp. 23–41; note, "Racial Matching and the Adoption Dilemma," *Journal of Family Law* 17 (1979): 333, 356–58; Michael Bohman and Sören Sigvardsson, "Outcome in Adoption: Lessons from Longitudinal Studies," in Brodzinsky and Schechter, *The Psychology of Adoption*, pp. 93, 100–106; Triseliotis and Hill, "Contrasting Adoption, Foster Care, and Residential Rearing," pp. 107–20.

32. Barth and Berry, *Adoption and Disruption*, pp. 24, 29; Barth and Berry, "A Decade Later," pp. 13, 16, 21, 27–30.

33. Bohman and Sigvardsson, "Outcome in Adoption," pp. 93, 100–106.

34. Leslie M. Singer, et al., "Mother-Infant Attachment in Adoptive Families," *Child Development* 56 (1985): 1543, 1550.

35. Kenneth Kaye sums up the evidence in "Acknowledgment or Rejection of Differences?" in Brodzinsky and Schechter, *The Psychology of Adoption*, pp. 121–22. Bohman and Sigvardsson, in "Outcome in Adoption," looked at early-adopted children born to a group of "antisocial or otherwise socially handicapped parents" (parents with a very high incidence of criminality and alcohol abuse) and found that in their teens, the children compared well with a control group from the nonadoptive population. The authors concluded that "the long-term prognosis for adopted children is in no way worse than for children in the general population" (p. 104).

36. Stein and Hoopes found that it was the quality of parent-child relationship, rather than adoptive status, that predicted adjustment; Leslie M. Stein and Janet L. Hoopes, *Identity Formation in the Adopted Adolescent* (New York: Child Welfare League of America, 1985), pp. 34–42, 46.

37. Kathryn S. Marquis and Richard A. Detweiler, "Does Adopted Mean Different? An Attributional Analysis," *Journal of Personality and Social Psychology* 48 (1985): 1054–66. The authors, together with Stein and Hoopes, concluded that the negative findings contained in so much of the adoption literature were explained by the fact that most other studies were theoretical in nature or focused on clinical rather than community populations of adoptees. Brodzinsky faults Marquis and Detweiler on methodology and for failure to take into account certain empirical studies involving nonclinical populations; "Looking at Adoption

Through Rose-Colored Glasses," *Journal of Personality and Social Psychology* 52 (1987): 394–98. But Brodzinsky's discussion of these other studies gives little attention to the adoptees' age at placement or other preplacement factors relevant to adjustment.

38. See Eaton, "Adoption *v.* Reproductive Technologies"; Sartor, "The Biological Link," pp. 24–27.

39. See Charlene E. Miall, "The Stigma of Adoptive Parent Status: Perceptions of Community Attitudes Toward Adoption and the Experience of Informal Sanctioning," *Family Relations* 36 (1987): 34, 37; Bohman and Sigvardsson, "Outcome in Adoption," p. 94, which states that adoptive families' "minority status" and "special existential situation" may create considerable stress; Kaye, "Acknowledgment or Rejection of Differences?" p. 140, which asserts that the fundamental differences between early-adopted and nonadopted children, apart from the disappearance of significant figures from their lives, are the "hurts and embarrassments caused by a social stigma and by people's cruelty"; Kirk, *Shared Fate*, a classic work describing adoptive families as constituting a minority group that lacks the support of social and historical traditions common to biologic kinship relations.

Stein and Hoopes, *Identity Formation*, asked their group of adopted adolescents how it felt to be adopted. Most indicated that it produced no ill effects and was not that different from being raised by birth parents as far as they could tell. One commented, "It's not adoption that is the problem but what other people think of adopted kids" (pp. 60–61).

40. Compare Kaye, "Acknowledgment or Rejection of Differences?" pp. 140–41, which finds that families of early-adopted adolescents tend to emphasize the normalcy of their situations rather than the differences, and concludes that this emphasis should be understood as healthy rather than pathological.

41. By contrast, Kaye (ibid.) emphasizes that both adopted and biologic children develop self-esteem problems if they do not experience a sense of "belonging" in their environment, and that the adoptee is different primarily in that he "has a real historical loss of ties to which to attribute the problem or in which to see hope of rectifying it" (p. 142).

42. See Marquis and Detweiler, "Does Adopted Mean Different?" pp. 1063–64, which speculates that positive findings about the

adoptive parenting relationship may be related to the adoptive parents' particularly strong motivation to become parents; David M. Brodzinsky and Loreen Huffman, "Transition to Adoptive Parenthood," *Marriage and Family Review* 12 (1988): 267, 276, which discusses other apparent benefits associated with adoptive parenting. Laraine M. Glidden's work reveals that the choice to adopt a child with developmental disabilities is associated with greater parental well-being than being the birth parent of such a child. See Glidden, "Adopted Children with Developmental Disabilities: Post-Placement Family Functioning," *Children and Youth Services Review* 13 (1991): 363–77; Glidden, "The Wanted Ones: Families Adopting Children with Mental Retardation," *Journal of Children in Contemporary Society* 21(1990): 177–205. See also Katherine A. Kowal and Karen M. Schilling, "Adoption Through the Eyes of Adult Adoptees," *American Journal of Orthopsychiatry* 55 (1985): 354–65, which finds that adoptees report feeling chosen or special twice as often as they report feeling uncomfortable with the fact of their adoption.

43. Mothers who are denied abortions are described as feeling an extremely high level of anger and resentment toward their children, who are in turn described as "much likelier to be troubled and depressed, to drop out of school, to commit crimes, to suffer from serious illnesses and to express dissatisfaction with life than are the offspring of willing parents"; "Study Says Anger Troubles Women," *New York Times*, May 21, 1991, p. C-10.

9. HIGH-TECH REPRODUCTION: IVF AND ITS PROGENY

1. Advertisement, *Boston Globe*, March 21, 1989, p. 92.
2. See, e.g., conflicting resolution of these issues in the various judicial decisions in *Davis* v. *Davis*, 15 Fam. L. Rptr. 2097, aff'd, 16 Fam. L. Rptr. 1535, aff'd, 18 Fam. L. Rptr. (Tenn. 1992).
3. See related discussions in Bartholet, "Parenting Options for the Infertile," pp. 523–30, and Bartholet, "In Vitro Fertilization," pp. 253–60. An overview of the law is contained in "Developments in the Law," *Harvard Law Review* 103 (1990): 1519, 1525–32.
4. See American Fertility Society, "In vitro fertilization-embryo transfer (IVF-ET) in the United States: 1990 results from the IVF-ET Registry," *Fertility and Sterility* 57 (1992): 15.

5. In GIFT (gamete intrafallopian transfer), the sperm and egg are placed in the fallopian tubes for fertilization, and in ZIFT (zygote intrafallopian transfer), the eggs are fertilized in vitro and the resulting zygotes are placed immediately in the tubes. The hope in both cases is that the tubes will then deliver the embryos to the uterus as in natural pregnancy. ZIFT encompasses other variations on the theme, such as PROST and TET.

6. It is said that among such couples there is a 20 to 25 percent chance of achieving a pregnancy after trying for one month.

7. See, e.g., U.S. Congress, Office of Technology Assessment, *Infertility: Medical and Social Choices* (Washington, D.C.: Government Printing Office, 1988), pp. 128–31, 303.

8. See American Fertility Society, "In vitro fertilization: 1990 results," p. 17. Five percent of all IVF pregnancies were ectopic; 22 percent resulted in live multiple births, with other multiple pregnancies resulting in spontaneous abortions and stillbirths; 13 percent of live deliveries were preterm.

9. See Ismail Kola, "Commentary: Embryo and Fetal Abnormalities in IVF," *Birth* 15 (1988): 145–47; American Fertility Society, "In vitro fertilization: 1990 results," p. 18.

10. A number of states now mandate insurance coverage, and some insurance companies voluntarily provide it. Many patients and doctors obtain reimbursement for some aspects of the IVF process, such as hormone treatment, simply by submitting the claims without informing the insurance company that the treatment was related to IVF. See U.S. Congress, *Infertility*, pp. 148–55.

11. See House Committee on Energy and Commerce, Subcommittee on Health and the Environment, *Fertility Clinic Success Rate and Certification Act of 1991: Hearing on H.R. 3940*, 102nd Congress, 2nd sess., Feb. 27, 1992, Richard F. Kelly, written testimony, p. 1, note 2. More than $1 billion was spent in 1990 for infertility services as a whole.

12. See review of the literature in Eaton, "Adoption *v.* Reproductive Technology."

13. Ibid. See also Charlene E. Miall, "The Stigma of Involuntary Childlessness," *Social Problems* 33 (1986): 268.

14. The doctors have measured "success" on the basis of the number of IVF patients out of the group who go through the embryo transfer process who are able to become pregnant. They do not

include the many cases in which women who start a cycle of IVF treatment never get as far as embryo transfer, or the many cases of women who manage to become pregnant but lose the fetus after a few days, weeks, or months or give birth to a dead child. Another problem is that the success rates that have been generally touted are often those at the most successful clinics in the country, rather than those at the average clinic, the clinic that is advertising, or the clinic that is promoting its services to a particular patient. See generally U.S. House of Representatives, Subcommittee on Regulation, Business Opportunities, and Energy, *Consumer Protection Issues Involving In Vitro Fertilization Clinics,* 101st Congress, 1st sess., March 9, 1989, p. 1; and Robert Pear, "Fertility Clinics Face Crackdown," *New York Times,* Oct. 26, 1992, p. A-15.

15. See, e.g., House Committee on Energy and Commerce, *Fertility Clinic Success Rate,* testimony of Richard F. Kelly: "The success rate formula that is least likely to mislead consumers is one that takes into account all significant negative results. Thus the starting point . . . should be the rate of live births per stimulation cycles" (p. 7).

16. See U.S. Congress, *Infertility,* p. 182; U.S. House of Representatives, *Consumer Protection Issues,* p. 2. The 12 percent figure is based on statistics in American Fertility Society, "In vitro fertilization: 1990 results," pp. 16–17, indicating 2,345 live deliveries out of 19,079 stimulation cycles. Actual success rates may well be lower, since the IVF-ET Registry has data only for clinics that volunteer their results; there is reason to believe that nonreporting clinics are less successful.

17. American Fertility Society, "In vitro fertilization: 1990 results," p. 19, Table 3 (calculations based on live delivery per stimulation cycles).

18. Ibid., pp. 22, 24: "We are certainly not seeing a breakthrough in increased pregnancy rates or deliveries."

19. See American Fertility Society, "Revised Minimum Standards for In Vitro Fertilization, Gamete Intrafallopian Transfer, and Related Procedures," *Fertility and Sterility* 53 (1990): 225; American Fertility Society, "Guidelines for In Vitro Fertilization, Gamete Intrafallopian Transfer, and Related Procedures," *Fertility and Sterility*

56 (1991): 194; Ethics Committee, American Fertility Society, "Ethical Considerations of the New Reproductive Technologies," *Fertility and Sterility* 46, supplement 1 (1986): 15. Clinics that choose to join the Society for Assisted Reproductive Technology, an affiliate of the AFS, are required to adhere to the 1990 and 1991 standards and to submit data to the IVF-ET Registry.

20. See U.S. House of Representatives, *Consumer Protection Issues*. An earlier hearing took place in June 1988.

21. The AFS collected clinic-specific information for the first time in 1989; this was reported in 1991.

22. See American Fertility Society, "In vitro fertilization: 1990 results." The clinic names are available in a document that has not been published or distributed to libraries or other places where consumers would have easy access to it. However, it can be purchased from the AFS.

23. Fertility Clinic Success Rate and Certification Act of 1992. See generally House Committee on Energy and Commerce, *Fertility Clinic Success Rate*. The most significant state legislation under consideration is a bill introduced in Massachusetts, H. 2452, 177th Gen. Ct., 1992 regular session, which has a similar focus on basic consumer protection measures. This kind of legislation would be helpful in giving public health agencies the authority to establish *and enforce* minimum standards, but the standards at issue are extremely limited in scope. A recent bill in Virginia (Virginia Code section 54.1-2971.1 (1991)) requires the patient to execute a disclosure form containing relevant information about the clinic's success rates before IVF treatment commences.

24. For examples of feminist opposition to IVF, see Gena Corea, *The Mother Machine: From Artificial Insemination to Artificial Wombs* (New York: Harper & Row, 1986); Patricia Spallone and Deborah L. Steinberg, eds., *Made to Order: The Myth of Reproductive and Genetic Progress* (London: Pergamon, 1987); Margarete Sandelowski, "Compelled to Try: The Never-Enough Quality of Conceptive Technology," *Medical Anthropology Quarterly* 5 (1991): 29, 34; Michelle Stanworth, *Reproductive Technologies: Gender, Motherhood, and Medicine* (Minneapolis: University of Minnesota Press, 1988); and Gena Corea, et al., eds., *Man-Made Women: How New Reproductive Technologies Affect Women* (Bloomington: Indiana

University Press, 1987). In July 1985, a group of feminists formed FINRRAGE, the Feminist International Network of Resistance to Reproductive and Genetic Engineering.

25. See House Committee on Energy and Commerce, *Fertility Clinic Success Rate*. Most feminist critics have emphasized the need for regulation. See Robyn Rowland, "Of Women Born, but for How Long?" in Spallone and Steinberg, *Made to Order*, pp. 67, 79–80, and Lori B. Andrews, "Alternative Modes of Reproduction," in Sherrill Cohen and Nadine Taub, eds., *Reproductive Laws for the 1990s* (Clifton, N.J.: Humana, 1989).

26. See, e.g., Andrews, "Alternative Modes of Reproduction."

27. Feminists have produced a powerful critique of the notion that women's pursuit of IVF treatment can be understood as choice. See Christine Crowe, " 'Women Want It': In Vitro Fertilization and Women's Motivations for Participation," *Women's Studies Forum* 8 (1985): 547–52; L. Koch, "IVF — An Irrational Choice?" *Issues in Reproductive and Genetic Engineering* 3 (1990): 235; Gena Corea, et al., "Prologue," in Spallone and Steinberg, *Made to Order*, pp. 7–8; Robyn Rowland, "Of Women Born, but for How Long?" p. 79.

28. See R. Blackwell, et al., "Are We Exploiting the Infertile Couple?" *Fertility and Sterility* 48 (1987): 735.

29. Informed consent requirements could be expanded to guarantee that consumers are given adequate information about both their medical options and such nonmedical alternatives as adoption. Some states have enacted special informed consent provisions governing the treatment of cancer, out of concern that women with breast cancer have a right to know about the less extensive therapy options available to them.

30. See, e.g., Jocelynne A. Scutt, "The Politics of Infertility Counseling," *Issues in Reproductive and Genetic Engineering* 4 (1991): 251.

31. Resolve purports to be neutral with respect to the various options open to the infertile, but has done little to change the attitudes and policies that give adoption its status as a last resort. Moreover, it has made mandated insurance coverage for IVF its major legislative priority, and has expressed little criticism of the kind of problematic IVF practices discussed above and little support for any protective legislation. Many feminists have expressed concern that Resolve's approach may have been inappropriately

influenced by the fact that it receives significant funding from a company that produces many of the infertility drugs used in the IVF process.

10. MODERN CHILD PRODUCTION

1. Like many, I consider "surrogacy" and "surrogate mother" inappropriate terms for describing the arrangement and the role of the woman who bears and gives birth to a child. These terms have been promoted by those who are sympathetic to such arrangements in order to minimize the significance of the birth parent. However, since "surrogacy" has been largely accepted in common parlance, I will use it here, even though "contract parenting" seems to me a preferable term.

2. On egg donation and sale, see American Fertility Society, "In vitro fertilization: 1990 results," pp. 21–22, 24, which reports that in 1990, sixty-seven clinics, or 37 percent of all those reporting, performed embryo transfer using donated eggs — a substantial increase over prior years; and Mark V. Sauer and Richard J. Paulson, "Understanding the Current Status of Oocyte Donation in the United States: What's Really Going On Out There?" *Fertility and Sterility* 58 (1992): 16, a report on a survey that documents the wide availability of egg donation programs in the United States and describes methods of paying egg providers.

3. The total cost of these arrangements to the contracting couple is about $30,000 to $40,000.

4. The well-publicized Baby M. case helped trigger concern. The highest court of New Jersey ruled in that case that commercial surrogacy arrangements violated state adoption law rules that prohibit baby-buying, protect biologic parenting relationships, and mandate that placement decisions be made in the best interests of the child; *In the Matter of Baby M*, 537 A.2d 1227 (N.J. 1988).

5. See the Uniform Status of Children of Assisted Conception Act, approved by the National Conference of Commissioners on Uniform State Laws on Aug. 4, 1988, and by the American Bar Association House of Delegates on Feb. 7, 1989, which presents two alternative model laws, one validating surrogacy arrangements and the other voiding them; *Family Law Reporter* 15 (Feb.

21, 1989): 1195. For general information on legal developments regarding surrogacy, see "Developments in the Law," *Harvard Law Review* 103 (1990): 1519, 1546–51.

6. "Developments in the Law," pp. 1519, 1532–37.

7. See George J. Annas, "Fathers Anonymous: Beyond the Best Interests of the Sperm Donor," *Family Law Quarterly* 14 (1980): 11–13; U.S. Congress, Office of Technology Assessment, *OTA Brief: Artificial Insemination Practice in the U.S., Summary of a 1987 Survey* (Washington, D.C.: Government Printing Office, Aug. 1988).

8. There have been an estimated three to four thousand surrogacy births in the past fifteen years, including some eighty to a hundred gestational surrogacy births; "Babies and Contracts," *Newsday*, Oct. 15, 1990, pt. 2, p. 4.

9. See Corea, *The Mother Machine*; Barbara Katz Rothman, "Motherhood: Beyond Patriarchy," *Nova Law Review* 13 (1989): 481. Some feminists, however, promote these arrangements on the grounds that they expand parenting options for the infertile and expand reproductive choice for women; see Lori B. Andrews, "Surrogate Motherhood: The Challenge for Feminists," *Law, Medicine, and Health Care* 16 (Spring 1988): 72–80.

10. See, e.g., Margaret Jane Radin, "Market Inalienability," *Harvard Law Review* 100 (1987): 1849, 1928–36.

11. Anita Allen, "Surrogacy, Slavery, and the Ownership of Life," *Harvard Journal of Law and Public Policy* 13 (1991): 139–40, note 9.

12. A 1990 survey revealed that a large number of all those IVF clinics providing egg donation services set no upper age limit for recipients. Of those that did, the range was from thirty-five to fifty-five years, with a mean of forty-four years. Sauer and Paulson, "Understanding the Current Status," p. 17.

13. See Radin, "Market Inalienability," p. 1930.

14. See Baran and Pannor, *Lethal Secrets*, pp. 54–73, 86–98, on sperm donors and donor offspring; Phyllis Chesler, *Sacred Bond: The Legacy of Baby M* (New York: Times Books, 1988), p. 47, on birth mothers in surrogacy arrangements.

AFTERWORD

1. Sociobiologists describe adoption as a "mistake," a "misfiring of a built-in rule." As Dawkins puts it in *The Selfish Gene*, "The generous female is doing her own genes no good by caring for the orphan. She is wasting time and energy which she could be investing in the lives of her own kin, particularly future children of her own." But Dawkins also writes that human beings have the capacity to defy their genetic programming and to deliberately cultivate altruism. See p. 101, 200–01.

2. See O'Flaherty, "Financial Support for Adoption," which describes recently proposed federal legislation that would expand support and makes related recommendations. For information on private sector support, which, although still limited, is growing, see National Committee for Adoption, *1989 Factbook*, pp. 213–14; Bureau of National Affairs, *Adoption Assistance: Joining the Family of Employee Benefits* (Washington, D.C.: BNA, 1988); and National Adoption Exchange, *Adoption Benefits Plans: Corporate Response to a Changing Society* (Philadelphia: NAE, 1984).

INDEX

DATE DUE

NOV 25 94			
FEB 18 '95			
March 17			
JAN 27 '96			
MAY 26 1998			
AUG 2 4 1999			
OCT 2 6 1999			
FE 17 '03			
FE 28 '04			
MR 11 '09			

Demco, Inc. 38-293